Avenues to Beauty
Eight Essays in Aesthetics

By the same author

Studies in the Metaphysics of Bradley
George Allen & Unwin, London
and Humanities Press, New York, 1967
(Muirhead Library)

The Winged Form: Aesthetical Essays on Hindustani Rhythm
Sangeet Natak Akademi, New Delhi, 1979

Aesthetical Essays
Chanakya Publications, Delhi, 1981

Ever Unto God: Essays on Gandhi and Religion
Indian Council of Philosophical Research, New Delhi, 1988

Swinging Syllables: Aesthetics of Kathak Dance
Sangeet Natak Akademi, New Delhi, 1991

Art and Philosophy: Seven Aestheticians
Indian Council of Philosophical Research, New Delhi, 1994

Hindustani Sangeet and a Philosopher of Art:
Music, Rhythm, and Kathak Dance
vis-à-vis Aesthetics of Susanne K. Langer
D.K. Printworld (P) Ltd., New Delhi, 2001

Hindustani Music and Aesthetics Today:
A Selective Study
Sangeet Natak Akademi, New Delhi,
and Hope India Publications, Gurgaon, 2009

Avenues to Beauty

Eight Essays in Aesthetics

S.K. Saxena

Formely Professor of Philosophy

University of Delhi

Sangeet Natak Akademi

New Delhi

D.K. Printworld (P) Ltd.

New Delhi

Cataloguing in Publication Data — DK

[Courtsey: D.K. Agencies (P) Ltd. <docinfo@dkagencies.com>]

Saxena, Sushil Kumar, 1921-
Avenues to beauty : eight essays in aesthetics / S.K. Saxena.
p. cm.
Essays; previously published.
Includes bibliographical references.
ISBN 13: 9788124605332
ISBN 10: 8124605335

1. Aesthetics. 2. Aesthetics, Indic. 3. Hindustani music – Philosophy and aesthetics. I. Title.

DDC 701.17 22

ISBN 13: 978-81-246-0533-2
ISBN 10: 81-246-0533-5
First published in India in 2009

Published by:
Sangeet Natak Akademi
National Academy of Music, Dance and Drama, India
Regd. office : Rabindra Bhavan, Feroze Shah Road
New Delhi - 110 001
Phones : (011) 2338 7246; 2338 7248; *Fax* : (011) 2338 2659
E-mail : sangeetnatakak@bol.net.in

and

D.K. Printworld (P) Ltd.
Regd. office : *'Srikunj,'* F-52, Bali Nagar
New Delhi - 110 015
Phones : (011) 2545 3975; 2546 6019; *Fax* : (011) 2546 5926
E-mail: dkprintworld@vsnl.net
Web: www.dkprintworld.com

To

Mr Abhijit Chatterjee

Preface

THIS little preface is at once a double delight. It enables me, first, to express my gratitude to one who deserves it; and secondly, to assure readers, just as happily, that the pages that follow present a good deal of such varicoloured and (I hope) sensible material — and in such a way — that poring over them is likely to be not only pleasurable all along, but a vehicle of some new insights, if only where hard analytic thinking is buttressed with apt references to details of fact. This is perhaps truer of the essays on "Music and Silence", "Attenborough's 'Gandhi'", and the "Rasa Theory" than of the rest. However, the remaining five too are essays in the way of our present-day scholarly concern with the arts which is philosophic in two clear ways. It abstains from glib generalizations and is specially keen on clarity of thinking, and hence also on a very watchful use of language, without being indifferent to the evidence of actual art and artistic practice. Here, I may refer specially to my two essays on Hindustani rhythm, "Aesthetic Theory and Hindustani Rhythm" and "Hindustani Rhythm and an Aesthetical Issue", which are related alike to contemporary aesthetics and aestheticians. Instead of merely appealing to our long tradition of solo tablā-playing, the first one *argues,* at fair length, why rhythm may be regarded as an independent art even from the viewpoint of current aesthetic thinking, and the second one is just as reasoned a protest against the view that the time that we find in music *cannot* be regarded as *sui generis.*

All this, however, is attributable not only to my own interest in how contemporary aesthetics could be fairly related to Hindustani sangeet, but to Mr Abhijit Chatterjee's standing invitation to keep contributing to the journal which he edits for Sangeet Natak Akademi, namely, *Sangeet Natak* — at *vilambit* pace, to be sure — but so meticulously that the off-prints which I have all along received are not only good to look at, but also impressively free from printing mistakes, and have sometimes duly shown a needful, gentle chiselling, so to say, of my original writing.

It is this editorial hospitality, covering a period of about twenty-five years, which has enabled me to think out the way to *a quite new discipline*, namely, a *truly contemporary* aesthetics of Hindustani sangeet. Mr Chatterjee himself is not quite aware of the value of the impetus he has given me. But I see it clearly that it has been of great help to me not only generally, but in providing a fair part of the present content of the book. So the dedication it carries is surely not a mere ritual. Nay, it epitomizes gratitude.

However, what lends value to a book is not its content alone. Its look also counts, and here I feel indebted not only to Mr Vijay Jain who has designed the jacket with his customary finesse, but to Mr Susheel K. Mittal of D.K. Printworld who has taken pains to minimize the number of printing errors and to choose fonts which are not only easy on the eye but good to look at.

S.K. Saxena

Contents

1

Aesthetics Today

In our country it is common to think of *aesthetics* as Saundarya Śāstra, that is, as the systematic study of beauty. This view may perhaps be said to be closer to how aesthetics began than to what it is today. It was Baumgarten who first visualized aesthetics as an independent philosophical discipline. But the book in which he did so (*Philosophical Meditations on Some Requirements of the Poem,* 1735) was "very literally a defence of the relevance of sensuous perception."[1]

It tried to maintain that the senses, specially the eye and the ear, produce a certain type of knowledge. The noteworthy point here is that philosophical aesthetics, which is today brimming with intellectual ferment, originated as a plea for the value of sensibility, not as a theory of art.[2] Today, on the other hand, the focus of this subject is on art; and, what is more, beauty (or *saundarya*) is no longer regarded as a *necessary* feature of art; *meaning* alone is given that distinction, though not in the sense of verbal meaning alone. This is so because, unlike meaning or significance, *beauty* cannot be said to cover all good art. Even such a mild predicate of appeal as "pleasant" cannot be applied to Goya's *Disasters of War* or to Picasso's *Guernica.*[3] Neither work tickles the eye, and so they cannot be

1. Kai Hammermeister, *The German Aesthetic Tradition,* Cambridge University Press, 2002, p. 4.
2. Ibid.
3. Harold Osborne, *The Art of Appreciation,* London: OUP, 1970, p. 41.

said to be *beautiful* in the ordinary sense of the word. Yet both are universally regarded as great works of art. *Guernica* is acclaimed primarily because it is meaningful in the sense of being expressive of the artist's own indignation and revulsion at the "cruelty and injustice" involved in the destruction of Guernica (a town in North Spain) by German bombers during the Spanish Civil War. This expressiveness, however, is very far removed from the way a frown may express anger or irritation, automatically, that is, *without any effort* on the part of the person who looks angry. It is a quality of the work's structural details — of some shapes that are unusually angular. In Picasso's hands this very angularity has become a symbol or indirect index of ferocity,[4] and it is obviously *the result of his creative effort.*

Be that as it may, aesthetics is no longer regarded as the *śāstra* of *saundarya.* Even a casual look at its contemporary literature bears out the point. One of the better known books on the subject, *Aesthetics — A Critical Anthology,* for instance, opens its General Introduction as follows:

> Aesthetics is a term commonly used to refer to such diverse matters as theories of beauty and the elegance of a logician's axiomatic system. Philosophically, the term has a far more precise designation. Today, those philosophers called aestheticians are concerned with two general enterprises — the theory of art and the theory of the aesthetic that emerged in the eighteenth and nineteenth centuries from the theory of beauty.[5]

The Cambridge Dictionary of Philosophy is a little more enlightening:

> Aesthetics . . . [is that] branch of philosophy . . . [which]

---

4. Harold Osborne, op. cit., p. 263.
5. George Dickie, Richard Scalfani, and Ronald Rabbin (eds.): *Aesthetics — A Critical Anthology,* Boston and New York: Bedford/ St. Martin's, 2nd edn., 1989.

> examines the nature of art and the character of our experience of art and of the natural environment. . . . Questions specific to the field of aesthetics are: Is there a special attitude, the aesthetic attitude, which we should take toward works of art and the natural environment, and what is it like? Is there a distinct . . . [kind of] aesthetic experience, and what is it? Is there a special kind of value that we can call aesthetic value, comparable with moral, epistemic, and religious values? . . . Aesthetics also encompasses the philosophy of art . . . [Here,] the most central issue . . . has been how to define "art". . . .[6]

However, insofar as good anthologies, original works and dictionaries appear only now and then, it is mainly the regular, leading journals of aesthetics that may be allowed to determine our understanding of what aesthetics *today* is; for they alone can keep all along abreast of the latest directions and concerns of aesthetical thinking. Luckily, the two leading journals — *The British Journal of Aesthetics* (*BJA*) and the (American) *Journal of Aesthetics and Art Criticism* (*JAAC*) — both here speak almost identically, and so their conception of what aesthetics is may well be put collectively as follows:

> The term "aesthetics" is to be taken to include all studies of *the arts* and related types of experience from a philosophical, scientific or other theoretical standpoints including those of psychology, sociology, anthropology, cultural history, art criticism and education. The term "the arts" shall include all branches of art, both of fine art and of practical arts.[7]

It is here noteworthy that both journals give pre-eminence to aesthetics regarded as a *philosophical* study of the arts. Today, in fact, such a way of looking at the arts is commonly regarded

---

6. Edited by Robert Audi, Cambridge University Press, 2nd edn., 1999, pp. 11-12.

7. The reference here is mainly to the front inside cover of the *Journal of Aesthetics and Art Criticism*, U.S.A., hereafter referred to as *JAAC*.

as a signal intellectual achievement of the twentieth century, quite as notable as philosophies of science, logic, and mind.[8] So our emphasis too in this essay will be on *philosophical* aesthetics, as against the other ways of looking at the arts, though a brief reference to those ways will have to be made, if only with a view to highlighting the uniqueness of the philosophical approach. The word *philosophical,* specially where it occurs with *art,* may appear rather daunting to readers in general and to lovers of art in particular. But, we may note, there is nothing esoteric about philosophy today. Reflection on supersensuous realities like God and the *ātman* are no longer its primary concern. In the words of William James, philosophy today is simply "a peculiarly stubborn attempt to think clearly";[9] and, we may add, so is philosophical aesthetics in its concern with art.

It would however be wrong to confine our study of aesthetics to Western art and the contemporary modes of aesthetic thinking in the West. We must also pay due attention to some of the more important aspects of *our own traditional thinking in this context;* for, though it never assumed the form of aesthetics regarded as a unified theory of all the arts, it has given us quite a few rich insights in respect of some individual arts such as drama, dance and poetry. In this connection it is interesting to note that the value of some age-old Indian concepts and theories of art, art activity and art contemplation has been recognized by quite a few leading aestheticians of today. Thus, see the following from Susanne K. Langer's *Feeling and Form:*

> Some of the Hindu critics . . . understand much better than their Western colleagues the various aspects of emotion in

---

8. S.K. Langer, *Problems of Art,* London: Routledge and Kegan Paul, 1957, pp. 2-3.

9. Cited by Brand Blanshard in his book, *On Philosophical Style,* New York: Greenwood Press, 1969, rpt., p. 13.

> the theatre, which our writers so freely . . . confuse: the feelings experienced by the actor, those experienced by the spectators, those presented as undergone by the characters in the play, and finally, the feeling that shines through the play itself — the vital feelings of the piece. This last they call *rasa;* it is a state of emotional knowledge which comes only to those who have long studied and contemplated poetry. It is . . . not like mundane feeling and emotion, but is detached, more of the spirit than of the viscera, pure and uplifting.[10]

Harold Osborne too speaks of the Indian doctrine of *rasa* as "the most complex and the most subtle of emotional theories of appreciation."[11] Further, he believes that even apart from "the metaphysical and religious framework which is common to very much of Indian thought" the doctine in question "is capable of supplementing the rather meagre insights of Western thought."[12] What is more, in conformity with the contemporary demand for internationalism in aesthetics, he rightly invites our attention to *the distinctive features* of traditional Indian thinking on art and art experience. Some of these may be quickly outlined here, just for the sake of providing a more balanced overall view of aesthetics:

a. As compared to their Western counterparts, the aestheticians of ancient India have put deeper emphasis on the subjective aspects of our experience of art. It would, of course, be wrong to suppose that these aspects have been totally ignored by aestheticians in the West. Some of them have, in fact, taken care to emphasize that contemplation of great works of art is "life-enhancing" in the sense that when we are able to concentrate on a work of art which makes very heavy demands on our percipience in revealing its total form,

---

10. S.K. Langer: *Feeling and Form*, Routledge and Kegan Paul, 4th Impression, 1967, p. 323.

11. Harold Osborne, *The Art of Appreciation*, p. 116.

12. Ibid., p. 204.

"we are keyed up to more than ordinary vitality and alertness,"[13] and that the occasion which art contemplation provides for the successful exercise of trained and discriminating perception gives us *a kind of delight* which distinguishes aesthetic pleasure.[14] But all this is neither so deep nor so exalted as the Indian view that "both the creative function of the artist and the practice of appreciation are . . . modes of personal devotion demanding systematic mental discipline akin to the various forms of psychic self-control taught by *yoga* in quest of spiritual enlightenment. [Here] the pleasures of art are . . . believed to culminate in transcendental bliss akin to the spiritual rapture of mystical or metaphysical union with the Absolute."[15]

The very climate of India was such that everything was perforce to be invested with the holy spirit of religion. . . . Even the most mundane activity [could here be] viewed as religious. . . . In the widest sense [that is, as somehow reinforcing one's commitment to the divine] dance and drama, music and painting, are [to the traditional Indian] so many ways of divine worship. It does not mean, as is generally supposed, that art was a handmaid to religion, that the aesthetic approach was subordinated to dogmas of religion . . . (but only that) artists in India were religious in their personal lives and took their vocation so very seriously that they deemed their work to be on a par with the hardest disciplines like *yoga*.[16]

---

13. Harold Osborne, op. cit., pp. 208-09.
14. Ibid.
15. Ibid., p. 204. It may here be noted, following Osborne, that writing which likens aesthetic experience to religious mysticism is "not entirely unknown to the West." John Dewey, for instance, speaks of "the mystic aspect of acute aesthetic surrender, that renders it so akin as an experience to what religionists term ecstatic communion." John Dewey, *Art as Experience*, New York: Capricorn Books, 1958, 7th Impression, p. 28.
16. Osborne, *The Art of Appreciation*, p. 288.

b. Further, in spite of its insistence on the closeness of art to religion, traditional Indian thought looks on entertainment as a quite legitimate function of art. This may seem to be no more than ordinary good sense;[17] but it is important, for (as Osborne points out) it may well serve "as a corrective to a too rigorous austerity, a too rarefied exclusiveness, which at any rate have lent a certain one-sidedness to most European aesthetic expositions."[18]

c. Finally, Indian thought has seldom lost sight of the fact that the artistic impulse in man is closely allied to the sheer delight in all created things. "The *Nāṭyaśāstra* of Bharata . . . the most important source-book of Indian aesthetic thought, begins with the story that the gods approached the Creator with the request for a diversion which should delight their eyes and ears alike."[19]

At this point, however, a word of caution is necessary for understanding what aesthetics really is as an intellectual discipline. Quite a few of us feel tempted by the idea that insofar as it deals with art and beauty, aesthetics must be a very pleasing subject. Now, the focus of aesthetics today is admittedly on art. It is also true that a substantial amount of art is beautiful, and that aestheticians today are perhaps *not as generally* sceptical about the relation of art to beauty as they were till recently.[20] Yet the study of aesthetics is certainly not as directly pleasing as the sight of a rainbow or of the "cup of wonder" that we occasionally see in a little child's eye. Nor is a work of art bound to be beautiful. Many works of modern art do not tickle the common man's eye. Awareness of this fact may disappoint those who are about to begin their study of aesthetics. But it

17. Osborne, op. cit., p. 205.

18. Ibid., p. 204.

19. Ibid., p. 205.

20. That is, till before the appearance of Mary Mothersill's book: *Beauty Restored*, Oxford: Clarendon Press, 1984.

would steady them a little were their attention also invited to the fact that literary works like *Rāmāyaṇa* or *Kāmāyanī* (by Jai Shankar Prasad) cannot be credited with the *immediately seizable* beauty of an architectural marvel like Taj Mahal, though their own status as great works of poetical art is quite beyond question. Very often we admire a work of art because of what it says or signifies, as against how it looks. Today, indeed, theoretically the most stimulating kind of aesthetics is its philosophical genre; the *meaning*, and not the merely sensuous charm of art is here the main concern; and if a study of this subject yet gives us some intellectual delight, as it surely does, it is mainly because it makes us see (or check) a little better either (a) the meaning (or range) of a concept or of a theory relating to art, or (b) the intricate character of art experience itself.

Illustration is here easy. Take, to begin with, the *theory* that art is essentially a kind of expression, a theory which has certainly dominated the history of aesthetics.[21] Perhaps most Indian classical singers would not only agree to, but also insist on, the view that music is nothing if not an outpouring of the singer's own heart (or feelings). The *rasika* too is here very likely to agree. The music *critic* may even be able to make us see that the expressiveness of a particular recital is due to its regulation of vocal volume, so that a semblance of the rise and fall of feeling is effectively evoked.[22] But the *aesthetician's* help

21. See, here, the following: "The expression theory of art, in one form or another, has dominated the aesthetic scene for the past centuries as much, perhaps, as the imitation theory had done previously." John Hospers in his essay, "The Concept of Artistic Expression", in: *Introductary Readings in Aesthetics* (ed. by Hospers himself). The Free Press, Collier MacMillan Publishers, 1969, p. 142.

22. I have here in mind some of the greatest vocalists of modern India, specially the late Ustad Abdul Karim Khan and Pandit Omkarnath Thakur.

yet remains necessary. As a philosopher, his concern with music (as with art taken generally) is much fuller than that of the layman, the *rasika* and the critic. It is he who is expected to make us realize that music is not mere singing, but also the music of instruments which is generally admired for qualities other than expressiveness; that even within the region of classical vocal music, the overriding criteria of excellence are sweetness to the (trained) ear, fidelity to the *rāga* and *tāla* chosen, structural beauty of *sthāyī-antarā* and *taans*, and effective execution; and that therefore expression (of feeling) cannot be regarded as the very *essence* of music. Expressiveness in our music is in fact rarely admired unless it appears as an occasional and quite unforced enlivenment of music that is already possessed of the other qualities listed.

Consider, now, an aesthetic *concept*, say, the concept of *form*. It is of course the task of a critic to make us see how exactly the details of (say) a poem's content are organized in relation to one another. But the meaning of artistic *form*, taken generally, is not his (the critic's) *direct* concern. It is the aesthetician who argues how, in the region of art, *form* means neither what it does in the context of things — say, their outlines or abstractable shapes — nor even the identifiable sub-type of an individual art — such as *ghazal* and *mercia*[23] in the region of Urdu poetry — but the intense inner unity of a work of art's content.

Here, if in passing, a hint may be given as to how some new awareness of artistic details and aesthetic possibilities can be had if we did aesthetics in relation to *Indian* art. The

---

23. *Mercia* may be likened to elegy in English poetry. It is a song of mourning. *Ghazal* holds the pride of place in Urdu poetry today. But, originally, it is a Persian and Arabic verse-form, of not more than 18 couplets, the first two lines and the even-numbered lines rhyming together; and it is mainly amatory and bacchanalian in character.

integration of different human figures in a single representational painting — say, by regulating the line of their *looks* — is widely known. But when we turn to classical Indian sculpture (or dance) we are often struck by the way *the whole bodily* posture is made to lend point *to a dainty (yet meaningful) little gesture or mudrā.* Again, as we follow the changing ways in Western painting, we may come to think of impressionist art as *merely opposed to* that which is expressionistic. But the first few minutes of *ālāpa* on the (*vichittra*) *vīṇā* are a clear *blend of both.* Here the generally fluid form not only provides aesthetic experience by projecting undivided *impressions* of the *rāga*'s distinctive character, but is variously *expressive,* say, of a yearning tenderness or deep-seated tranquillity, though because of music's inherent demands — say, of identifiable form and tonal sweetness — the artistic devices of exaggeration and distortion are just not possible here. Finally, whereas our *ālāpa* of the *dhruvapad* manner is a surpassing example (in singing) of what Walter Pater meant by "pure music," our rhythm is a whole world of purely formal charm, of sounds that have a minimum of (graded) tonal variety, but which can yet be the subject of a quite new aesthetics, *the aesthetics of mnemonic syllables,* which has happily begun to engage the attention of scholars in India.

But, to turn again to the present, what exactly is philosophical aesthetics? An obvious, though not very enlightening answer is: it is "simply the philosophical study of art."[24] Now, it would make us see the nature of such aesthetics a little better if we began by marking it off, quite briefly, from some other kinds of aesthetics. Consider, to begin with, what is known as *psychological* aesthetics. Some of the questions it addresses may be listed as follows:

---

24. Antony Flew, *A Dictionary of Philosophy,* Pan Books Ltd., 1984 edn., p. 6.

Is a man's excellence as an artist related to his Intelligence Quotient? How is creativity a "magic synthesis" of the primitive, irrational forces of the unconscious with the logical, cognitive processes of the conscious mind? Can creativity be cultivated? If yes, what are the controllable factors on which it depends? Does the intake of mind-altering drugs like mescaline and L.S.D. somehow add to the artist's creative power? Again, if he is about to set out on a big creative venture, would it help if he prefaced it with a day or two of quiet relaxation? Silvano Arieti points out that a measure of "aloneness" may here be necessary. But he hastens to add that it need not be accompanied by any painful feeling of loneliness, and that it is quite different from that persistent shyness which is generally brought about by one's own psychological problems.

The psychological, however, is not the only non-philosophical way of looking at the arts. Sensible questions can also be put from the viewpoint of socio-cultural conditions. Some of these questions, which are generally left out by a present-day *philosopher* of art, may be put thus:

How can we explain the sudden resurgence of both *ghazal/bhajan*-singing in our country today? Is it because attendance at such concerts is a good way to at once appear socially important and to have some quick and easy entertainment; or is it traceable to the fact that neither lovers of Hindi nor of Urdu want to lag behind in their open admiration of music and poetry? Why is it that most of the better *ghazal* singers still hail from Pakistan? Does the socio-cultural setting in which an artist is born and brought up determine not only his choice of a specific musical genre but his performing ability too? And, to turn to our dances, why does the Lucknow Gharānā[25] of Kathak dance pay greater attention to softness and delicacy of

---

25. A *gharānā* is a traditional school of music or dance, generally having a particular family as its focus.

expression than, say, the representatives of the Jaipur school? Is it because of the patronage which the Lucknow school received from Nawābs who were generally fond of a peaceable life of love and luxury?

Nor is *metaphysical* aesthetics, which chooses to relate art and beauty to ultimate Reality, unfamiliar to us in India. In fact, a good deal of our traditional theory of art has been frankly metaphysical. The variform *mithuna*[26] figures that fill the walls of our older temples in such abundance are said to symbolize the union of soul with God; and music has for long been regarded in India as a disciplined worship of *Nāda-Brahma* or the Absolute as *Nāda* or primal Sound. In our own day, Vinoba Bhave has spoken of beauty as the grace of the Lord granted to prayerful and ceaseless endeavour.

Now, we may not at once say that such thinking is quite without value. But the trouble is that there is no way to see what this value really is; for we are at a loss to see what precisely such writing means. Philosophical aesthetics is different. In philosophy, today, we hesitate to speak too freely of an ultimate, supersensible Reality; and our emphasis, in principle, is on clarity of meaning. In this basic sense indeed — that is, as an attempt to clarify our ideas — philosophy is perhaps of special relevance to the arts, for our talk about them is quite often glib. Very freely, for instance, we declare that Indian music is *spiritual*, without taking care to clarify what exactly this word can be taken to mean in the context of music,[27] a great deal of which does not use any elevating or even

26. *Mithuna* signifies loving *couples*, as distinguished from erotic *groups*. *Mithuna* had been part of Indian artistic repertoire since the first century CE.

27. See, here, my essay: "The Spiritual and Hindustānī Music" in *Sangeet Natak*, official journal of Sangeet Natak Akademi (New Delhi), nos. 131-132, 1999, pp. 3-14.

thoughtful language. Therefore, as serious and detailed thinking about matters relating to art, philosophical aesthetics is indeed a demand of the day.

Yet a suspicion is likely to linger. One could protest that though it may be right to philosophize about matters which call for understanding, art is essentially an object of relish; and that therefore it seems improper to do *philosophy* in relation to art. Why indeed should we labour to link two quite disparate things? The doubt is however easy to dispel. Art is not merely, or even essentially, an object of mere enjoyment. It is, in this context, important to see that the "tasting" (or आस्वादन) of which our *rasa* theorists speak is no mere indulgence of the tongue, ear or the eye, but the relish of a connoisseur and a mental activity (*manasāsvādana*). The metaphor of tasting is only meant to emphasize the utter immediacy and personal character of aesthetic experience. Nor is this tasting an expert act quite in the same way in which a professional tea-taster tastes and checks a particular blend of tea. The *rasika* — or one who can experience *rasa* — is believed to be a person who is equipped with a fair *knowledge* or *understanding of the technique* of an art, along with a well trained ability to register the specific finenesses of — and artistic devices employed in — a work, such as the artist's unremitting adherence to *svara* and *tāla* in the case of music, or the accord of verbal meanings with the very sound or even disposition of words in the case of poetry. How indeed can any work of art be fully enjoyed unless it is contemplated discriminatingly? However, such an effort may not be easy for the average listener or reader. The *nigāh* (or discriminating perception) which a knowledgeable lover of the arts is expected to have and to exercise is indeed no isolated act of immediate attention, but an ability — acquired through long and loving communion with art, and even with artistes — to follow and admire the projection or embodiment (in actual works) of some principles which are freely talked about and discussed by the makers and "consumers" of art. It is a known fact that our poets, musicians, and dancers feel greatly encouraged by applause *at the right turn* of phrase, rhythm or melody; and that this perception of rightness is possible only for the knowledgeable.

Such a seizure of artistic significance is indeed not just a sensuous activity. Nor is *a work of art* ever meant for uncultivated perception. It calls for understanding and so is not intelligible to one and all. This is why questions such as the following, "what does it say" or "what is it about," are often freely put by us, especially with regard to a work of modern art. How then can we object to philosophy of art (or philosophical aesthetics) which discusses such questions with the throughness they demand? Nor is there any warrant for supposing that the moment we set out to *understand* what a work of art is or means, our *relish* of it is necessarily impoverished. As we have already said, the artists themselves expect their works to be praised discriminatingly; and it is quite common experience that the more conversant we become with the technique of an art, the deeper does our appreciation of creations in its region become. The alternative is to be content with just being baffled or vaguely excited by the mere surface appearance of a work of art.

Such facts are enough to justify philosophical aesthetics. A look at the problems it addresses highlights its value further. These are essentially the same as those of general philosophy: that is, problems relating to meaning, reality, truth, value and knowledge. Of all these theoretic concerns, the question of meaning is today of pre-eminent value, for we now see it clearly that whatever be the question that faces us, we cannot even try to answer it properly unless we first take care to understand what it means. In contemporary aesthetics this question is specially important also because, as we have already pointed out, meaning or significance is today regarded as a more essential feature of art than beauty. A work can very well be good as art without being beautiful or good to look at, but it cannot claim any artistic excellence if it does not "say" something, or is otherwise significant, say, by way of lifting us above our everyday concerns for a while; by giving us some insight, maybe, into the life of feeling; or by simply teasing or refining our perception. So an important question of philosophical aesthetics is that of artistic meaning.

This question is indeed quite basic; for the meaning of *art* itself calls for some reflection. The point is easy to explain. The meaning of the words which are being used right now can also be conveyed by means of their Hindi equivalents, which means that their (English words') meaning cannot be said to be inseparable from their present (English) character. But, on the other hand, how can the meaning (or the net impact or significance) of a particular poem, painting or music composition be shifted, whole and entire, to a different set of words, colours, notes and rhythm? To take a simple example, the dictionary meanings of *glistening* and *glimmering*, are almost identical; but in a poetic line which speaks of the sea, a beach and the waves one cannot possibly replace *glimmering* with *glistening*, for only the former's phonetic quality has a slightly undulating feel which goes well with the image of waves.[28] And, to turn to our classical music, is it not an admitted fact that a properly structured *bandish* (composition) blooms (or खिलती है, as we say in popular parlance) at — and so is

---

28. The reference, here, is to the following lines of Matthew Arnold's poem. *Dover Beach:*

The sea is calm to-night,
 . . . , the moon lies fair
 . . . , on the French coast, the light
Gleams . . . , the cliffs of England stand
Glimmering and vast . . .
Listen, you hear the grating roar
Of pebbles which the waves draw back and fling . . .

aesthetically inseparable from — *its* own specific *laya* (or aesthetic pace)?

But of course this is not the only way to see the value of the question of meaning in respect of philosophical aesthetics. A whole list of terms that we freely use in our talk about art requires deeper analysis, for their various meanings are not always clearly distinguished. Here are some such words: art, expression, feeling, form, creation, *rasa,* and aesthetic experience; and problems here easily arise when we try to determine the meaning of these concepts philosophically, that is, in a clear and self-consistent way. For the sake of brevity, however, only one of them may here be picked for attention: the concept of *art*.

What does "art" *mean?* The question is by no means unnecessary, for we in fact use the word in different senses, and these may suggest quite different lines of enquiry. One common meaning of the word is a distinct kind of object, *an object* of art. This is the intended meaning when, say, a critic points to an abstract painting — which may look quite odd and unmeaning to a layman — and insists: "*this is art.*" Another familiar use of the word is art in the sense of an activity, or art as the making of art. This is the obvious meaning when, for instance, we talk of promoting the practice of art along with the study of science and computers in our schools and colleges. Finally, "art" may be taken to signify works of art *taken generally,* as when we speak of an institution as The National Museum of Art. All these meanings are of value to us, for they all excite aesthetic thinking, if differently. Thus, to begin with the first meaning, if "art" signifies a *distinct* kind of "thing," the meaning clearly is that it is not an everyday object. But the moment we say so, at least two questions arise. If "art" *is* something and yet not in the way of things of daily use, how is it *real* at all, and how are we to *know* that it is art, and not a thing of daily life? These are both questions of *philosophical* aesthetics, for they relate to reality and knowledge. Further, should any one venture to suggest that a work of art is a distinctive something because, quite unlike our everyday objects, it is an "expressive form" or a source of disinterested *delight*, another philosophical question may be put at once. How can we be sure as to the *truth* of such general characterizations of art? Our rhythm is an independent art too.[29] A good solo *tablā* recital can be an important item in a whole session of classical music. But nobody will be found admiring it as follows: "How *expressive* the playing was!" On the other hand, if Picasso's *Guernica* is regarded as a superlative painting, it is surely not because it gives some immediate delight to the eye but because one comes to see, by exercising discriminating attention, that the artist has here used to perfection such subtle devices as making the very "unusual angularity" of shapes as "the equivalent of ferocity."[30]

The truth indeed is that, in one respect or another, the various attempts to seize the *essence* of art alike seem questionable. But what they all necessarily assume — that is, the work of art's *reality* in some sense of the word — cannot be denied. The assumption, however, is not only necessary, but invites enquiry. Is a work of art real in the manner of an everyday object? A thing is extended, and so has its "place" in actual space. It is also generally useful or is at least usable. Now, we *can* speak of art too in these everyday ways. Thus, when we say: "Put this painting in that corner" we obviously think of it as a thing that can be handled, carried and placed. We can also so put it that it may cover an ugly patch in the wall, in which case it would become *useful* too in the everyday

29. In support of this particular view quite a few arguments have been given in my essay on Hindustānī Rhythm which appeared in the summer 1976 issue, vol. 16. no. 3 of *The British Journal of Aesthetics*. (hereafter referred to as *BJA*) and is also reproduced in this book as essay no. 4.

30. Harold Osborne, *The Art of Appreciation*, p. 263.

sense of the word. But it is clear that in all such talk about, or dealing with, the work no attention is paid to its quality *as art.* Artistic perception would here begin only when, say, the lines, figures and masses in the work are carefully noticed, and when an effort is made to see how they all make for some unified impact or significance. Here, how the work can help us in practice is not the question at all. If a man so decides, he *can* surely use a small piece of sculpture as a paperweight, but in so doing he would in no way be concerned with its value *as art.*

But though it is surely not a mere thing, a work of art cannot be said to be wholly unreal, or a mere abstraction like number. A measure of remoteness from sheer fact may well be necessary for a good deal of art. But even where it is totally non-representational — or a very negation of surface appearances, as in the hands of the Russian expressionist painter, Wassily Kandinsky[31] — art produces specific aesthetic sensations in the spectator, or a kind of shock effect on him, maybe because of its bright colour and emphatic brushwork. On the other hand, a number as such is never seen to have the same effect on us. Further, quite unlike a number, art often amazes and delights us by virtue of its beautiful form and its magical or "virtual" elements. The literally moveless and often quite limited canvas of the painter may well be able to project a semblance of *movement* and *infinite recession* or *distance.* The former, for instance, is "seen" in El Greco's *Resurrection*[32] where Christ seems to be *rising* back to life; and the latter, in *The Boat Padma* by Gaganendra Nath Tagore.

It would here be relevant to see, in brief, how the question

---

31. 1866-1944. Kandinsky is regarded as the first painter to develop an entirely abstract style.

32. This painting may be seen in: *El Greco* (by Lionello Puppi), A Dolphin Art Book, London: Thames and Hudson, 1967, Plate 49.

of art's reality has been discussed by some important theorists of art. Of course, a mere look at works of art and literature is enough to make us see that a work of art cannot be said to be real like a material object. As a rule, things serve some practical purpose. Works of art, on the other hand, are only meant to be contemplated. But Susanne K. Langer explains the difference in a way which is not at all so obvious, but is yet not quite without sense. According to her, a work of art is a symbolic expression of how life feels. Being alone is one thing; feeling lonely or deserted is quite another; and Langer insists that art is uniquely important because it captures and projects not only the actual things and happenings, but their subjective impact which is quite as real. Arthur Danto has yet another way of distinguishing *creations in the region of music* from material objects. The former, in his view, are "logically incombustible" in the sense that whereas all material objects can be destroyed by sufficiently intense heat, the burning of the notation of a composition will do nothing to harm the music itself.[33] But, then, are we to accept the *ideal* theory of Croce and Collingwood, which says that all works of art are, in essence, the *artist's own intuition,* which is at once (spiritual) expression too; and that what is called (overt) expression is only a secondary and practical activity? We can hardly say, yes; for the acceptance of such a view would be simply to miss the vital truth that most works of art reveal what they do by means of, or rather in terms of, their uniquely shaped *material* or *perceptual* elements. What is more, the specific character of its material not only determines (and largely delimits) the expressive power of an art, but (along with other factors) contributes to its distinctiveness. Thus, whereas on the one hand, our rhythm, with its wordless material of mnemonic syllables, cannot tell a

33. Nelson Goodman, *Languages of Art,* Indianapolis: Hackett, 1976, chapter III. But, one may ask, what about paintings and literary works? *They* cannot be said to be "incombustible" in this sense.

story or express an emotion, it is on the other hand exactly this material, comprising many Hindi letters but not in the way of (meaningful) language, which separates this art from other arts and makes it a virtual paradigm of *pure* art. Oppositely, the *art* of drama uses quite a few different materials — say, language, gestures, music, and dance. So it is infinitely capable of representation and expression, as against rhythm which can only be made *to add to* the expressiveness of some other artistic element, say, *abhinaya* in our dances. It is therefore clearly improper to underestimate the value of materials in art. Luckily, there is a kind of middle view too which seems to do justice to both aspects of art — the material and the non-sensuous or spiritual. Arthur Danto believes that "the relation of [say] a sculpture to the shaped material of which it consists is analogous to the habitation of the human body by a soul." According to this view, the non-material something which distinguishes a work of art from a mere thing "is not, as on the ideal theory, located in the artist, but in the work itself; it is not found in the human soul, but rather animates a piece of bronze or a canvas charged with pigments."[34]

We may now turn to the second meaning of "art." If art is a distinct kind of activity, it is so partly because the agent is here no ordinary person, but an individual who has trained himself in a particular way and has his own way of looking at things. This is of course common knowledge. But when we focus on this simple fact, the need is at once heightened to reckon with the *artist's* own point of view and experience in discussing questions about art. His (art-)activity, however, is distinctive not merely because he is its source, but because it can be objectively marked off from other major fields of human

---

34. Crispin Sartwell's essay "Aesthetic Dualism and the Transfiguration of the Commonplace" in *JAAC*, Summer 1988, p. 461. This view has been called "aesthetic dualism."

endeavour, say, craft, morality, science, and philosophy.

Art-Craft *differences*:

1. Of all these human concerns it is craft which is necessarily related to art. Therefore, how the two *differ* has to be carefully thought out. They cannot be said to be utterly dissimilar. Both call for a considerable degree of skill. Both, again, involve the manipulation of some given material — be it stone, pigment, clay, or wood. What is more, both produce objects of value. But, and now we turn to distinguish the two, whereas a product of craft is generally important mainly because it is practically useful, a work of art is of value because it expresses or communicates a feeling or some meaning, *and is therefore meant to be contemplated rather than used.* Art is never mere craftsmanship, but craftsmanship *as harnessed to a special end*: "the creation of . . . visually, audibly, or even imaginatively perceivable forms"[35] that seem to be expressive or otherwise significant, say, by virtue of their ability to provide disinterested delight or some other kind of non-sensuous satisfaction to a knowledgeable contemplator. The difference is in fact reflected in our everyday parlance. It is usual to speak thus: "a craftsman *produces* goods, but *creates* a thing of beauty"; "a builder *erects* a house, but *creates* an edifice if the house is a real work of architecture, however modest." An artefact as such is merely a combination of material parts, or a modification of a natural object to suit human purposes. A work of art, on the other hand, is more than an "arrangement" of given things . . . something emerges from the tones or colours which was

---

35. S.K. Langer, *Problems of Art*, p. 111.

not there before," and the ground of value is here this emergent form, semblance or significance.[36]

2. Further, as he sets out to exercise his skill, a craftsman has a fairly clear idea of the details of the particular object — say, a table — which he proposes or has been asked to produce. The method of making too is fairly prefixed; and but for very few changes that may be demanded by some unsuspected detail — say, a knot in a piece of the wood being used — the act of making itself is on the whole foreseeable. The "making" of *art* is a quite different activity. It is rarely notable for the kind of foreseeing and pre-determination that distinguish mere craftsmanship. Even the making of a film may not be regarded as the slavish execution of a prefixed script; and there is plenty of good sense in the view of Vera Chytilova,[37] a well-known contemporary Czech director, that the making of a film is not the mere illustration of its script; that the latter is only the provisional foundation of a film; and that during its (subsequent) making quite a few such changes may have to be made as are a clear departure from the script. Further, we have it on the authority of Herbert Read that Picasso rarely knew "in advance what he . . .[was] going to put on the canvas, nor . . . [would] he decide what colours to use . . . [the crucial thing here being] a renunciation of the will and a surrender to the promptings of the unconscious."[38] And should we seek a senior (Indian) classical musician's opinion on the

---

36. S.K. Langer, *Feeling and Form,* Routledge & Kegan Paul, 3rd Impression, 1963, p. 40.

37. Expressed in the course of an "interview" during our 12th Film Festival, January 1989.

38. W.G. Archer, *Indian and Modern Art,* George Allen & Unwin, 1959, p. 60.

matter, he would insist that at the moment of opening a recital what he decides (and knows he is going) to do is simply the treatment of a particular composition in a specific *rāga-tāla* setting; that, in respect of the details and disposition of the musical filling, what he knows only is that they are nowhere to be allowed to flout the demands of the specific melody and rhythm (or *rāga* and *tāla*) chosen; and that such (mere) generalities relating to the order of presentation have also to be kept in mind as the precedence of *sthāyī-antarā* over *bahlāvā, baṛhat* and *taan*s, or of *vilambit* in relation to *drut* compositions. But, he would hasten to add, exactly how many times the *bandish* is to be sung (or played), which particular *taan* is to have priority over others, the precise moment of switching over to the *drut* composition, or the exact length of time for which the voice is to tarry at the *tār shadj,* — all this is quite undecided as one begins, and has to be left to the impulse of the moment. Further, there is here a positive feature which explains why the progression of our music cannot be predetermined in detail. Where a musician performs in the presence of some *rasika*s, he is generally quick to register their reactions; and just as the making of a painting is (in general) not the breathless execution of a prefixed plan, but a sensitive response to, and determination by, what the presently completed detail of the work itself seems to demand or suggest, so the musician — if he is not a mere craftsman — depends for the next step quite often on how exactly the immediate *svara-samūha* sounds, and also, if but occasionally, on how the *rasika*s react to the details of ongoing music.

3. Further, the good that the arts do to us is not the same as what we gain from the crafts. The latter cater for

our specific *needs,* say, for food, shelter, clothing and ornament. Builders, weavers and jewellers are therefore of obvious value to society. But the making, contemplation, and appreciation of works of art relate to our attitudes, states of being, and cognitive/affective capacities. By creating a work of art the artist gets the deep, inner delight of effective self-expression which he cannot possibly equate with any other gain. As for the *rasika*s, they too can benefit richly from contemplation of works of art. It is an admitted fact that aesthetic experience relieves tensions and checks destructive impulses, refines perception, and "develops . . . imagination, and along with it the ability to put oneself in the place of others" which is so essential even for the maintenance of good inter-personal relations in daily life. What is more, on entering the world of art we may at the same time get closer to our fellow-beings:

> If two people listen to the same music or see the same painting, insofar as they have learned to make similar responses, they share an experience. All shared experience helps to bring people together in friendship and mutual respect. Aesthetic objects . . . represent a quintessence or distillation of certain qualities of experience, and any two people anywhere who enjoy one of these qualities will have a bond between them.[39]

Now, it is clear that if the way we have distinguished art from craft is accepted, much that is commonly classed as art may have to be called craft and vice versa. Quite a few of our Kathak dancers perform but mechanically, providing only a *laboured* exposition of rhythm. The TV serial *Nukkaḍ*, on the other hand, has been generally a *captivating* performance by a well conducted team, though merely because of this one

39. M.C. Beardsley, *Aesthetics — Problems in the Philosophy of Criticism*, Harcourt, Brace & World, Inc. 1958, p. 575.

consideration the whole genre of TV serials cannot be regarded as a new art-form. At the same time it would surely be wrong to insist that just because Kathak has for long been regarded as a major form of our classical dance, its exponents must *all* be called artistes, and that *those who participated in the serial* in question can at best be called good craftsmen, if not entertainers, just because such *presentations* have not yet come to be commonly regarded as art. Whittick is indeed right when he contends that *any* activity which aims, in the main, at the creation of a new aesthetic experience should be regarded as an art, and that the traditional list of five fine arts is a bit too narrow. Kant included landscape gardening too among the fine arts, and he is here justified. For,

> when a landscape gardener arranges trees, lawns, shrubs, flowers, water and perhaps sculpture in a park, or in the ground of a mansion, he is working primarily with aesthetic intention, and with a feeling for colour, line, mass, light and shadow, very much as a painter.[40]

Art-Craft Relation

1. Though the primary aim of a craftsman is to produce articles which serve some everyday purpose, he can, if he so desires, easily invest them with beauty and some quite new decorative features, and so turn them into possible objects of aesthetic regard. Indeed, though they are obviously meant to cater for our primary needs, vessels and cloths of everyday use have always been more than mere objects of utility. In the Indian tradition specially:[41]

---

40. Arnold Whittick, "Towards Precise Distinctions of Art and Craft", *BJA*, Winter "84, p. 51.

41. The extract that follows has been taken from Krishna Chaitanya's critical piece "A halation of beauty" in The Hindustan Times of 14.6.1987. The bracketed portions in the quote are all insertions, barring the first one.

> There has always been interaction between arts and crafts . . . For all we know, weavers may have tried to make their fabrics more and more transparent because of the erotic fantasies of poets who tried hard to discern the form of the beloved through the drapery that covered her. The *haṁsa lakṣaṇa sāṛī* [with a border showing a row of swans] is described in Sanskrit texts and can be seen in Ajantā . . . [and] the very rich decorative patterns in grille and inlay . . . [that distinguish the tomb of Aurangzeb in Aurangabad] . . . have been adapted for fabrics and furnishings.

Yet such instances of relatedness are hardly enough ground for denying that art is not quite the same kind of activity as craft. Both sides of the matter have to be kept in mind. The *fact* that there is craft *in* every art is one thing; the *view* that art may be generally regarded *as a* kind of craft is quite another.[42] There is nothing odd in a book's being entitled: *The Craftsmanship of Keats;* but many would join Collingwood in objecting to the view of Plato and Aristotle that poetry too is a craft.[43] No student of Hindi literature would agree that just because he appears to be much more conversant with the rules of prosody, Keshav may be regarded as a better poet than Sūrdās. Art includes craft; but it does not stop there. Craft is here used for a quite distinct end; namely, the creation of forms which are (at least) pleasing in themselves; its role here, though undeniably essential, is hence but subsidiary.

To conclude, art and craft are not only related to, but distinct from, each other. As a kind of skill, craft is present in every art. Further, motifs and images from the region of art have been freely availed of by craftsmen to beautify their own work. Yet, on the whole, the distinction holds, and is clear and

---

42. S.K. Langer, *Feeling and Form,* p. 384.
43. R.G. Collingwood, *The Principles of Art,* Oxford: Clarendon Press, 1955 Reprint, p. 18.

overriding. Any kind of activity that aims at creating forms of intrinsic charm or significance, or any class of artefacts which are commonly expected to evoke disinterested delight may be said to be art. Craft, on the other hand, is skill exercised essentially in creating objects of utility.

Our main concern, however, is art's relation to *philosophy*, not only because the kind of aesthetics we have picked for attention is philosophical, but because, in view of the obvious fact that art is *directly attended to and enjoyed* in galleries and concert halls, the propriety of seeking to relate it to a highly *intellectual and often abstract* subject like philosophy may be easily questioned.[44]

Now there is no doubt that art is quite different from philosophy. Philosophy just cannot be done without a careful use of language. The bulk of art, on the other hand, does not use the verbal medium, literature and vocal music[45] being the only arts that build upon words. There *are* people who would like even painting and sculpture to be regarded as *a kind of* language on the ground that, after all, works in the region of these arts also appear to "say" something. But what could this suggestion really mean? If the words, *a kind of*, are taken to suggest that art is not language *as it is commonly understood*, our insistence on the art-philosophy difference would remain unaffected. In case the words in question are taken to imply only that art too *is expressive* (more or less) like language we may not object to the emphasis on expressiveness taken quite generally; but we would surely have to reject the suggestion, in case it is actually made, that non-verbal art is expressive *in the way of language*. For, whereas in the everyday use of language, verbal meaning is detachable from the particular words which

44. I say (only) "*often* abstract" because existentialism and phenomenology cannot be said to be abstract.

45. That is, all singing barring *ālāpa* of the *dhruvapad* manner.

presently convey it — insofar as it can be conveyed by synonymous words from a quite different language — the meaning, or rather the *import* of a particular work of art cannot be accurately provided by any other work, for the simple reason that the distinctive perceptual elements (or "perceptua") of any work of art are integral to its overall meaning. The way in which a work of art is related to what it "says" is indeed to be clearly understood. It does not merely transmit or convey, but is *an embodied revelation of its meaning.* Art is not the mere index, but the necessary locus of its meaning. Precisely for this reason it would be patently wrong if the words "a kind of" are deleted from the proposed view we are discussing and it is categorically said that art is a language. To comprehend the meaning of written or spoken language we have to proceed in a determinate before-after order; but where what we seek to get at is the "meaning" of, say, a painting or sculpture, we are free to begin with a notice of whichever part of the work catches the eye, though of course every detail of the work must be attended to ultimately.

There is a good deal more that *distinguishes* art from philosophy. The purpose of philosophy is to clarify our ideas, and to determine the truth of our views by means of analysis, discussion and argument. The process of art-making too involves a good deal of thinking and self-criticism. But the aim of such ideal activity, here, is not to clarify, refute or support a theoretical position in the way of philosophy, but to ensure better performance or to make the work better organized or more expressive or truly representational. For instance, where a Kathak danseuse prepares and rehearses for a forthcoming recital, and checks the *pace* of a particular pattern or the *sequence* of the various numbers that she proposes to include in the recital, her objective is (a) proper projection of the *form* of the pattern — so that it may neither appear flaccid nor huddled because of the excessively slow or too quick sequence of the constituent syllables (or *bols*) — and (b) greater impact of the individual numbers achievable by so putting them in a before-after order that their distinctive character may be heightened by virtue of contrast, as of *vilambit* with *drut* or of *śṛṅgāra* with *vīra rasa* numbers. The painter too must carefully check as to which two colours, if used adjacently, would appear to go well together.

Such agreeable adjacence, of which a clear instance in our music is provided by the working of *saṁvāda*, may be called *aesthetic* consistency. It is quite different from logical consistency which is of paramount value to the philosopher. The former is the mutual agreeableness of two details of *fact* in respect of their *sensuous* character, say, look in the case of colours or sound in that of musical *svaras*. The latter (or logical consistency) is an understood accord of verbal *meaning*. In art, as already pointed out, congruence or harmony simply means that the elements of the work appear to go well together — to direct contemplation. To say that *shadj* and *madhyam* seem to belong to each other in a *rāga* like *Kedāra* is to admit the working of *aesthetic* consistency. Philosophically, on the other hand, if we object to such talk: "A is the *best* student in the class, but B is also *as good* as A," we protest simply because the meaning of the word "best" — that is, "better than *everyone else*" — prevents us from saying that the best can have an equal too. Here, our appeal is to logical consistency.

Yet it is neither possible nor desirable to keep philosophy away from art. Philosophy today is not so much a subject of study with a distinct subject matter as a sustained and systematic attempt to clarify our ideas. Matters relating to art are in fact freely discussed by critics, educators and artistes themselves. How then can we object if philosophy offers to improve the quality of this ongoing debate? Concepts like *form*, *feeling* and *expression*, which occur so freely in our talk about art, are often misconstrued, and so the assistance of philosophy should only be welcome to all those who are really serious about understanding art.

In contemporary aesthetics, indeed, what we find generally dominant is analysis of theories of art — say, as form, expression, or as symbol — and of certain concepts related to or within art: for instance, the concept of the *work of art,* and the concepts of representation, illusion, intention, and meaning within the arts. This is however only the focus, not the whole ambit of present-day aesthetics which (we have seen) is visualized very widely today. It is regarded as a serious, academic and many-sided concern with *the arts.* The viewpoint of philosophy is only one of the many approaches here listed. In other words, *philosophical* aesthetics is only a form or part of aesthetics taken generally. But whatever be the kind of aesthetics, its subject of study is held to be *art*; and today the word "beauty" is often left out.

This omission, however, is not quite fair. It is true that a good deal of contemporary art cannot be said to be *beautiful* in case the word is taken to mean: "of immediate appeal to sense." But, on the other hand, it is equally true that there *are* numberless works which seem to be paradigms of beauty. Further, the beauty of nature cannot be kept out of the purview of aesthetic experience, which is freely discussed in books on aesthetics. Historically, aesthetics has always been importantly concerned with beauty: and today, specially since the appearance of Mary Mothersill's book: *Beauty Restored,*[46] aestheticians are perhaps not as averse to the concept of beauty as they were till a few years back. In India too, as we know, *saundarya* (or beauty) has always dominated thinking about art. Therefore it seems demanded that philosophical aesthetics be regarded as the philosophy of art *and beauty.*

46. Oxford, Clarendon Press, 1984.

The supplement, *and beauty,* would, on the one hand, make our understanding of aesthetics adequate to its traditional character; and, on the other hand, provide not only for the possible disjunction of works of *art* from *beauty,* but for distinct lines of enquiry demanded by the two concepts. As the philosophy of *art,* aesthetics is concerned with such specific questions as the following: the nature and definability of art; the ontological status of a work of art or the relation of art to Being; the place of art in the entire panorama of human activities, for art is a distinctively *human* phenomenon; and, above all, the meaning and truth of aesthetic discourse. And where it focuses on *beauty,* philosophical aesthetics studies such problems as the nature and effects of beauty, and analysis of the whole "hierarchy" of the concepts that are cognate to the beautiful, namely, the graceful and the pretty, the grand or the majestic, and the sublime. A discussion of this "hierarchy" would naturally come up against the question as to how or in what precise respect one concept differs from the others; and an inquiry will also be needed into "the ways in which the beautiful in its wide . . . sense is different from and . . . related to the good, the true, and finally to being itself."[47] All these lines of enquiry cannot possibly be pursued in this essay, but it would surely be of help to see, if in brief, how even the more abstract ones of these can give us some interesting ideas.

Consider, for instance, the relation of art to *Being* as Heidegger visualizes it. It is common to look on works of art as *objects that we see in galleries and museums.* But this is only a secondary relation of art. Originally, a work of art is *a revelation of Being.* Here, we may note, *Being* is to be taken not in any transcendental (supernatural, mystical) sense, but simply as what is there historically, that is, in a specific time-place setting; and "revelation," as projection of the essential or typical

47. C.W. Nwodo's essay, "Philosophy of Art Vs Aesthetics", in *BJA,* Summer 1984, pp. 200-01.

functional reality of an object. Accordingly, Heidegger values Van Gogh's painting, *Two Shoes,* not because it is the faithful representation of a particular pair, but because it is revelatory of the pressure and distortion that the peasants' shoes generally suffer as they trudge — day in, day out — through craggy and uneven pathways straggling across the fields. The farmers themselves only use the shoes; they do not focus on the shoes' functional *career.* The painting does it — and projects the truth effectively. The point of what Heidegger here says is borne out by Van Gogh's own report on the logic of his creative effort in producing another notable work:

> I have tried hard to paint (*The Potato-Eaters*) in such a way that the spectator is immediately struck by the idea that these people, eating potatoes in the lamplight, have dug them up with the same hands with which they are now taking them out of the dish; that they are real workers . . . have literally earned their food. . . . I was not interested in creating something that somebody might think "good" or "beautiful" . . . I . . . have searched for *the ultimate pattern* and . . . it might prove to be a *real peasant picture.*[48]

As a real pesant picture, we may note, this work has a general relevance, and a whole segment of farmers' real life is captured on the canvas — "the same hands" growing potatoes, digging them up, eating them, the dim lamplight (we may add) not quite revealing the soil that still clings to the hands. All in all, it betokens the labour that precedes the humble meal. However, though the point we have just tried to make is not without sense, its relation to Being is not the only way of looking at art. How its *beauty* is related to the good and the true is also a fit object of philosophic enquiry. Consider, for instance, Maritain's view that "the beautiful is not a kind of truth, but a kind of good; the perception of the beautiful . . . is

48. M.E. Tralbaut, *Van Gogh — A Pictorial Biography,* London: Thames and Hudson, 1959, Italics added.

not so much a kind of knowledge as a kind of delight."[49] The meaning here may not be easy to seize, but a little close attention is enough to show that what Maritain here says has a ready appeal. It is of course not easy to *define* beauty, but one thing is clear. Whatever strikes us as beautiful *delights* us; we just like it and feel impelled to call it *good*. On the other hand, relating beauty to truth or knowledge is never so easy or natural; it calls for some effort, is a strain on the mind; and so is removed from that immediate appeal which is always the impact of whatever strikes us as beautiful.

Such philosophic reflection, however, is not the only discriminating way of being concerned with art. Art appreciation and art criticism are two other ways which involve both percipience and analytic thinking in varying measure. Yet they both should and *can* be distinguished from philosophical aesthetics.

> Instead of *reflecting* on the nature, significance, or reality of works of art, *art appreciation* consists largely in looking at . . . [or in some other way contemplating them] on different occasions *and in different moods*, so that one may gradually come to *enjoy and savour* everything in a work of art that is there to be enjoyed and savoured. This appreciation may involve lectures, demonstrations [*or lec-dems*, such as the ones which are organized by Delhi's own *Spicmacay*], and informal conversations with others; but it may also be *silent*, consisting only of *repeated exposure* to the works of art.[50]

The keywords in the above extract are actual and "repeated exposure" to works of art; for by focusing on these two words we can easily see what art appreciation really is. Take the case

---

49. Jacques Maritain, *Art and Scholasticism and the Frontiers of Poetry*, tr. J.W. Evans, University of Notre Dame Press, p. 26.

50. John Hospers, *Introductory Readings in Aesthetics*, New York: The Free Press, 1969. Italics and bracketed words added.

of music, for instance. Just as a child is enabled to distinguish sweet from sour taste by actual tasting, so a listener is enabled to mark off a lower note from a higher one by actually listening to the music himself. It is true that the child may learn to use the *word "sweet"* for the eatable (which really has this taste) by following its parent's habitual use of specific words for particular articles of food; but what *sweet taste* itself really is, for which the *word "taste"* is used, has to be sensed by the child on its own. Similarly, a *rasika* (or trained listener) may well try to help a tyro by saying (while pointing to a particular note): "Look! this *svara* is a little higher than the one you have just heard"; but the actual difference has to be perceived by the lay listener himself. This explains the traditional Indian emphasis on the metaphor of *tasting* in respect of art appreciation. We have to listen to music ourselves and repeatedly if we are to perceive even minuscule differences between the pitch of two adjacent notes; and this is quite as true of perceiving even the slightest changes of tempo. The Indian word for such percipience is *nigāh* or the ability to see not only the differences or changes we have just referred to, but even the slightest suggestion of transgression of the grammatical limits of a *rāga*. No amount of reading books on music can replace this personal *and repeated* contemplation of actual music. A talk on music can only *invite our attention* to specific details, segments or genres of music. Truly to see how all these actually sound, flow, or interrelate is to be marked by the listener himself. Nor does a *lec-dem* necessarily explain why the opening line of a song is called *sthāyī* or *when* it is to be regarded as a good specimen of its type.

Such interpreting and evaluating are the task of *art criticism* which always uses language and (unlike art appreciation) can never be "silent." What is more, if a critical write-up on a work of art — say, on a poem or painting — is successful, "it will enable the reader to see in the work . . . many features, *lines of connection, and subtleties of detail* that he did not perceive before." To illustrate the point it would be better to turn to poetry in preference to the other arts, just because works from their regions cannot be presented here. So let us consider the following lines from Shakespeare's *The Winter's Tale* (Act IV, Scene IV):

> . . . daffodils
> That come before the swallow dares and take
> The winds of March with beauty.

Here, without the expert help of a literary critic an ordinary reader is likely to content himself with a grasp of the merely literal meaning of the words which is easy to get. Such understanding, however, cannot be the source of any delight (as distinct from merely cognitive apprehension) because there is no *obvious* charm here of impressive language or lilting rhyme. But see now what the following critical interpretation reveals:

> As against the swallow that *dares* into the scene from afar, the daffodils just *come* or arrive on the scene gently, without any fanfare, so to say. The word *dares* supplements the image of the long-winged *migratory* bird, on the one hand; and balances it against the flowers' gentle appearance (because they only *come*), on the other — providing a kind of aesthetic relief. A swallow's meteoric streaks into the blue can easily coerce attention, but the daffodils' quiet act of just taking "the winds of March with beauty" is likely to be missed or only vaguely noticed by a passer-by; which is probably why the poet has chosen to picture it. But the real charm of the lines dawns upon the reader's mind only when he visualizes that a flower which only takes (or receives) the caressing winds cannot but lend itself to them; and that, therefore, a gentle and (so to say) unmurmuring *swaying* of the *diffodils* is the real import of the lines, though of course the charm tends to dissipate in the very course of being so accounted for, analytically. It should now be clear how (as we have

said in an extract already cited) criticism can make us see some "lines of connection" and "subtleties of detail" that are very likely to be missed by uncritical attention.

Music criticism can also be of similar help. Take the case of a Ravi Shankar-Ali Akbar (*sitār-sarod*) *jugalbandī*, for example. There is hardly any lover of Indian music who has not been fascinated by such music, but its inner knitwork — and so the secret of its charm — as also, if incidentally, the true aesthetic function of a *jugalbandī*, are revealed to us only by critical write-ups such as the following:

> . . . The two performers . . . try to reinforce each other's effects by matching playing in one octave with similar or simultaneous playing in the other; and by trying to articulate audibly what the partner's playing as it ends, demands by suggesting, either as continuance or as a repartee (*sawāl-jawāb*). The one reinforces, completes, or just caps with the dainty singleness of just one note, the meaning or the manner of the patterns of the other. *Sometimes it appears as if one heaves a sigh and the other lends a tear to it.*[51]

This extract, we may note, is a critic's actual reaction to a particular recital by the two maestros, though it is generally relevant to their usual playing too, as a duo. Philosophical aesthetics, on the other hand, does not *confine* itself to individual works or some select genres of art; and as a branch of philosophy, it raises and discusses the time-honoured basic questions of philosophy, in respect of art — questions (as we have said earlier) of meaning, truth, reality, knowledge and value. It is true that neither art criticism nor philosophical aesthetics can do without language; but whereas the former only uses some concepts without worrying as to what they

51. S.K. Saxena, "Essentials of Hindustānī Music" in *Diogene*, 45, Paris, 1964.

really mean, the latter — that is, philosophical aesthetics — takes pains to clarify these concepts at length, — concepts like the aesthetic, beauty (or aesthetic value), meaning . . ., representation; expression; . . . [and] art. . . .[52]

Such concepts, it is obvious, relate to art in general, and are not confined to any particular form of it. This indeed is what distinguishes aesthetics clearly from criticism which focuses, as a rule, on individual works of art. At the same time, aesthetics is by no means quite unrelated to criticism. The two *are* related, first, because we cannot do aesthetics until we have some critical statements to work on; and, second, because, as *metacriticism*, aesthetics becomes a natural demand of critical statements when we try to clarify what they really mean. To illustrate, were we faced with statements such as the following: "art is a symbolic expression of the forms of human feeling" (Langer), aesthetical thinking may easily begin by asking as to what exactly is meant here by: *symbol* (as against *sign* and *signal*); *expression* (as artistic, not physiognomic); and *feeling in general* as against specific, designable emotions (such as joy and sorrow). Similarly, where a critic admires a picture as one which shows a *profound sense of reality* we may naturally wonder as to what exactly the word *reality* here means.

> [It] may mean the surface appearance of things, the sense qualities that are open to immediate inspection: smells, tastes, textures. A "profound sense of reality" could then be a strong interest in sense appearance, a fascination with it, a desire to reproduce it. . . . This . . . [interpretation] fits the French impressionists, but not the . . . Gothic and Byzantine artist . . . [to whom *reality* means] a . . . supernatural world known not through sense experience but through intuition or pure reason.[53]

---

52. John Hospers, *Introductory Readings in Aesthetics*, p. 2.

53. M.C. Beardsley, *Aesthetics — Problems in the Philosophy of Criticism*, New York: Hartcourt, Brace & World Inc., 1958, p. 5.

In other words, *aesthetics as metacriticism* is critical thinking about the concepts (and criteria) which a critic merely uses but does not himself clarify.

But, one may ask, is the *meaning* of our talk about art — that is, of the words it comprises — the only concern of philosophical aesthetics? Does it have nothing to do with our actual *experience* of contemplating art? The answer, affirming philosophy's positive interest in art contemplation, is provided by the *phenomenological* way of doing philosophical aesthetics which may now be distinguished from the *linguistic* approach.

The analytic approach, associated in particular with Bertrand Russell and the early work of Wittgenstein, maintains that analysis of language is the basis for resolution of philosophical issues. It therefore attaches great importance to clarity of meaning and protests against glib generalizations which merely ignore differences of verbal meaning and so also the diversity of facts that words signify. How these two emphases actually work is easy to illustrate:

a. Consider, for instance, the following high-sounding tribute:

> . . . The music of Lourie is an ontological music, in the Kierkegaardian style, one would also say "existential." It is born in the singular roots of being, the nearest possible juncture of soul and spirit.[54]

Now, we cannot say anything about the truth or falsity of this compliment unless we are first somehow enabled to see what the words here used really mean. Yet this meaning is precisely what we here find very difficult to determine. It would make perfect sense if someone said, "He put himself into the song." The meaning, then, would clearly be: he sang wholeheartedly.

---

54. E. Elton (ed.), *Aesthetics and Language*, Oxford: Basil Blackwell, 1970, p. 2.

But the words that the extract cited uses make it patently unclear on the whole. The ontological is that which relates to Being; "existential," in philosophy, means "based on personal experience," "concrete" as opposed to "abstract." Up to this point we may perhaps agree to grant some meaning to the utterance; for it does make sense to suggest that music gains in quality where, instead of being an exercise in mere technique (and so "abstract") it is full of some feeling recollected (maybe) from a deeply personal experience (and is in that sense "concrete"). But the words that follow: "born . . . soul and spirit" serve only to prevent us from regarding the extract as having a determinate meaning on the whole. We may even agree to distinguish *soul* from *spirit* (as we are required to by the word *and* conjoining the two as "soul *and* spirit"), for whereas *soul* may be taken as that immaterial part of man *which is believed to survive the body after death* (that is, as *ātmā*), *spirit* may be interpreted merely as *prāṇa* or that life-principle which animates the body of living things. But the words "*nearest possible juncture* of soul and spirit" posit our ability to discriminate between varying degrees of closeness between soul and spirit. Such a suggestion can only bewilder the reader.

b. Take, next, the following emphatic thesis of Clive Bell:

> The representative element in a *work of art* may or may not be harmful; *always* it is irrelevant.[55]

Now, what do the words, *a work of art,* here mean? If we take them *along with "always"* (as we are required to — mark the semi-colon which *conjoins* the two segments of the sentence) they could only mean: "*every* work of art which has a representative element." But to suggest that the representative element is always irrelevant to the aesthetic value of *every* work of art which has it (that is, the representative element) is simply to miss *the difference between the various arts* because in some of

55. Clive Bell, *Art,* Grey Arrow Edition 1961, p. 36.

them, as in landscape painting, the element in question is undeniably important. So the thesis in question only bespeaks an aesthetician's excessive craving for generality. Do not the characters, situations and happenings — which our epics, *Rāmāyaṇa* and *Mahābhārata represent* (in the sense of bringing clearly before the mind, or setting forth in words) — provide a rich and impressive content to them, instead of impairing their value as literary works? Does not the greatness of Michelangelo's works painted on the ceiling of Sistine Chapel depend very importantly on *the exalted character* of the subjects they *represent*? It is surely this quality and not merely the size or extent of the whole superlative effort that Goethe had in mind when he remarked: "Without having seen the Sistine Chapel no one can form an appreciable idea of what [not merely how much] one man can achieve."[56]

Yet, though scrupulous attention to the *language* that we use in aesthetic discourse is surely necessary to ensure clarity of meaning, it is by no means enough for a proper understanding of our *total concern with art*. The creation and contemplation of art and our non-verbal responses to it — that is, how it evokes semblances of feeling, quickens our imagination, and how it relates to our life-experience as a whole — all this has also to be taken into account. It is precisely this need which is met by the *phenomenological* approach to aesthetics. How this approach is distinctive can be easily brought out, in spite of the fact that, insofar as they both arose as a challenge to idealism, phenomenology has generally tended to work along with existentialism.

One basic emphasis of phenomenology is on the need (a) to philosophize without any presuppositions or theoretical bias, and therefore to dwell upon the phenomena of art (as

56. Rolf Schott, *Michelangelo*, London: Thames and Hudson, 1st edn., 1964, p. 38.

experienced) without sundering their delicate tissues through analysis; and (b) to neither reduce nor elevate art to something which it is *not* in actual fact. For example, where a painting actually looks warm in its colours and vibrant in its brushwork to the contemplating eye, phenomenology would like us to just keep insisting that the work looks so, instead of *contriving* the explanation that, insofar as what we call warmth and vibrancy (or energy, animation) in real life cannot be actually there in a picture which is literally lifeless, the qualities in question are only our subjective reaction (fictitiously) superimposed on the picture; for, so to explain the experience will be only to divide its actually felt singleness into two artificial halves. The manifest seamlessness is its truth, and the aesthetician has to hold on to it. Indeed, if even in respect of the everyday perception of an object we cannot determine the precise contribution of the percipient and mark it off from what the thing itself presents, how can we overcome this inability in the case of aesthetic experience where the focusing of attention is generally more intense and the subjective responses — comprising half-blown impulses and imaginings, all quickened by the work — far more varied than in the case of perceptions of daily life? It is not that phenomenology forbids us from registering the *details* of an aesthetic experience. What it insists on only is that our use of language here should be "illuminative" rather than disintegrative. Thought just cannot work without marking differences in its object, but it can yet avoid sundering the object's unity and regarding it as a mere aggregate of separate parts.

Phenomenology itself makes some very helpful distinctions. One of these opposes *intention* to (what it chooses to call) *intentionality.* An intention is a plan. It is more or less fixed in the sense that one is expected to stick to it generally. Further, the aim of an intention is some attainment that is *yet to come.* Intentionality, on the other hand, is one's involvement with what is present *here and now.* Now, to turn to the *creation* of art, what seizes its essential logic is *intentionality,* not *intention.* The making of a work is very rarely the quite slavish execution of a predetermined plan. It may well be that as he sets out to create a work of art the artist has a vague, general plan in his mind. But when creation actually begins he (as a rule) focuses on the detail just accomplished, registers *its* aesthetic demand, and then proceeds accordingly, with the result that when the work is completed it may turn out to be quite unlike its vaguely prefigured character. To conclude, it is the concept of intentionality, as against that of mere intention, which enables us to explain the *emergent* character of those works of art which are truly creative.

Finally, insofar as we have spoken of the joint working of existentialism and phenomenology, we may dwell upon and clarify two points: first, how the (combined) aesthetics of existential phenomenology can deliver some basic truths about art-experience; and, secondly, how the linguistic-analytic and phenomenological approaches are both required for an adequate understanding of the facts of art and art-experience. Now, as for the first point, here is one clear truth provided by existential phenomenology: a work of art (as contemplated) presents experience as unbroken or pre-judgemental. In other words, no clear distinctions are here drawn between what we feel, think or imagine, or even between what is now presented to us, and its colouring by reminiscence. As for the equal necessity of the (other) two approaches we are dealing with, the following example from the region of music should serve. Suppose, while listening to the basic composition (or *bandish*) of a *khyāl* recital, *as it is gently accelerated in pace* by the singer, we are struck by the sudden appearance of a kind of bloom in the *sthāyī* as it arrives sharply and designedly at the *sama,* and are therefore moved to say: "See, how well it has come to bloom!" (देखिए ! कैसी खिली है स्थायी). Now, how exactly are we to make sense of or interpret these words of acclaim? The correct answer would be that here the *right verbal understanding* can be had *only if* we make the attempt all along *in the context of actual listening,* and discriminatingly, that is, with the help of experience (if any) of repeated exposure to such music in the past. The point may be clarified as follows:

Suppose, as we make the remark in question, it is also heard by a fellow listener who has no idea of what classical music really is. How will *he* understand our words of acclamation? Naturally, he would do this (if incorrectly) in the light of *his* own everyday experience and so look on what he has heard as a mere complex of varying sound and pace, and not *as art.* He is therefore very likely to think that we made the remark (in question) just because we noticed a certain expansion or distension in the music, because in everyday parlance (as against our talk about music *as art* to which he is alien) the word खिलना commonly evokes the image of an object's unfolding itself, or gaining a little *spread* or *distension.* But such interpreting will be clearly untrue to what has actually happened. By gently forcing the pace of singing a little, the vocalist has in fact *shortened* the intervals between the *svara-samoohas* and the *mātrās* (tonal phrases and beats) *reducing* the overall extent of the *bandish,* and thus making it and its inner linkages *more easily manifest to contemplation.* It is this increased ease of apprehension, aided of course by the literal liveliness of a slightly quicker pace, that makes the *sthāyī* appear to bloom. Of course, a major inner detail that the quickening of pace may here serve *to vivify* is the relation of the *sama* to the *way* the basic line (or *sthāyī*) attains to it. Because of the overall shortening, the preceding *svaras* now appear to be *heading for* the *sama* which therefore comes to look like the target of the passage, and so gives one the distinct impression of a little tension released, because of due attainment of what the *sthāyī* itself appears to demand, *that is, arriving at the sama.* In other words, instead of spreading out or becoming a little flaccid, the *sthāyī* which now appears to "bloom" has in fact become shorter (in musical space); and also, because of this little compression, more easily evident in its overall form and inner details. So the viewpoint of immediate and discriminating *experience* of music, or the phenomenological approach, is here essential for the right *understanding* of what the "blooming" of a *sthāyī* really means. Surely, the blooming of a flower, as the *visible* opening of its petals, is not the same as the *intelligible* bloom of a work of art's segments, occurring as improved *manifestness* of its knitwork and design. And should we decide to *speak* of the semblance (or the "blooming') evoked, we will have to be careful in our choice of words. The right words here will be: "स्थायी ज़रा सिमट गयी है" not "स्थायी ज़रा सिकुड़ गयी है!" As demanded by what we have called the linguistic-analytic approach, our speach has to be adapted precisely to the apprehended character of fact.

2

Embodiment and the Quest for Key Aesthetic Concepts[1]

I SEE some serious defects in the thesis of "embodiment." In this article I have tried to expose them, with due regard (I hope) to the theory and fact of art. Towards its close, I have proposed — quite briefly, and with but some show of reason — a new definition of art as creative invocation, with a view to setting up *presence*, in place of other words, as the key concept of aesthetics.

Reid regards "embodiment," not expression, as "the key-idea in the aesthetics of art."[2] Now, any concept which claims to be central to aesthetics has to meet some basic requirements. It must keep close to "the *fact* of creative art,"[3] or be a "first order"[4] word. On the other hand, it has to be of help to aesthetic *theory*. Is Reid's word, *embodiment*, able to meet these demands? Is it, as he believes, truly *preferable* to "expression?"

---

1. This essay first appeared in *Contemporary Indian Philosphy*, Series Two, ed. Margaret Chatterjee, London: George Allen & Unwin, 1974, pp. 194-214.
2. L.A. Reid, *Meaning in the Arts*, London: George Allen & Unwin, 1969, p. 95. Hereafter, throughout the essay, this work is referred to as *M.A.*
3. Ibid., p. 27.
4. Ibid., p. 200.

Our first task, obviously, is to see what "embodiment" means. The claim that it is "a defining characteristic formulated after careful examination of *all* kinds of art"[5] can be weighed only later. Now, at least once, Reid directly equates embodiment with "unity of form and content."[6] I find he also speaks of the one-many involvement that characterizes *all* art.[7] Are we then to *identify* "embodiment" with the form-content, one-many unities which are known features of good art? Perhaps yes; but then we miss not only what distinguishes Reid's view, but a crucial point of his disagreement with Langer. We must mark the "special" meaning that he gives to the word, "embodiment," that is, inseparable fusion (in art) of the ideal with "material," of "meaning," with perceptua.[8]

II

The Rival Concepts: Reid's Arguments

I may now turn to the details of Reid's arguments.

The first contrast that he draws is as follows:

> . . . "Embodiment" suggests the thing directly before us, while "expression" has the unfortunate tendency . . . to direct our thoughts *otherwards*, to feelings or ideas which are expressed.[9]

Let us see if it is really so.

---

5. L.A. Reid, op. cit., p. 224 (my italics).
6. Ibid.
7. Ibid., p. 235.
8. This *is* a "special" meaning of "embodiment" because it does not seem to follow from the word *directly*. "Embodiment" as creative or "emergent," as something which comes to "happen" only when artistic creation is completed — rather than as the gradual *act* of embodying according to a prefixed plan (Ibid., pp. 80-81) — is not a "distinctive" meaning. It would certainly not *distinguish* Reid's view from that of Langer.
9. M.A., pp. 77-78 (my italics).

Consider the concepts, first, as meaningful words. Does "embodiment," thus regarded, "*suggest* the things directly before us?" It does not; for, we are here interested only in meaning, and this does not require anything to be "directly" before us. The suggestion in question arises only when some "seeing" in the mind's eye here surreptitiously enters, with some felt insistence on what is thus "seen." Otherwise, what "embodiment" *means* simply is that some content or meaning is embodied in a form or medium. "Expression," too, as a word, implies a distinction (and relation) between "what is expressed" and "that which expresses." But in both cases the distinction falls within, or rather *is* the meaning; and in the case of neither word is there any going *otherwards*.

I suspect in the extract cited a dual vitiation of argument by spatial imagery. "Embodiment" is turned, without notice, into *an* "embodiment" that we *find;* and "otherwards," in the case of expression, into the spatial "outside."[10]

From meaning let us now turn to fact — to "things" that are expressive or embodiments. Consider, first, "things" that are non-aesthetic, say, the "seeing" of "character in a person's face."[11]

This is, in Reid's view:

> . . . neither to perceive his body only nor to apprehend his character through his body, but to apprehend one single embodied person with distinguishable aspects. If I apprehend someone as sad, . . . I am not aware just of . . . feelings or a body behaving, but of a person — sad. . . .[12]

Now here, again, I see some confusion.

10. It is only this imagined spatiality which makes the protest seem pointed.

11. *M.A.*, p. 76.

12. Ibid.

It *is* correct to say that here I neither perceive the person's "body only" nor merely his feelings. Nor is the awareness simply one of "a body behaving." To say, here, that I "apprehend his character *through* his *body*" would also be inaccurate; for the fact in question[13] is the "seeing of character *in* a person's *face.*" But, one may add, to describe this "fact" as the apprehension of "one single embodied person with distinguishable aspects" would be just as wide of the mark. For, the emphasis of attention is *ex hypothesi* on the face; and its being non-identical with the body and with what it expresses is here certainly experienced, if only as felt. This is why the percipient himself would speak of the experience in some such words: "He looked sad," or: "I saw grief writ large on his face." No one would here think of saying: "I apprehended one single embodied person."

From the outside, and quite generally, it is certainly true that the object of experience is here "single" and undivided. But to say so is, in this case, at once to miss the specific, inner character of the experience, that is, how (or what) the object really appears to the percipient; it is merely to reduce the phenomenological to the existential.

A little more attention to words may help us in dealing with (a possible form of)[14] the objection under review *in the context of art*. Ordinarily, we speak of seeing character *in* a person's face, not of apprehending it "*through* his body." Unlike the latter — which may evoke the image of a squeeze, and make some of Reid's objections to "expression" seem valid — the former way of speech certainly keeps close to the undivided singleness of fact. But when my look *has* lingered at a very sad

13. *As I* have taken it.

14. The objection is: "expression" takes us away from the work. Its "possible form" that I here discuss is: what is expressed is pressed out of the work, and so if we say that a work is "expressive," we — with its "meaning" — move away from the work.

face — and, here, the sadness *is* "embodied" — would it at all appear *unnatural* if, turning a little discursive, I said that the face seemed expressive of deep, inner gloom? We must answer in the negative, unless it be assumed that *all* expression is "expression *through*." Such an assumption would be quite unwarranted; for, a simple meaning of "to express" is to "reveal."[15] Yet, some such supposal is clearly implicit in Reid's following protest:

> . . . feeling-import and "surface" are . . . in aesthetic experience so *inseparably* one that in this context it [would] sound artificial to say that art is projecting or expressing something else — "feeling."[16]

I disagree. What is (in fact) expressed is not necessarily *separated* from that which expresses; and the "separation" may not even be suggested when we *say* that something is expressive. Thus, when a face strikes us as, and is said to be *expressive* of sadness, whether we take the word as "expressive *of*" or as "expressive *to*," there is hardly any danger of misbelieving that the "sadness" exists apart from, or is in any way "loosened" from the face. Why should it be otherwise in the case of works of art?

Reid, we may note, does not deny expressiveness to the *elements* of art. But he is anxious to uphold the autonomy of *the total work*; and so he insists that the *materials* and the *elements* are so well organized *in* the work that the whole appears single and self-contained:

> . . . "Expressiveness in it melts into the wholeness of the individual form which you see. . . ."[17] "It has never been

15. Hospers rightly wonders if *this* meaning of "express" has received due attention in aesthetics. John Hospers: "The Concept of Artistic Expression", included in his *Introductory Readings in Aesthetics*, New York: The Free Press, 1969, p. 151.

16. *M.A.*, p. 63. My italics.

17. Ibid., p. 109.

> suggested in this book that in embodiment expression is annulled — only that expression is not the key criterion of the aesthetic."[18]

Now, I must at once say this baffles me. To hold with regard to, say, poetry that it takes up words (all of them meaningful) and weaves its wondrous magic with them, transfiguring sense into a whole of sheer verbal radiance;[19] and that yet what it produces in the end is *embodied meaning* rather than "*expressive form*," — this is, in my view, a mere assertion rather than the reasoned attainment of a truth.

Why does Reid have to speak thus? Evidently because of the fear that if meaning is "expressed" it would, so to speak, spill its locus, making the *work* itself self-transcendent. But the fear and the purpose it subserves are both here suspect. The autonomy of art is not the finality of a thing's rigid outlines. It is the seeming self-completeness of a *work* that we find satisfying. The *autonomy* here is a fullness that is felt. There is no risk of spilling, for there is no measured extent. And expression, we have seen, is not always an *activity* of *pressing out*. In art and psychophysical embodiment alike, it may well be a mere *mode or quality of being or appearing*. Where Reid protests that in the case of abstract drawing, so long as the process of creation is determined by what is found drawn[20] on

18. *M.A.*, p. 160.

19. Ibid., pp. 158-9. Reid openly speaks of "the work of art" as a "qualitative individual *charged with meaning* . . . [and as thus] able to *reveal* in its own important way." Ibid., p. 248: my italics. I invite attention to: *charged with* and *reveal.*

20. Ibid., pp. 108-9. Reid *here* underestimates the artist's *active* role in creation. Elsewhere (Ibid., p. 125) he himself protests against the (possible) attempt on the part of some artists to unduly minimize their own part in artistic creation. The truth, as Coleridge suggests, is that the mind, as engaged in composing, suffers "alternative pulses of active and passive motion."

Owens Barfield, *What Coleridge Thought*, London: OUP, 1972, p. 78.

the "paper," the artist cannot be said to be "expressing" himself, the word is used, quite properly, in the sense of an activity. But when a face is said to express sadness, the meaning simply is that the face *looks* sad. And whereas we may agree that (self) *expression* is not (quite) adequate to the *making* of a work, we may insist — without contradiction, by availing of its meaning as seeming — on applying the word to the work as *completed*.

I can here appeal to some of Reid's own instances. In the case of (Barbara Hepworth's) abstract drawing, determination of creative activity by the material character of lines and curves *results in* a new form "with its own special life";[21] and of the sculptures of Henry Moore it is just as true that they *say* something as that it is, in every case, the stone which says it.

Every work of art, I admit, is an "embodiment" if the word be taken to mean a deep, indivisible fusion of all that is there in the work; but all this blending is, in my view, subsidiary. Though needful admittedly, it *only makes for* the emergence of art; and if the work is finally aesthetic, it is only because of its ability to invite and hold disinterested attention; or, because of its expressiveness, far more frequently than only because of its striking quality.

Reid may be right in insisting that music does not *express* excitement or relaxation if the word is taken to mean "detach from the heard sounds." But he is wrong in suggesting that (some) music simply *has* the qualities in question, if the "having" referred to is mere containment. I am not sure if *all* good music can be said to be essentially expressive. But there *is* a kind of soulful music which does not merely have but *seems to teem with feeling*; and to such music as contemplated[22] the word "expressive" would be clearly apt, and "embodiment," quite irrelevant.

---

21. *M.A.*, p. 108.

22. As against our *explaining* why the music appeals.

It is however not merely cases of actual art, but some valid emphases in Reid's own view that make me question his choice of *embodiment*. I may put the matter thus:

Our concern here is with *the aesthetic* in art. *This* is revealed only in actual aesthetic experience. So, Reid rightly insists, in our quest for key aesthetic concepts we have "to keep close to the *fact* of direct contemplation of art." Such contemplation, or at least its "moment of . . . achievement," is "*natural* . . . absorption in the fullness of artistic meaning."[23] But if this so, and if it is proper — as it obviously is — to hold that the knowledge of art and "aesthetic testing" are (or involve) a kind of "indwelling,"[24] should not art be credited with a built-in openness in relation to "the discriminating percipient?"[25] We can only say "yes." But then, this "openness" must be *directly* provided for in a concept which claims to be pivotal in aesthetics. Does "embodiment" do this, and is not "expression" *in this respect* preferable?

This mere wonder, however, is hardly enough. In our critical concern with what is expressive, its relation to the percipient is not the only line of enquiry. "Expressive *how*" and "expressive of *what*," the manner and the content of expression, these are here just as proper concern of thought as "expressive to." But within the limits I must keep, and in accordance with the *present* concern of this essay — which is simply to meet one objection to "expression" — only the following may here be said about the content[26] of expression:

It is true that, as Reid insists, no critical language is quite adequate to the fact of art as *directly* contemplated — a "fact"

23. *M.A.*, p. 88. My italics.

24. Ibid., pp. 220, 234.

25. Ibid., p. 85.

26. The question as to the *manner* of expression is being wholly left out. It is, in my view, too intricate to admit of a summary account.

which is complex and yet without full-blown distinctions. But this is the understood negation to which all critical talk about[27] art is, in principle, subject. It is no special barrier to the language of expression; and if we only bear it in mind, quite generally, as we distinguish in words the life-content that a work "expresses," we keep to the "fact" in idea, even though in speech we move away from it. It is by no means very difficult to remember that whatever life-meanings "critical" dissection now lays open to view were, in aesthetic contemplation, all felt as mere accents in (or of) a complex, individual whole.

2. From the viewpoint of "content," however, there is another protest which Reid makes pointedly:

> "Expression" suggests, at least in some of its uses, events which had some sort of complete existence before they were expressed and became known in expression, whereas the aesthetic meaning which is embodied has no complete existence till it is born in embodiment.[28]

Now here too, I fear, Reid takes sides. Of embodiment he speaks in relation to its "aesthetic meaning"; but *expression* he considers in its "non-aesthetic" uses. Some of these uses of the word (expression) certainly suggest the complete existence of content even before "expression"; but so does "embodiment" in its everyday meanings. We speak freely of souls as embodied or of virtue made manifest in overt activity or attitudes. But in no such case we ever think that embodiment actually *makes* the content embodied. Alternatively, if "expression" too is taken in its special aesthetic uses, it may not at all suggest the complete existence of any content before (its) expression. To Susanne Langer, for instance, what is expressive is an *apparition*; and of this, she insists, *all* "elements" are created. What the expressive apparition says, *its* import, is quite new substance.

---

27. "About," not "of," as Reid points out. *M.A.*, p. 217.

28. Ibid., p. 78.

I think the only *clear* superiority of "embodiment" over "expression" is that in respect of meaning it is closer to materialness. *Theories* of expression do not all underrate the material in art. But expression, as a *word*, does not suggest concreteness as directly as the rival word does. Here too, however, one can rejoin in favour of "expression." If this word seems a little too ethereal, does not "embodiment" appear a bit too material to be directly applicable to the essentially non-sensuous form of, say, poetry? Reid himself sees it clearly that, if it is to become relevant to the literary arts too, the word "embody" has to be "*stretched* to include the whole range of what we can imagine."[29]

As for the charge that is here made against *expression*, does the defect in question, I ask, vitiate Langer's *theory* of art? Reid thinks it does. But let us see:

3. The protest to which we now turn relates to Langer's (allegedly) "ghostly" language. Reid complains that words like "apparition," "virtual" and "illusory" belie the great value of art's material bases.

Now the question here is about the meaning of some words. So we have to see how they have been used. Reid himself refers freely to Langer's *Problems of Art*.[30] But where his purpose is directly critical, instead of citing her words as they occur in the book, he merely picks them and weaves them into his own running comments, making them appear as manifest warrant for the protest being made. Consider, for instance, what he says about "apparition":

> The distinction of "apparition," though legitimate, is a conceptual distinction — and as conceptual must be opposed

29. *M.A.*, My italics.

30. S.K. Langer, *Problems of Art*, London: Routledge & Kegan Paul, 1957. In all subsequent references to this book (in this essay) I have used the abbreviation *P.A.*, instead of the full title.

> to the "material." But this does not imply that the conceptual distinctions stand for *separate* ontological objects, that the virtual image of the dance ("a display of interacting forces," etc.) is something *cut off* from the motions of the dancers ("People running around and twisting their bodies").[31]

The charge is that Langer *separates* the material from the aesthetic, that is, from "apparition" or the "virtual" art-image.[32] (*Her own words* in this context have been put in brackets in the extract just cited.) But let us see them now in their original context:

> In watching a dance, you do not see what is physically before you — *people running around or twisting their bodies;* what you see is a *display of interacting forces* . . . forces . . . which . . . are not the physical forces of the dancer's muscles. . . . A dance is an apparition of active powers, a dynamic image. . . . The more perfect the dance, the less we see its actualities. . . . The virtual dynamic image . . . (as) a work of art is a composition of tensions and resolutions.[33]

Now, the beginning of this passage indeed seems odd. If in watching a dance I do not see what is physically before me, what do I *watch*? What *is* a dance *without* bodily movements?

The point of such sceptical question is, however, merely apparent. It arises by ignoring the overall sense. The keyword here is "physically"; and I get at the real meaning thus:

When does a dance strike me as *mere physical movement*?

---

31. *M.A.*, p. 84, My italics.

32. If this charge is true Langer will have to be credited with the impossible view that the dancer's figure does not appear solid at any moment of the dance.

33. *P.A.*, pp. 5-8, My italics. *These* are the words around which Reid builds his protest.

Obviously, when I do not follow it as a work of art at all.[34] In such a case, all that I see is someone "running around." Conversely, when I respond to the dance as required — that is, aesthetically — I do not see *mere* physical movement. This is, in my view, the simple meaning here. Langer does not say (how could she?) that in contemplating a dance as art we do not *at all* see the danseuse and her movements, but only that we do not see plain bodily movement of the everyday kind. What is seen (merely) *physically* before us is one thing; what is apprehended aesthetically is quite another. "People running around or twisting their bodies" in daily life surely do not describe patterns or keep to chosen rhythm.

And what exactly do I here see aesthetically? Obviously "a display of interacting forces"; for, this is what dancing as an art truly is. Does this "display" exclude the dancer's bodily movements? No, it does not; and it cannot. But the turns and glides are here all so organized, transfiguring actualities,[35] and the unity worked up is itself so significant — because of the rhythmic tension and "resolution" that characterize it — that movement as *merely* physical is nowhere seen.

But the dancer's own figure — does *it* not remain visible throughout? Certainly, it does; but (in principle) never merely as it actually is. Slender, bony fingers here at once make for some effect — which may be that of a bloom or sparkle or of mere postural invitingness. In two leading forms of Indian classical dance, Bharata Nātyam and Oḍissī, even the basic posture is *markedly* different from the way a person normally stands; and, what is more, it is so striking[36] in itself that it does

34. This really happened when I first saw a ballet. I only *saw* movement.

35. *P.A.*, p. 6.

36. "Beautiful" certainly in the case of *Oḍissī*, and at least striking in our other styles. It may here be noted that the dot under ḍ in *Oḍissī* makes it truer to how the word as spoken actually sounds to the ear.

not at all allow the mind to think of *any* everyday posture. Conversely, whenever the posture lapses into a purely normal bearing — say, on the breathless completion of a hectic rhythmic pattern by an average Kathak[37] dancer — "the work of art breaks, the creation fails."[38] In such cases, I may add, when the pattern is *being danced*, physical power may be directly manifest, instead of being "used up"[39] and swallowed in the "dance"; whereupon what remains to be seen is mere "gymnastics and arrangements,"[40] and the aesthetic at once disappears.

Langer, I conclude, does not "cut-off" the "dance" from actual movements. She only means that here they are not seen in themselves. The "dance" assimilates them and insofar as (on Reid's own view) "assimilation and transformation does not mean annulment or elimination,"[41] I fail to see any point in the "protest."

In relation to painting, the objection in question may be met as follows:

Considered as an art-image, a picture is an *apparition* — in the sense that it is "a piece of purely visual space . . . nothing but a vision."[42] From this single idea that the picture is meant only to be seen, two other concepts emerge. First, insofar as it "exists only for perception," a picture is a *virtual* entity, quite

37. Kathak is the classical dance of north India.

38. *P.A.*, p. 10.

39. Ibid.

40. Ibid. It *is* true to say that "the more perfect the dance, the less we see its actualities" (Ibid., p. 6), assuming, of course, that we make a *trained* audience. Dancers in India wear the most gorgeous dresses; yet, after the recital, the really knowledgeable in our audiences hardly remember anything about the dancer's *dress* if she or he has danced really well.

41. *M.A.*, p. 165.

42. *P.A.*, p. 28.

unlike actual things which can be *used* for practical purposes;[43] and, secondly, because it is utterly different from actual space,[44] the purely visual space that a picture has may be said to be *illusory*. Langer explains:

> To call the art-image illusory is simply to say that it is not material; it is not cloth *and* paint-smooches, but space organized by balanced shapes with dynamic relations. . . .[45]

Here, the keyword is "and"; and the meaning simply is that a picture is not merely the additive (or "material") unity of canvas and pigments. Langer would readily agree that a Van Gogh picture cannot be rightly contemplated unless we attend to its "vibrant paint-smooches" too; but she would hasten to add that if we regard them aesthetically we do not perceive the smooches as mere marks on the canvas.[46] Surely, "one does not see a picture as a piece of spotted canvas."[47] Actual space merely "contains" things and movement. Pictorial space is, on the other hand, organic; it at once appears made by the shapes and volumes it displays, as their interactive unity. This is why pigment and canvas, as *distinguished* materials, are not to be seen in pictorial space.[48]

It should now be possible to make sense of the remark of Langer on music which troubles Reid specially and which runs as follows:

---

43. Cf. *P.A.*, p. 5.

44. Unlike the purely visual space of a picture, actual space has real depth and acoustical properties.

45. *P.A.*, p. 34. My italics.

46. Cf. *M.A.*, p. 85.

47. *P.A.*, p. 127.

48. The moment we distinguish them, through an effort of analytic attention, pictorial space disappears, and what remains to be seen is merely the "additive" space of actual life. Cf. Ibid., p. 28.

> In artistic production, the composer's materials must be completely swallowed up *in* the illusion they create. . . .[49]

Langer here speaks of that thorough assimilation of *materials* in music which makes for its *elements* — sonorous forms that *seem* to move, and are *therefore* called "illusory." It is true that every musical phrase or composition builds upon some actual tones and duration; and that the way we perceive these "materials" vitally determines how we react to the music aesthetically. What is more, they can all be distinguished by an analytical effort of attention. But, and this is here the essence of the matter, if the music presented is to seem truly aesthetic the "materials" must all conduce to it with inextricable jointness, and directly, that is, *without at all appearing to assert themselves against the flow.* This is what it really means to say that in music its "materials" are "swallowed up." As illustration, notice may here be taken of a detail of practice which sometimes disfigures north Indian classical music without outraging its grammar. At times, a classical vocalist chooses to sing *in* an excessively slow and expansive rhythm-cycle, simply to show off his ability to hold on to a very reposeful (or *vilambit*) rhythm. In such cases, the exaggerated slowness at once protrudes and makes the singing seem flabby, and laboured. The "materials" here may be taken to be *svara* and *tāla;* and "composition," to signify *bandish* — say, a *sthāyī-antarā* twosome. Now, where the materials seem merely put together, and are therefore simply found as they are in themselves, as in a *lakṣaṇa geet,* the music is rarely, if ever, admired for compositional excellence. On the other hand, where the whole form dominates and the *bandish* seems swinging, contemplative or at least self-completing, no detail is actively noted in its merely grammatical character. The *svara*s here appear as musical phrases that yearn or relax or gently swirl around, or pave the way to, the pivotal notes.[50]

---

49. *P.A.*, p. 39. My italics.

50. In so appearing, the *svara*s become *elements* and cease to be mere material.

The *sama* is seen here as the *target* of a musical flow, and not as a mere first beat. *Rāga* and *tāla* alike here appear "upgathered" as one. I do not deny that in listening to classical music we often look for single (salient) notes, in accordance with the individual nature of the *rāga* being rendered. But rarely, if ever, are we so disposed without the definite hope that they will be treated *in requisite ways.* The *gandhār* of *Darbārī* is to seem *āndolit* (oscillating); and the *madhyams* of *Kedāra* or the two *niṣāds* in *Miān-kī-malhār* also admit of a way of (beautifying) treatment which changes their mere, actual adjacence on the scale into a gentle, almost reverent *probing* for tonal details in the inside of the melodic flow.

It would therefore be wrong to regard the talk of "materials" being "swallowed up" as mere rhetoric. I would even say it is *demanded* by a question that is crucial. How is the sensuous related to the aesthetic in actual contemplation of art? To say simply that the two are compresent[51] or *in*separable will just not do. It would be a merely external way of speaking and take no notice at all of the positive, inner harmony of the work which may even seem *self*-active in the case of occurrent arts.[52] Nor can we say that the material here overpowers the ideal; for the aesthetic object is no mere thing. The only way open is to say that here the aesthetic (or the virtual) *swallows up* the materials; or, from the other side, that the materials disappear *in* the aesthetic. This is precisely the logic of Langer's terminology; and her positive view undeniably is that the arts *use* the "materials," "to create something over and above what

51. According to Reid himself, the "side-by-side" image would here be as improper as the "either-or" one. *M.A.*, p. 84.

52. As to how, in the region of north Indian classical vocal music, the suggestion of self-activation is actually there in many good compositions, see my article, "The Fabric of Aamad — A Study of Form and Flow in Hindustānī Music" included in *Sangeet Natak* (Journal of the Sangeet Natak Akademi, New Delhi), no. 16, April–June 1970, pp. 38-42.

is physically there. . . ."[53] In no case does she sever, I repeat, the material from the aesthetic: she urges only that it is quite transmuted in the latter. I must mention here a proposal which may seem to favour Reid. Margolis suggests that it may be possible to relate art easily to other cultural aspects of human life if we seized and built on the idea that they all have two aspects, the ideal *and the physical* — as for example, the essence of religion *and* its institutions — which are distinct and irreducible, and yet quite inseparable.[54] But, it is easy to see, this hardly proves anything as to which of the two is superior in value — the bodily or the non-material.

4. Of the remaining arguments of Reid I shall now deal with only two: first, with the one by which he opposes the idea that art expresses the *forms* of life-feeling, and then with that brief bout of poetic criticism which (he thinks) warrants his choice of embodiment, rather then expression, as the right word for creation *as completed*. The first is a basic, though general, objection to Langer's view; and the second seeks to illustrate how poetry is embodiment.

(a) The essence of the former is provided by this extract:

> . . . If all feelings or complexes of feeling are [therefore] concrete and particular, how can their "forms" be other than concrete and particular too? And if so, how can the "form" of one kind of concrete feeling or complex of feelings, the feeling of "life," be projected into another form, the form of art?[55]

Now, the argument is here odd. Feelings, it is true, are all of them particular. But from this it does not follow that their "forms" too must be particular, unless by *form* we understand the mere "shape" or givenness, the psychological occupancy of

53. *P.A.*, p. 4.

54. Joseph Margolis, "A Strategy for a Philosophy of Art" in *The Journal of Aesthetics and Art Criticism*, U.S.A., Summer 1979, p. 446.

55. *M.A.*, p. 61.

a feeling as an event in experience. Langer uses the word *feeling* to cover "anything that can be felt."[56] So she may be taken to mean by it the direct or non-relational *manner* of experiencing any content or object;[57] and what she speaks of as "the forms of feeling"[58] may be taken to signify such general features as the rise and fall or sheer stowing of feeling, whether it be anger or sorrow or the mere excitement of an immediate prospect. Now, to turn to actual thinking, it is always particular. It is yours or mine, relating to this or that particular topic or situation. Yet no one protests when we talk about clarity or consistency of thought quite generally. Why should it be otherwise in the case of feeling? Reid himself finds it useful to speak of "dynamic elements." Of course, he insists that these elements are always found "involved in . . . reactions to life situations";[59] but once the reality of such general features is admitted, could we not say that they are found in art as well? For instance, who could miss *the rise and fall of feeling* in the music of the late Omkarnath Thakur? It may be noted, in passing, that even Hanslick, who resolutely opposes the relation of music to emotions, concedes the possibility that music *can* represent the "dynamic properties" of feeling: their "speed, slowness, strength, weakness, increasing and decreasing

---

56. *P.A.*, p. 15.

57. Langer indeed speaks of feeling "in the broad sense of whatever is felt" (S.K. Langer, *Mind — An Essay on Human Feeling*, Baltimore: The John Hopkins Press, 1967, vol. I, p. 4). This is also in accord with Reid's own view that feeling is "the *immediate* experience of everything that occurs in conscious psycho-physical life." (*M.A.* 148. My italics). I take the word "immediate" to mean "direct" and "non-discursive or non-relational." Langer, I may add, accepts Sheffer's idea of "unlogicized" mental life. *P.A.*, p. 125.

58. Or of "how (all) feeling rises . . . tangles or sinks . . . " S.K. Langer, *Mind — An Essay on Human Feeling*, op. cit., p. 64.

59. *M.A.*, p. 164.

instensity."[60] To be sure, these are all general features, and as such "forms" of feeling.

(b) This is not to suggest that Reid is indifferent to "the *fact* of creative art."[61] He in fact appeals to it as follows:

It may be true to say that the artist — say, a poet — *begins* by "expressing" his felt awareness of things, ideas and truths in terms of words.[62] But this "is only part of the story. The other half . . . of central importance"[63] is that such words are here used and in such a way that a rich and fresh unity is brought into being. The poem that results is "new embodied meaning,"[64] not a mere conjunction, but an interpenetration of words and what they suggest. The "meaning," insofar as it is now inseparable from the perceptible "weight and rhythm of sounding words,"[65] acquires a concreteness which it did not have before "embodiment," so that it is itself now really new or "emergent"; and the words do not merely convey,[66] but appear *charged with* meaning. "The "sound" and the "sense" are (here) aesthetically, completely inseparable."[67] This embodied singleness is (necessarily) belied when we say that the poem *expresses* a "meaning." Though initially admissible, "the language of 'expression' is untrue to the net embodiment

---

60. Hanslick, *The Beautiful in Music*, tr. Gustav Cohen, London & New York, 1891, p. 37. As for defects in Hanslick's arguments advanced to repudiate the relation of music to emotion, see the essay: "The repudiation of Emotion — Hanslick on Music" by Malcolm Budd in *The British Journal of Aesthetics*, vol. 20, no. 1, Winter 1980, pp. 29-43.

61. *M.A.*, p. 27. My italics.

62. Ibid., p. 98.

63. Ibid.

64. Ibid.

65. Ibid., p. 158.

66. Ibid., p. 159.

67. Ibid., p. 99.

— the complete poem — and is therefore merely provisional and incomplete."[68]

The issue here involved is clear. Can "expressiveness" somehow be regarded as the net, real character of a good poem? Now, the answer, I suggest, would turn on what precisely we here understand by "a poem," an "object" of aesthetic contemplation *or* of critical understanding.

The *judgement* that in good poetry "the "sound" and the "sense" are, aesthetically, completely inseparable" is a finding of critical analysis. It *is* true as analysis; but, insofar as it involves distinctions, it is not quite true — upon Reid's own general view — to the poem as aesthetically contemplated. I admit that *all* talk "about" art is subject to this inadequacy; but, and this what I here wish to emphasise, the judgement that a poem is "embodied" meaning in virtue of its indissoluble sound-sense unity, or an "embodiment" in the sense of an "object" that is directly *before* us, is not maximally close to the poem *as contemplated,* or — as Reid himself would put it — to the "operation" of embodiment.

I may refer here to some of his own truthful remarks on the lines he picks from Milton's *Samson Agonistes*:

> Feeling carries the imagination to the point of identity with the tragic realization as it flows relentlessly along. . . . We know the poignancy of the situation Milton is depicting through our participating feelings as we could not know it by detached intellectual cognition alone.[69]

Now, I ask, if the overall manner of experience is here that of feeling, and what is "known" (as felt), the poignancy of the situation; and if, further, the focus of attention is on the *distal*

---

68. *M.A.*

69. Ibid., p. 159.

feelings,[70] how exactly is it wrong to say that, as it seems to direct contemplation, *the poem* expresses[71] Samson's agony? Reid would of course object to the word "expresses." But then, what other words shall we use? Presented "before" us? No; Reid himself here cannot say "yes." For he holds, quite rightly, that "the words do not just picture, or tell us about, Samson's agony . . . we *participate in it.*" But if that is so, if the feeling that is "shown" is at once felt by us, it is clearly truer to hold that, as an *aesthetic* object, a poem is expressive *to us* than to say that it is a sound-sense unity which is directly *before us*. What can persist in disturbing us here is only the old prejudice that all expression is a pressing-*out*.

Reid rightly insists that all talk about art has to keep close to the undivided fact of aesthetic experience. But from the viewpoint of this requirement it should be easy to see that critical admiration of the details of the way in which a poem is duly organized — say, of its sound-sense fusion — is not really *the point of transition* from embodiment as "enjoyed" to embodiment as analyzed. What comes earlier in the wake of aesthetic experience is simply the clear realization that the work I contemplated seemed[72] imbued with some feeling, some semblance of life. Here, as remembrance, the "fact" remains visible; and though it is now seen (in the main) from the outside, its aroma persists, preventing the work from getting quite divided from the subject. This is what I mean by "the point of transition."

In our common talk about the main forms of experience — immediate or felt and mediate or discursive — we tend to forget that the one can in fact be seen as dallying with, before actually becoming the other. And here, indeed, in the *passage*

---

70. *M.A.*

71. "Expresses" as a presentation that is felt, not as ejection from within.

72. "Seemed" as merely "seemed to *be*," not as implying a contrast with truth or reality.

from aesthetic "indwelling" to the extraversion of theory of which I speak, we half objectify the "fact"; and, without quite abdicating it, just get set on the road to analysis. The work's felt charm is now on the wane, but it has not yet deserted us; and, by its very haunting recession, it fetters and feeds the "how" of embodiment, or the urge to unravel the fabric of art.

Embodiment and the Arts

From the context of its opposition to "expression" I now turn to consider "embodiment" in relation to the arts and "genuine aesthetic experience."[73] Of the arts which elude the grasp of "embodiment," I choose some forms (and features) of the music of India.[74] The following brief remarks should here serve:

(a) As a paradigm of pure music, our *ālāpa*[75] of the *dhruvapad* manner is the most distinctive part of our classical singing. Like every other genre of classical Indian music, it too has to conform to a *rāga* or melody-type. But, as rightly contemplated, a good *ālāpa* recital is (on the whole) not a merely objective unity of form and content; it is rather a musical atmosphere — "one intense diffusion, one serene Omnipresence"[76] — which seems so *disembodied* from the plural details of the *rāga* and suffuses our being with such overwhelming completeness that a conscious judgement as to the propriety and fullness of *rāga*-rendering is made only when the spell has weakened or disappeared. The best word for such an ethereal, yet compellingly effective

73. *M.A.*, p. 225.

74. In this article wherever I speak of Indian music, I have its *north* Indian forms in mind. Generally, however, what I have said on the subject is applicable to the entire classical music of India.

75. *Ālāpa* is effective singing (and playing too) *without* rhythmic "accompaniment" and language.

76. Shelley, *Epipsychidion*, lines 94, 95.

"apparition" is, in my view, "presence" in Marcel's sense. "Expressive *form*" would here be inapplicable *if*, following Kant, we agreed that "form" necessarily implies some limitation.[77]

(b) Indian music is "occurrent" not merely because we see it *being made* (by the artiste), but because, by virtue of some inner features of composition or rendering, it may seem to be *making itself*. The latter suggestion is, in general, manifest as follows. In small, intimate gatherings of knowledgeable listeners — where our artistes, as a rule, feel freer to perform — the music does not merely occur "before" us as a set predictable movement, but grows directly in accordance with our response to it, which is often quite audible.[78] To say of such music that it "embodies" significance would be only to miss its free, improvisatory character which is here obvious and commonly admired.

(c) All this is clearer in the region of our rhythm.[79] Here, a solo recital which is not merely competent, but winsome as art is one which througout teems with suggestions of creative freedom and vitality. Thus, some patterns may end a little before *or* after the fixed location of the

---

77. On the other hand, if the word *form* is taken in its usual aesthetic sense — that is, as proper inner organization — *ālāpa* may well be said to be a form. It is surely no haphazard singing.

78. The suggestion is not that the musician throughout performs with his eye on the audience, but only that a felt awareness of correct audience-reactions vitally determines the growth and quality of his music.

79. As to the propriety of the (Indian) view that rhythm is *an independent art*, see my article "Form and Content in Hindustani Rhythm" in *Sangeet Natak*, no. 18, October–December 1970, pp. 5-19. The chief "materials" of our rhythm are mnemonic syllables like *tā, dhā, dir, dhir*. These are *never* used for any non-aesthetic purpose — in which respect, I think, rhythm excels music.

sama, the first beat of the cycle, not marking it directly — as is the common requirement[80] — but suggesting it by the very designed quality of avoidance. Form is here brought out by the drummer's very refusal to be merely correct;[81] and the patterns in question may seem a little coy, or ebullient, self-assertive. But, it is needful to note, our experience is here at once the felt awareness of a sweet, flowing wilfulness,[82] not of "embodiment" which in itself suggests some inertness.

Even generally, in playing *any* pattern the drummer may, with guarded abandon and distinct aesthetic gain, shorten or withhold one syllable or tarry at or displace another, against their set speed and location, without of course failing to mark or suggest the *sama*.[83] And when the playing quickens, the drummer may unleash a torrent of patterns that climax at the *sama* brilliantly and are made to reach it variously. They are all themselves designed, it is true; and they keep to a measure. But the playing as it seems, directly and on

80. North Indian rhythm runs in cycles. The first beat, called *sama*, is doubly important. From it we set out, and to it we return, completing a round. The ability to come back to the first beat with split second accuracy *and in a well-designed way* is a normal requirement. Avoiding it *designedly* can make for added beauty.

81. Cf. Stephen Spender, *World within World*, London: Hamilton, 1951, pp. 313-14.

82. I am not sure if Langer's view is here quite transcended. "Feeling" seems usable, but "form" would be untrue to the experience in question.

83. The basic rhythm-cycle and the patterns flowing along with it — or, for a brief while, away from it — but in every case appearing to manifest its character as an aesthetic anchor of creative measure and variety — this is, in general, the essence of a solo exposition of Indian rhythm. The overall requirement is due observance of the speed and extent of the rhythm-cycle chosen. The *way* this demand is met can, however, vary infinitely.

the whole, is an upsurge of the very spirit of creative freedom, a flooding of embankments, as it were; and to speak of it as "*embodied* meaning" would in my view be wrong, for it would suggest that the "object" contemplated is a kind of fixedness. One might as well say of a waterfall that it "embodies" a flow or is "embodiment."

To me it is indeed clear that Reid's word misses much that distinguishes quite a few aspects of musical performance and presentation as *we* know them. Some of these features, noticeably occurrent, are: the drummer's competence in respect of बोल काटना, बोल बनाना, दाब गांस; and the intentional softening of the sound of drumming when the singer (the main performer) weaves a resonant phrase in the *mandra* or the Kathak wishes a subtle turn of *laya* in footwork to be clearly noticed.

I here feel impelled to make a few more remarks on the relative value of the concepts in question, before I propose a new one with perhaps better claims to centrality in aesthetics:

(d) Reid, we have seen, appeals to the evidence of Barbara Hepworth, by way of arguing that it is the *perceptual* character of the lines rather than any "form of feeling" that guides the further course of creation in a drawing. But, I rejoin, there is no dearth of artists who believe that it is the specificity of a feeling that determines *the choice of the medium itself*. Consider for instance, the following from Satish Gujral:

> I have used almost every medium possible: glass, ceramic, metal, papier maché, oil paints. It all depends on the feeling I get, and right now I have a feeling for wood.[84]

84. "The Return of Satish Gujral" in the *Sunday Standard* (New Delhi), November 30, 1980.

> There are feelings which claim paint, and feelings which claim wood or metal. Wood fascinates me (today) . . . . (It) has a warm feeling and very interesting texture — it breathes.[85]

(e) Further, the definition of art as creative aesthetic embodiment does not visibly provide for the fact that, however creative he may be, the artist does not work in absolute isolation from life, and that he cannot but draw upon elements which lived reality furnishes, though such abstraction for creative manipulation is doubtless far removed from mere imitation. Reid, on the other hand, seems eager to heighten the *difference* between life-feeling and the feelings that we find in art:

> Strictly speaking, the forms of the feelings of life-situation *cannot be* expressed or projected into art-situations. "Expression" and "projection" seem to be the wrong words . . . for formulating the *essential* nature of art. What happens is that in creating a work of art a new complex object comes into being, and in our aesthetic experience of it we come to have new feelings, and new structures of feeling, which are not projections of the forms of life-feeling . . . not just "how vital and emotional and intellectual tensions feel . . . " but new and fresh vital tensions, relevant and specific to the meaning specifically embodied in this thing here before us, nowhere else and never before.[86]

Langer, on the other hand, is always careful to emphasize the art-life *relation*, though she studiously opposes the view that looks upon imitation as the essence of art.[87] Thus, she defines works of art as

85. "I Live for Today", Balwant Gargi's encounter with Satish Gujral in *The Hindustan Times* (New Delhi), 30 November, 1980.

86. L.A. Reid, *M.A.*, pp. 61-62.

87. Langer, *P.A.*, p. 95.

"images of the forms of feelings"[88] and uses "feeling" (I repeat) to cover not only emotions, but whatever may be felt or directly experienced. The most elementary problem of the artist, in her view, is that of "symbolic transformation of *subjectively known realities* into objective semblances that are immediately recognized as their expression in sensory appearances."[89] Or see, again, her following clear words:

> What is the work of art for . . . ? To express its creator's ideas of immediate felt life. To set forth directly what feeling is like.[90]

(f) The flux of our life as felt suggests another point. *Embodiment* means "giving a shape or body to" or to incarnate. The word gives no direct hint as to what is called the *development* of a theme or idea in a work of art. Langer's word, *expression,* is not so inadequate. In fact, if we go by the full phrase, expression of *felt life,* provision is at once made for the idea of developing details of content; for, life is in fact "a natural process of . . . tensions, balances, rhythms . . . it is these that we feel, in quietness or emotion, as the pulse of our own living."[91] This is why Langer finds it natural to say that in a work of art "each aspect of feeling develops as one develops an idea."[92] To have a feeling is to experience it, and experience is often the awareness of a flow, maybe as mere succession.

Towards a New Concept

Can any *new* word be chosen to cover all art as *directly*

88. Langer, *Mind — An Essay on Human Feeling,* op.cit., XVIII.
89. Ibid., p. 157. My italics.
90. Ibid., *P.A.*, p. 8.
91. Ibid., p. 8. Italics added.
92. Ibid.

experienced? I think it is possible; and here is my word: *presence.*[93] No single word, it is true, can meet all the requirements of a key aesthetic concept. But, as I shall presently argue, "presence" is preferable to both expression and embodiment. Art, I believe, is the creative invocation of (what is, in principle) a presence.[94] But, let me explain:

With its commonly acknowledged contrast with mere making, "creation" here provides for three important truths: the "emergent" quality and unity (or form) of art, and the interplay of process and product in creation. "Invocation" suggests the transcendent, almost magical quality[95] of the work. To invoke is to call up a being or an influence that is "higher"[96] or benevolent. Again, as in the case of invoking a deity or its blessings, what is invoked is not on the whole (or essentially) material. It is a presence, as Marcel understands it. It is no mere object, far or near, but is at once a felt influence. So, in speaking of art as a "presence" we provide, as required, for the immediacy of "aesthetic object," without any suggestion of ghostliness;[97] and also without turning the "object," I must

93. I borrow the word from Marcel. See Ch. IX (pp. 251-68) of the first volume, *Reflection & Mystery* of his *The Mystery of Being*, Gateway Edition, Chicago, Illinois: H.R. Company, 1960.

94. A work of art is the result of creative activity. Because of its emergent quality it may be said to be an invocation. It *can* become a "presence" the moment it is rightly contemplated. But in actual contemplation, the work *is* a presence. Here, what is needed is just disinterested attention, no creation as ordinarily understood.

95. See *M.A.*, pp. 81, 88-89. Magic, we may note, is concerned with the presential side of things.

96. The idea of invoking a *higher* being or influence goes well with some of Reid's own words here: "Ladder," "climb," "upper." *M.A.*, p. 34.

97. A *presence* is not "a sort of vaporized object" (Marcel, op. cit., 255), but an "object" which at once influences us. *This* would be my answer to the protest that "presence" is too frail a word for solid

→

add, into something that is merely *before* us, — a suggestion which infects all talk of "embodiment." Again, in relation to the *non*-sensuous form of the literary arts, "invocation" and "presence" seem clearly superior. They do not here need the refinements of meaning which "embodiment" clearly does.[98]

Finally, insofar as a presence is said to *radiate* influence or to *vibrate* with meaning, we at once meet the requirement that (its) "meaning" is neither to be separated from nor kept merely confined to the work of art. Such a way of speaking implies not only that "meaning" emanates from within the work, but that it flows freely towards those who are open and eligible. A presence is received, felt, or "gathered to oneself."[99] Such words are, in my view, truer to art *as contemplated* than "embodiment," "meaning," "individual," "seizing" or "grasping the meaning of," which all smack of things and thought. To be subject to a "presence" is at once to be *permeable* to it. It is no active dealing with a thing or person for any practical end. Yet, as experience, it is vital and rich. In its remoteness from art *theory* the direct contemplation of art is indeed "a time to be silent";[100] but, as felt from within, it is an *active* self-opening and an inward quickening. Yet, whatever be the precise form of this "activity" — a passage from words to feeling imagery or the indrawn sweetness of intense musicality — it is always a disinterested self-subjugation to the other.[101] It is *this*, rather

→ arts like sculpture and architecture, *not* any appeal to such facts as the tendency in modern sculpture to look upon surface as skin alone. As for architecture, must not a palace (as art) impress us at once with its majesty; and a church, directly with its seeming holiness?

98. *M.A.*, pp. 78-79.

99. Marcel, op. cit., p. 255. The idea that a presence is "gathered to oneself" serves also to redeem overemphasis on the *outgoing* character of aesthetic experience. Cf. *M.A.*, p. 261.

100. Ibid., p. 89.

101. This is communion, not mere communication. Cf. Marcel, op. cit., pp. 252, 255.

than any judgement of value, that makes the "object" contemplated, Art or Nature, always appear "higher" than the man contemplating it; and perhaps it is only as this humility of self-opening to what is felt as benign, and not merely useful, that a genuine element of the aesthetic (as experienced) may be said to permeate all true religiousness.

3

The Aesthetic Attitude

THERE are many today who speak of a crisis in aesthetics. Indeed, the distinction between art and non-art is in question as never before. Even those who are unsympathetic to the avant-garde[1] movements agree that such developments pose a positive challenge. In respect of "aesthetic contemplation" too it is today objected by many that, though it is doubtless of value in private experience, it hampers the social functions that art is called upon to carry out today. Yet we cannot summarily dismiss the concept. For if we do, what would replace *disinterested perception*[2] of which we all are so easily capable? On the other hand, however, the very possibility of *such* perception may be called in question. This is exactly what is done by George Dickie in his well-known essay "The Myth of the Aesthetic Attitude" though in a recent work he admits the contention of Stolnitz that the concept of "aesthetic disinterestedness" is logically central to and distinctive of the era, viz. the eighteenth and nineteenth centuries, in which modern aesthetics arose; and that it "encouraged extraordinary catholicity in the denotation

---

1. These movements stand for such trends in the region of art as employ techniques which are markedly experimental or in advance of those that are presently current.

2. The reference here is to: "Crisis in Cracow" in the *Newsletter of The American Society of Aesthetics*, vol. I, no. I, Spring 1980.

of "aesthetic object."[3] I therefore seek in this essay to discuss Dickie's objections to the view of Stolnitz that the aesthetic attitude is "disinterested and sympathetic attention to and contemplation of any object of awareness whatever, for its own sake alone."[4]

The present chapter has two clear sections. The first develops my answers to Dickie's protests; and the second formulates and critically deals with what some *other* aestheticians have said against my rejoinders. The essay reproduces, with but some minor changes, the discussion of my article, "The Aesthetic Attitude", in *Philosophy East and West*.[5]

It is today common to say that art may be good even if it repels the eye or conflicts with our set moral attitudes. We are asked to care for art's own values; to look at it aesthetically. But is the aesthetic attitude really specific, or is its distinctness merely assumed? It is this single question that I will discuss in this essay. I will refer, on the one hand, to Bullough, Stolnitz, and Vivas — three powerful advocates of the distinctiveness of the aesthetic attitude; and, on the other, to some objections to the same, mainly, George Dickie's.[6] I hope to show that the protests are faulty.

3. J. Stolnitz, "The Aesthetic Attitude, in the Rise of Modern Aesthetics" in *The Journal of Aesthetics and Art Criticism*, U.S.A., Summer 1978, p. 409.

4. Stolnitz, "The Aesthetic Attitude" in *Introductory Readings in Aesthetics*, ed. John Hospers, New York (PB), The Free Press, 1969, p. 19.

5. Hereafter referred to also as *PEW*. See the following by me for the full debate: "The Aesthetic Attitude" (*Philosophy East and West*, 28, no. I, Jan. 1978), "Reply to My Critics" (*PEW* 29, no. 2, April 1979) and "The Aesthetic Attitude: Reply to some new criticisms" in *PEW*, April 1980.

6. George Dickie, "The Myth of the Aesthetic Attitude" in *Introductory Readings in Aesthetics*, pp. 28-44.

According to Bullough, the essence of the aesthetic attitude is the psychological process (or act) of *distancing*. The meaning is that, because of its own captivating quality and/or the contemplator's deliberateness, the object is put "out of gear" with, or "distanced" from our "practical needs and ends."[7] We here open up to the object's own charm, instead of regarding it as a mere springboard for our personal reveries. To quote Bullough's well-known example, the jealous husband who, at a performance of Shakespeare's *Othello*, keeps thinking of his own wife's odd behaviour, is attending not really to the play as such, but to its *relation to his own life*. His attitude is not duly "distanced," and is therefore not aesthetic. His involvement in the play is merely personal.[8] When one feels delighted by a play merely because his daughter plays a leading role therein; or by a record of *shahnāī* music just because it is being played on his own stereo, the inner fabric of the play or the music is not given due attention, and hence the attitude here cannot be said to be aesthetic, basically.

It is important to mark what the requirement of "not getting personally involved" really enjoins. It does not say that the playgoer is not to identify himself with the characters in the play "or be vitally interested in what happens to them." What is here demanded only is that the onlooker is to avoid *such* involvement of his personal life with the problems or characters of the play as may tend to replace "a careful viewing *of the play itself*." His attention should not turn to himself. Here we may borrow an instance from Hospers to make the point clearer:

7. Edward Bullough: "Psychical Distance" in *A Modern Book of Esthetics*, 4th edn.; ed. M. Rader, New York: Holt, Rinehart Winston, 1973, p. 371.

8. John Hospers, "The Esthetic Attitude" in *A Modern Book of Esthetics*, 4th edn., p. 398. It may be noted in passing that, according to our *rasa* theory, authentic aesthetic experience liberates us from *nijasukhaduḥkhādivivaśibhāva* (or preoccupation with our own joys and sorrows).

> When a man is actually involved in a shipwreck, he just does whatever he can to save himself. He cannot here lavish attention on the details of the sinking. When, on the other hand, he watches a movie about it at some later date he may give it very close attention, and even feel fascinated by the turbulent waters and the ship's final lurch. Here, it is obvious, he does not have to do anything to save himself. "However much [he] may identify with the sufferers, [he is] not [now] personally involved in any sense that is geared to action."[9]

All this is easy to follow. But is distancing a separate act? And does it give uniqueness to aesthetic awareness? We must here reckon with a protest of Dickie:

A. The jealous husband at the *Othello* performance is, according to the followers of Bullough, "*under-distanced.*" An onlooker who is concerned mainly with the technical details of the play's presentation is, on the other hand, "*over*-distanced"; he does not at all get into the inside of the play, so to say. But these are (says Dickie) both simply cases of not attending to the play or of not attending to it adequately. Does, then, the requirement of (due) "distancing" simply mean that we *should give close attention to the play?* If yes, why can't we put the matter in these simple words? Why do we have to speak of the process of "distancing"? To introduce the technical terms "distance" . . . (and some others) . . . does nothing but send us "chasing after phantom acts and states of consciousness."[10] It is improper to use the terms "to distance" and "being distanced" to refer "to *special* kinds of acts and states of consciousness."[11]

Now, I may counter the protest thus:

The key word here is "special." Its one meaning is "exceptional," or unusual, specially in a good sense; and *in this*

9. John Hospers, op. cit.

10. Dickie, "The Myth of the Aesthetic Attitude", p. 30.

11. Ibid. Italics added.

sense, I believe, "psychical distance," as *Bullough regards it,* is certainly "special." See the way he himself puts it.

> The working of Distance is . . . not simple, but highly complex. It has a negative, inhibitory aspect — the cutting-out of the practical side of things and of our practical attitude to them — and a *positive* side — the elaboration of the experience on the new basis created by the inhibitory action of Distance.[12]

It is only occasionally, I may add, that we abstain from regarding things in relation to our purposes, so as to see the charm and details of the objects themselves. Roger Fry is certainly right when he says that under the stress of our everyday life, "we learn to see only so much as is needful for our purposes."[13] So, if the suspension of our practical concerns — along with the dawning of some richer awareness — does occasionally take place, it must be said to be a "special' occurrence. It *can* happen in real life too, if only in exceptional situations; and when it does, it reveals new charm in what is thought commonplace. I find it here helpful to cite an occurrence described by Bullough himself:

> . . . A fog at sea . . . for most people . . . is an experience of acute unpleasantness. . . . It is apt to produce feelings of peculiar anxiety, fears of invisible dangers. . . . Nevertheless, [it] can be a source of intense relish and enjoyment.
>
> Abstract from the experience . . . its danger and practical unpleasantness . . . direct the attention to the features "objectively" constituting the phenomenon — the veil surrounding you with an opaqueness as of transparent milk, blurring the outlines of things and distorting their shapes into weird grotesqueness; . . . notice, the curious creamy smoothness of the water . . . and, above all, the strange solitude

12. Bullough, "Psychical Distance", p. 370.
13. Roger Fry, *Vision and Design,* London: Chatto and Windus, 1920, p. 24.

> and remoteness from the world, as it can be found only on the highest mountain tops; and the experience may acquire . . . a flavour of such concentrated poignancy and delight as to contrast sharply with the blind . . . anxiety of its other aspects. This contrast, often emerging with startling suddenness, is like a momentary switching on . . . of a brighter light, illuminating the outlook upon perhaps the most ordinary and familiar objects — an impression which we experience . . . It is a difference of outlook, due — if such a metaphor is permissible — to the insertion of Distance.[14]

What we have in cases like the above is not just close attention, but *such heightened awareness as comes in the wake of a temporary suspension of the everyday attitude and so discloses much new material.* It is such special awareness that "distance" signifies. It is not the distance of actual space; and so when Bullough speaks of "the insertion of Distance" his manner (admittedly) is metaphorical. But the experience it refers to is a quite genuine one. Further, when we try to contemplate a work of art intently we have often *to try* to prevent attention from going back to thoughts of daily life and concerns; and to focus it on the object being contemplated. "Distancing" *has often to be done;* and its use as a verb, to which Dickie objects, is therefore legitimate. Nor is "being distanced" a mere use of words. The getting of freedom from the yoke of everyday worries and interests is not a "phantom state of consciousness," but positive experience, a kind of feeling released.

"Under-distancing" is our common problem when we contemplate art, for it is not easy to turn away from our daily concerns; and "over-distancing" occurs, say, when a listener at a concert of classical Indian music keeps wondering what particular *rāga* (melodic type) is being presented.

B. Stolnitz emphasizes the *disinterestedness* of the aesthetic

14. Bullough, "Psychical Distance", pp. 369-70.

attitude. He interprets the word to mean that, here, there is "no concern for any ulterior purpose"[15] and that we attend to the object for its own sake. It is obvious that the italicized word, disinterested, cannot be taken to mean "without or deficient in interest," for it is common knowledge that the aesthetic attitude is one of intense attention.

However, many diverse protests have been made against the alleged *disinterestedness* of the aesthetic attitude; and it seems necessary to deal with two of the major ones:

(a) Hospers contends that whereas it is perfectly proper to speak of judging in a disinterested (or impartial) way, it makes little sense to speak of *perceiving* in this way.[16] To this we could readily answer that the word "disinterested" also means "unselfish" or "not influenced by private feeling or considerations"; and that, as already brought out, the aesthetic attitude is *disinterested* in the sense that the way we here perceive is unrelated to personal, practical needs.[17]

(b) Dickie's protest here is more elaborate. We may put it thus:

The idea of *disinterested* attention to the arts would be sensible only if we could sometimes be said to attend to them in an *interested* way. But many of the so-called "interested" ways of looking at the arts are "just different ways of being *distracted* from (say) the play."[18] This is so, for instance, when the onlooker is a play-goer who likes a dramatic performance mainly because *his* daughter has a key role therein (personal satisfaction); or the play's director beams at the way *he* has been able to solve its technical problems (intellectual satisfaction); or the moralist

15. J. Stolnitz, *Aesthetics and Philosophy of Art Criticism*, Boston: Houghton Mifflin, 1960, p. 35.

16. Hospers, "The Esthetic Attitude", p. 399.

17. Incidentally, *this* is the sense in which the delight of beauty is *disinterested* according to Kant.

18. Dickie, "The Myth of the Aesthetic Attitude", p. 33.

feels happy at the prospect that the play is likely to have a good effect on the viewers' conduct (moral satisfaction). These are all really cases of not attending to the play. So there is nothing like interested *attention*. But if this is so, the opposite concept of *disinterested* attention is also invalidated. The fact (in Dickie's view) is that though it is possible for us to be more or less attentive to a work of art, to attend to it for various reasons, and to be distracted from it in a variety of ways,[19] the way to attend (positively) to the work is only one; and that is neither "interested" nor "disinterested" but just close attention. The critic too "differs from other percipients only in . . . [his] motives and intentions and not in the way he attends to art."[20]

Now, this objection may be met as follows.

First, consider some of Dickie's own words:

> Of course, there is no reason to think that in any of these (three) cases (of non-aesthetic satisfaction visualized above) the distraction or inattention must be total, although it could be. *In fact,* such inattentions often occur; but they are so fleeting that nothing of the play, music or whatever is missed or lost.[21]

I see, in this extract, much that is questionable. To speak only of what is here regarded as a matter of *fact*, Dickie means (and says) that the distraction or inattention in question is (often) such a fleeting occurrence that it does not detract from one's awareness of the art object. But if it is but a passing and harmless occurrence, how can the word *distraction* be used suitably for the attitude of, say, a musicologist, who *all along* listens to a music recital with due care to be sure, yet merely to determine — and report, say, to the radio authorities — its technical accuracy in respect of *rāga* and *tāla* (or melody-type and rhythm),

19. Dickie, op. cit., p. 32.
20. Ibid., p. 39.
21. Ibid., p. 33.

and is therefore very likely to miss the evocative or expressive quality that may be quite a feature of the music? Listening with an ulterior purpose is at once to attend from a specific point of view, may be quite keenly; and this, the point of view, determines one's notice throughout, and necessarily entails indifference to some other aspects of the music.

I conclude, therefore, that *interested* attention to art is not the same as (momentary) distraction.

Second, there is reason to doubt Dickie's insistence that the way to attend is only one. As one instance of (what may be called) *interested* attention, he himself cites the case of the reader who reads a poem as history and suggests that, instead of attending *differently* from an ordinary man, this reader "is simply attending to an aspect of a poem."[22]

Now here a question may be put at once. If the reader in question wishes to glean historical information from the poem, and if an average man wants simply to enjoy the poem quite generally, how can we say that their attention is yet of the same kind? Dickie, however, does say this, and with emphasis. He holds, we may recall, that though the motives of attending can vary — and "the attending [itself] may be more or less close"[23] — the way in which we attend or the kind of attention is only one.[24] But this is surely odd. The act of *attending* is an application of the mind. It is getting and remaining set to be aware of, or to know the given; and it commonly includes choosing a *particular* point of view.

Further, if the awareness can be more or less close, and the knowing may reveal this or that aspect of the object, how can *attention* be said to be of only one kind? It is not a mere torch which is just directed (casually) at an object and which (yet)

22. Dickie, op. cit., p. 36.

23. Ibid., p. 37.

24. Ibid., pp. 32, 36-37, 39.

remains unaffected by the angle from which it is used and by the character of the thing lit up. It is always a specific way of directing the mind at the given, and what it reveals of the object is at once its own filling too of some determinate awareness.

It indeed seems proper to hold that art can be attended to in different ways. Where our concern with a work is determined by some ulterior purpose — as when we seek to determine the social conditions it reflects — attention is clearly "interested"; and if we dwell on (or within) the work alone, we do so disinterestedly.

C. The disinterested quality of the aesthetic attitude has also been taken to mean that attention is here "intrinsic" or "intransitive." But here one may ask, does it make sense to speak of, say, reading a literary work of art *transitively?* Vivas believes it does; and as an instance of transitive attention, he cites the case of readers who may approach a poem "as diagnostic evidence of the author's neuroses."[25] But Dickie here protests that:

> This is a case of using information gleaned from a poem to make inferences about its author rather than attending to a poem. If anything can be said to be attended to here it is the author's neuroses (at least they are being thought about). This kind of case is perhaps best thought of as a rather special way of getting distracted from a poem. Of course, such "biographical distractions might be . . . momentary. . . . On the other hand . . . [they] may turn into dissertations and whole careers." Such an interest may lead a reader to concentrate his attention (when he does read a poem) on certain "informational" aspects of a poem and to ignore the remaining aspects.[26]

25. Dickie, op. cit., p. 35.

26. Ibid.

Now, I see in the extract just cited the strain of a wrong emphasis, *and* an incorrect use of language. Dickie here begins by suggesting that "to make inferences about its author" is no attention to the poem at all. This is plainly wrong. One cannot possibly make the inferences in question unless the poem is attended to. Dickie himself (at the end of the extract) is forced to say, inconsistently, that the *attention* here involved is to certain "informational" aspects of the poem. But what is even more improper is a part of his remark on *biographical* distractions. They may take the form, he says, of even "whole careers." But, to be sure, devoting a whole life to the task of discovering the author in his works is not a mere distraction; it is rather a matter of *resolving to look at them with an ulterior purpose or from a particular point of view*. . . . It is, therefore, a case of positive attention, though surely "interested."

D. Two other objections of Dickie may here be dealt with. They both aim at showing how the concept of disinterestedness is harmful to aesthetic theory:

(a) The first of these is built around the following view of Stolnitz:

> . . . Whether an association is aesthetic depends on whether it is compatible with the attitude of "disinterested attention." If the association re-enforces the focusing of attention upon the object, by "fusing" with the object and thereby giving it added "life and significance," it is genuinely aesthetic. If, however, it arrogates attention to itself and away from the object, it undermines the aesthetic attitude.[27]

Stolnitz illustrates what he here means by citing two students' responses to the following poetic lines:

> Between the erect and solemn trees
> I will go down upon my knees;

27. Dickie, op. cit., p. 37.

I shall not find this day
So meet a place to pray.

One of the readers is here led to think of a "rugby forward running." The other reacts with the image of a cathedral. The rugby image, Stolnitz argues, diverts attention from the poem, and so is not an aesthetic association. On the other hand, the cathedral image *is* aesthetic; for it "is congruous with both the verbal meaning of the poem and the emotion and mood it expresses. It does not divert attention away from the poem." Therefore, it *is aesthetically relevant.*

Dickie here contends that aesthetic relevance in this case is really congruity with the meaning of the poem, *which is quite independent of the notion of disinterestedness*[28] and that therefore Stolnitz errs in thinking that in his account of what an aesthetic "association" is, the criterion of "aesthetic relevance" duly appears as derivable from the concept of the aesthetic attitude.

Now, much here depends on how Stolnitz conceives of the aesthetic attitude. It means, in his view:

> that we *do not* look at the object out of concern for any ulterior purpose which it may serve. . . . Our interest *comes to rest upon the object alone.*[29]

Dickie, in my view, is here able to protest only by ignoring the second (positive) emphasis in the extract just cited. For, if being "disinterested" (also) means *caring for the object alone,* and if (as in the case in question) the object is a poem, what could this caring mean except being guided by the *meaning* of the poem, unless of course the poem is regarded as a mere aggregation of some marks on the paper. Congruity with the meaning of the poem is in fact demanded by, instead of being independent of, the notion of disinterestedness.

---

28. Dickie, op. cit., p. 38.

29. J. Stolnitz, "The Aesthetic Attitude", p. 20.

(b) But does not the "attitude theory" overdo the independence of the aesthetic? Does it not (wrongly) suggest that aesthetic value is always independent of morality? Dickie thinks it does. He begins by citing the following words of Stolnitz:

> Any of us might reject a novel because it seems to conflict with our moral beliefs. . . . When we do so . . . we have *not* read the book aesthetically, for we have interposed moral . . . responses of our own which are alien to it. This disrupts the aesthetic attitude. . . . To maintain (this) attitude, we must follow the lead of the object and respond in concert with it.[30]

Here Dickie protests against this attempt 'to hold the moral . . . and . . . aesthetic aspects of the work of art (so) firmly apart.' He first feels encouraged by David Pole's thesis 'that the moral vision which a work of art may embody is *aesthetically* significant,' and then ends up by recording this own attitude to the matter as follows:

> My concern . . . is simply to insist that a work's moral vision is a part of the work and that therefore a critic can legitimately describe and evaluate it. I would *call* any defect or merit which a critic can legitimately point out an aesthetic defect or merit, but what we call it does not matter.[31]

Let us now attend to this extract at some length:

Nobody would deny that, as in the case of some novels, a moral vision can be an integral part of a work. We may also agree, in a general way, that a critic has the right to (or can "legitimately") describe and evaluate whatever is there in the work. But, while admitting the critic's right to deal with *everything* in the work, do we also mean that he is free to do this *in any way?* Dickie himself speaks of what "a critic may *legitimately* speak of"; and adds that any defect or merit which

30. Dickie, "The Myth of the Aesthetic Attitude", p. 41.

31. Ibid., p. 43.

is *so* pointed out can be called aesthetic. But, what does "legitimately" here mean — on its second appearance in the extract cited? If the meaning still simply is "relating to what is a part of the work," we get no light as to how the critic's *way* of dealing with the contents of a work is specific. And, I believe, it has to be specific if it is to make for a finding that is *aesthetic.* After all, it would not be the pointing of an *aesthetic* defect if the critic only drew attention to two such words in a novel as have been wrongly printed as one, though they are doubtless a part of the work. Dickie merely urges that, insofar as they are both *parts* of it, a work's *moral vision* may be called aesthetically good or defective quite as properly as its *degree of unity,*" but, as we have just pointed out, any kind of concern with the parts of a work cannot be called *aesthetic.*

What is it, one must ask, to deal with the "part" — say, the moral vision — *aesthetically?* In the absence of any answer by Dickie himself, we may proffer the common, if *negative,* reply that the concern in question does not consist in checking the "vision" *with our own moral views from the outside.* It may be noted that it is only this externalistic moral checking — this interposition of "moral . . . responses of our own *which are alien to it"* — to which Stolnitz (in his words cited) objects. He does not deny that a moral vision may be a part of a work's inner content. What he seeks, I conclude, is not a categorical separation of morality from *the aesthetic,* but a subordination of the latter to the moral beliefs *of the man who contemplates it.*

We may turn, in the end, to an objection which relates to the view that the aesthetic attitude is opposed to the "critical" way of looking at the arts. Stolniz holds that "whenever criticism obtrudes, it reduces aesthetic interest"; and that, though it is certainly necessary to read and listen perceptively and acutely, during aesthetic experience itself we must not "analyze [and] measure in terms of value-criteria."

Here Dickie protests that the opposition envisaged is not in fact true. Recalling his own experience of preparing for a panel discussion of some films, he tells us that making notes on their various aspects during their showing actually *enhanced* his appreciation of the films. There is hardly any "significant difference," he adds, between attending to a work "perceptively and acutely" — which, Stonlitz admits, is necessary for appreciation — and searching for reasons which make it aesthetically valuable. Nor need we suppose, as (in Dickie's view) Stolnitz seems to do, that making notes on what is contemplated leaves us with much less time for its "enjoyment." For, "*finding* a reason is an achievement like winning [not running] a race"; it does not take time. "It is done in a flash," like coming to understand. Surely, we hardly take any time in "seeing" that a note is off-key or on-key; or to notice that an actor mispronounces a particular word.[32]

Now, to this specific protest my rejoinder is ready. Everything here depends on what meaning we give to the key-words: say, *criticism* and *aesthetic interest*. The "criticism" which Stolnitz regards as being hostile to aesthetic interest is analysis *and measurement in terms of value-criteria.* Dickie thinks that this (or the finding of reasons) is not significantly different from perceptive and acute attention to a work. But, I think, the two are fairly distinct, and I may argue for my view as follows:

Consider the case of listening (knowledgeably) to an item of classical Indian singing. It is perceptive and acute if the listener does not miss the slightest deviation from *svara* (tone) and *tāla*, and is throughout alive to details of style and sctructure — for example, the power and fluency of *taan*s (patterns) coupled with perfect inner clarity of their constituent notes, or the (seemingly) self-completing design of the first line of the song (*sthāyī*). The perception of such details is indeed almost instantaneous, where the critic is knowledgeable and attentive.

32. Dickie, op. cit., p. 40.

But these are in themselves *mere material* for "critical" thinking and "measurement in respect to value criteria," *not explicit criticism* or in themselves "reasons" for final evaluation of the music. The ultimate critical write-up calls for a proper placement and viewing of these details in the economy of the whole, and may be also in the light of such overriding criteria of theory as might have been ignored because of the very constriction of notice that goes with the gripping quality of what meets the ear. Thus, when the recital is over and the critic sets out to prepare his write-up for the press, he may have to reflect that the *fluent and vigorous taans*, though admirable in themselves, were (in this case) not quite warranted by the gentle import of the text of the song — and thus violated the principle of sound-sense harmony — or by the tender emotion which the *rāga* rendered (say, *pūriyā*) is required to work up; and that, though the *sthāyī* and *taans* were all in themselves duly designed, the *torrent* of patterns tended to eclipse the *sthāyī*, so that instead of appearing figures against a recurrent ground, they seemed a mere network impairing, rather than adding to the overall balance and structural lucidity of the recital. In such critical thinking the value-criterion is coherence *of the whole;* and assessment of *this* kind is by no means instantaneously accomplished. This "finding" of *such* reasons for the grading of a music recital is an attempt *to think out and formulate* one's overall reaction, and *not the mere discovery of attentive perception.* Were the direct finding of keen listening the same as giving reasons, it would not have been necessary for the critic to check the perceptual details recorded with reference to his grasp of the concepts and principles of music; but this latter need is paramount in criticism.

And as for making notes on the work being contemplated, whether it harms aesthetic interest on not would depend on exactly how this noting is done. If, for instance, what is sought to be recorded is the manner of movement by which a note is (in the end) daintily touched, a quick linear image on the paper may not ruffle listening noticeably; but if the same is written out in orderly language, the loss may be sizeable. And, in any case, the risk is always there, in the case of *occurrent* arts in particular, that the moment attention shifts from listening to careful noting, the very next accent of beauty may be utterly missed or but weakly felt. If *aesthetic interest* (or experience) be taken to mean "rapt attention . . . [to] an object's immanent meanings and values in their full presentational immediacy,"[33] the critical attitude, in the express form we have emphasized, truly seems opposed to the *aesthetic attitude.*

I turn now to consider some criticisms of my views given above.[34] Coleman contends that though I have successfully captured their spirit, I have failed to "satisfactorily meet Dickie's criticisms of the aesthetic attitude."[35] Further, he advances "an alternative account."[36]

1. Let me begin by considering Coleman's charge of how I have failed to deal with Dickie's criticism:

(a) By "special states of consciousness" Dickie means such states as are *psychologically distinctive.*[37] I (on the other hand) take the words ('special . . . consciousness' merely) as meaning "exceptional or unusual in a positive sense."[38] So, I have *not* interpreted the words in question "in a way . . . [which could

33. This is the view of Vivas, cited by Dickie in "The Myth of the Aesthetic Attitude", p. 34.

34. And published in *PEW.*, 28, no. 1, January 1978 as the *The Aesthetic Attitude.*

35. Earle Coleman, "On Saxena's Defense of the Aesthetic Attitude" *PEW*, 29, no. 1 January, 1979.

36. Ibid.

37. Ibid.

38. Ibid.

be said to be] consonant with Dickie's remarks."[39]

Now, I admit that the words "exceptional" and "unusual" are no direct pointers to *psychological* distinctness. But, what *is* such distinctness? A general answer would be: distinctness in respect of experience, behaviour, attitudes. But this certainly fits the way I have sought to argue the distinctness of the aesthetic attitude, namely, as "not just close attention, *but such heightened awareness as comes in the wake of temporary suspension of the everyday attitude and discloses such new material.*"[40] I have also said:

> Nor is "being distanced" a mere use of words. The getting of freedom from the yoke of daily worry is not a "phantom state of consciousness," but positive experience, a kind of feeling released.[41]

(b) Coleman also feels disturbed by my following question: "Further, if the awareness can be more or less close, and the knowing reveals this or that aspect of the object, how can attention be said to be of only one kind?" He forthwith adds, with obvious approval:

> Surely Dickie is free to reply that attention can differ in degree but remain singular in kind.[42]

Now here, I rejoin, Coleman simply *misses* the opening "further" — which (in my essay) relates to the preceding: "attending . . . commonly includes choosing a *particular* point of view"[43] — and the words "reveal this or that aspect of the object," *and confines himself* to "more or less close" in my question. If, as I have *on the whole* maintained, the aesthetic

---

39. Earle Coleman, op. cit.
40. Saxena, "The Aesthetic Attitude", p. 83.
41. Ibid.
42. Coleman, p. 2.
43. Saxena, p. 85.

attitude (or attention) involves (1) suspension of everyday attitudes (practical and theoretical); (2) close attention to the object for its own sake; and (3) heightened awareness, maybe of "much new material," does it still make sense to insist that the aesthetic attitude does *not* seem distinct from the other attitudes? If we say "yes," what, I ask, *would* make the aesthetic attitude distinct, if it at all could be so? One cannot meaningfully deny the distinctness of an attitude unless it is understood what such distinctness generally is. The aesthetic attitude, I repeat, is distinct largely because of its disinterestedness, that is, its caring for the object as such. It is a case of attention which is not merely close, but intransitive.

I have read of a surgeon's failing to register the falling of a side part of the ceiling while operating on a tumour. Nobody would here doubt the closeness of attention. But this alone does not make it aesthetic; for what here determines notice is the purpose of a clean and ample excision, not the tumour's own form alone.

Nor do I see any difficulty in regarding disinterested attention as being distinct in kind. Here an analogy should help. Our close interest in people can be selfish *or* unselfish. The alternatives here signify a distinction of kind or quality. But if this is conceded, how are we justified in protesting that attention which is not determined by any selfish or self-referential end is not of a different kind?

I suspect that, as I have already hinted earlier, in a good deal of our present-day analysis of the matter, objections to *kinds* of attention rest on a vicious abstraction. We tend to think of attention on the image of, say, a mere torchlight which is itself quite independent of the person who wields it, as also of the things it illumines. The truth, on the other hand, is that to attend is to try to be, or just being actively aware; and that the point of view or attitude of the man who attends and what features or meanings are, in consequence, revealed in the object are all actual parts of the fact of attention. Therefore, I deem it proper to speak of *kinds* of attention. (This aspect of my view will, I hope, gain from the way I will later deal with comments of Snoeyenbos.)

But perhaps a consideration of Coleman's "alternative account" will still show how my view is mistaken. So let me see what this account is, and if it is really an *alternative*:

(2) Coleman wants us to speak not of disinterested attention or the aesthetic attitude, but of (1) "openness and sensitivity to nuances of content and subtleties of form,"[44] (2) "an apprehension hungry set,"[45] and of (3) such an adjustment of "the machinery of our bodies and . . . minds (as is) conducive to the perception of certain intrinsic properties of things, as also to the consequent *extraction* of satisfaction from the presence of those properties."[46] He believes that whereas the concept of "aesthetic attitude" does seem to suggest a *peculiar* or special psychological state,"[47] his characterizations, just listed, are free from this defect, and that "the aesthetic attitude model" which he here recommends "has the virtue of *accommodating* the rich varieties of aesthetic experience."[48]

But, I ask, how (if at all) does this "accommodating" appear possible? (1) — in the preceding para — seems confined to art, as against the simple beauties of (raw/quiet) nature, and (2) is inapplicable, even metaphorically, to the *serene* contemplation of, say, the expanse of the blue overhead. The word *extraction* too would here seem inapt, because it suggests overmuch effort ("getting" would be better, because it is wider in application).

---

44. Coleman, p .3.
45. Ibid., pp. 3-4.
46. Ibid., p. 4, italics added.
47. Ibid., p. 2, italics added.
48. Ibid., p. 4, italics added.

The remainder of (3) seems all right. But what does *it* say? Simply that the aesthetic attitude is attentive orientation ("attention," I need hardly add, is never there without some *bodily* adjustment) to the object's own properties. How is this an improvement upon "disinterested and sympathetic attention to and contemplation of an object of its own sake alone?" (Stolnitz). Does the alleged "alternative" give us any new idea? I fail to see any.

It may here be noted that, by way of interpreting the word "sympathetic" in his definition of the aesthetic attitude, Stolnitz himself speaks thus:

> When we apprehend an object aesthetically . . . we must accept (it) *"on its own terms."* We must make ourselves receptive to the object and *"set" ourselves to accept whatever it may offer to perception.*[49]

Is there any major emphasis of the "alternative" offered by Coleman which is not here provided for? It is here needful to add that what really makes his "alternative account" seem applicable to all kinds of aesthetic experience is the common factor of (disinterested) attention in his three characterizations. Otherwise, taken individually, they all fail to fit *every* case. This is why Coleman himself oscillates between terms which seem too passive or too active, moving from "receptivity . . . openness . . ."[50] to "apprehension-hungry," "extraction"; and finally coming to rest with "discerning receptivity."[51] But "discerning"

---

49. J. Stolnitz, "The Aesthetic Attitude" from *Aesthetics and the Philosophy of Art Criticism*, reprinted in *Introductory Readings in Aesthetics*, p. 21. Italics added.

50. Coleman, p. 3.

51. Ibid., p. 4. It is important to mark the way Stolnitz emphasizes the discerning character of the aesthetic attitude: "To savour fully the distinctive value of the object, we must be attentive to its *frequently* complex and subtle details. Acute awareness of these details is *discrimination*." (J. Stolnitz, "The Aesthetic Attitude", in *Introductory* →

is perhaps not quite true to the case of serene contemplation I have visualized earlier. On the other hand, "disinterested and sympathetic attention to and contemplation of . . ." is a way of speaking which, I believe, would fit, because of its very generality, *all* cases of aesthetic experience. Otherwise, if we try to seize all the details of such experiences, our definition of the aesthetic attitude will have to provide for such felt features as the "inhaling" of restful sweetness or elevation to the lonely regions of renunciation, both of which (in music) are quite possible effects of *dhruvapad* style *ālāpa*-singing[52] at its best.

(3) I may end my rejoinder to Coleman's criticisms by inviting attention to two more points. The first is his complaint that in allowing my view to be determined by Bullough's description of a fog at sea, I have (improperly) chosen a case which is, as Dickie points out in a book not cited by me, an atypical case.[53] Now, I admit that the case in question is not a common instance of the aesthetic attitude. One does not ordinarily contemplate such a situation aesthetically. But if we indicate the possibility of adopting a specific kind of attitude even in a very uncommon situation, is not its distinctness or reality *as attitude* — in opposition to things as given and the effect they commonly and effortlessly produce — at once thereby heightened? For instance, we do not commonly love those who hate us; but is not the reality of *ahiṁsā* (or non-violence) *as a positive attitude* magnified in the practice of one who seeks to be of help even to his enemies? So, I conclude, though the case in question is

---

→ *Readings in Aesthetics*, p. 23). How is this different from the first of the three requirements of Coleman I have listed? I invite special attention to the word "frequently" which I have emphasized. Stolnitz does not say "always." This makes *his* definition applicable even to the "simple" beauties of nature.

52. *Ālāpa* in north Indian classical vocal music means, in the main, singing without the aids of language and (beat-measured) rhythm.

53. Coleman, op.cit., p. 1.

admittedly atypical, reference to it seems essential to heighten the distinct positiveness of the aesthetic attitude.

The other point is a part of what Coleman says *against* Dickie:

> Dickie is wrong in asserting that there is only one way to pay *close attention*, for one may do so begrudgingly or . . . *with indifference.*[54]

This surprises me. How can anyone "pay *close* attention" to an object with indifference? But of course this has no direct bearing on my essay.

Let me now turn to the protests of Milton H. Snoeyenbos.

He begins by roundly complaining that my positive account of the aesthetic attitude is inadequate.[55] Perhaps it is, but I want to deal with his specific objections.

(a) The first of these may be put thus: To adopt the aesthetic attitude is to *take* (not merely *have*) an interest in the object. It entails that one is attending to the object. But, such attention

> is *interchangeable* [my italics] with terms denoting perceptual abilities. . . . To take an interest in, and hence to attend to, a painting is to look at it. Thus, irrespective of whether one is taking a historical or an aesthetic interest in *Posthorn*, one is attending to, i.e. listening to, the music. . . . The motives . . . people may have in taking an interest in the music may differ. One person is motivated to listen to the [music] in order to pass an examination, while another intends to focus attention on the harmony. But [this] difference in motive does not entail that taking an aesthetic interest involves a special kind of attention or perception [over and above listening].[56]

54. Earle Coleman, op. cit., p. 3. Italics added.
55. Milton H. Snoeyenbos, "Saxena on the Aesthetic Attitude", *PEW*, 29, no. 1, January, 1979.
56. Ibid., pp. 1-2.

I find this argument questionable from the third sentence onward. Is the act of taking aesthetic interest *strictly interchangeable* with terms denoting perceptual abilities? Shall we say that to attend to a painting (as art) is (the same as) — or merely that it *includes*, though necessarily — looking at, when it is known that all "looking" is not necessarily, "heeding"? Snoeyenbos talks of aesthetic properties; but is not the taking of interest in such properties of, say, a painting necessarily a looking *in a particular way*, or the exercise of a duly trained attention? Be it noted that here I speak of the aesthetic properties *of art*. It, of course, does not need any training to perceive a *cheerful* face; but the apprehension of the cheerful quality *of music* calls for (at least) an elementary training in rhythm. Aesthetic attention here always involves something over and above mere listening.

The training required, again, admits of varying points of view; and, I insist, of different *kinds* of attention. The average student (in my country) who listens to a piece of music with an eye to his annual test is concerned mostly with the merely technical details — the *rāga* (melody type) and the *tāla* (rhythm-cycle) — of the music; and with such of its features, generally, as call for mere recognition rather than penetrating awareness of its inner fabric, and dwelling within or flowing along with its form. Attention here is not merely superficial, but just technical; and it is clearly different from, though it can be — nay, it has to be — a part of attention as aesthetic. To speak of just one aspect of our music, rhythm, the examinee here just notices (by simple counting) the number of beats of *the cycle to which the composition* is set, not the latter's own inwardly designed access to the focal beat. To be sure, counting the beats of a cycle — in which, so to say, a composition is put — is not the same kind of attention (or perception) as feeling attuned with the cyclic quality which permeates the composition on the inside.

(b) This paves my way to meet the other (relatively pointed) protest of Snoeyenbos against Stolnitz, whom I have largely followed. It may be put thus:

> Consider a person who . . . attends [only] to the distances between all the actors in a play summed at 26 minutes intervals. Such a person may have *no* ulterior purpose, his sole intent is to attend to [the particular details]. He is *not* using or manipulating the object. His concern is *not* with the origins . . . of the object, or its interrelations with other things.[57] Yet, nobody would say that this man's attention or attitude is aesthetic. How is then Stolnitz justified in saying that "aesthetic interest is [merely] *not* to look at the object out of concern for any ulterior purpose which it may serve"? [The person visualized is] not trying to use or manipulate the object. . . . [It is not] apprehended with an eye to origins and consequences, its interrelations with other things.[58]

To this my answer is that the citation from Stolnitz included in the above (within quotes) presents only the negative aspect of his view, and that his full and explicit definition of the aesthetic attitude is:

> disinterested and sympathetic attention to and contemplation of any object of awareness, for its own sake alone.[59]

Our attention, we are told, is "sympathetic" if we "give the object the "chance" to show how it can be interesting to perceptiom,"[60] or if we "follow the lead of the object and respond in concert with it."[61] *This* is just not done by the man whose only concern is distances between actors. The aesthetic attitude does not *extract* any detail for attention. It indeed makes

57. Milton H. Snoeyenbos, pp. 4-5.

58. Ibid., p. 4.

59. J. Stolnitz, *Introductory Readings in Aesthetics*, p. 19.

60. Ibid., p. 21.

61. Ibid.

for a whole view. But this, I at once add, is not incompatible with my claim that specific interest entails indifference to some aspects of an object;[62] for at least the utilitarian aspect of the object *is* here clearly ignored. It may be noted that here I speak of aspects, *not of parts*, or of the ways in which an object may be regarded.

Let me conclude by making it quite clear how Snoeyenbos does not consider the view of Stolnitz in its fullness. The word "disinterested" is indeed interpreted by Stolnitz negatively, that is, as signifying that "we do *not* look at the object out of concern for any ulterior purpose . . . [that] we are *not* trying to use or manipulate the object."[63] But the next word in the definition, that is, "sympathetic" is (we have seen) given a clearly positive sense by Stolnitz. Snoeyenbos unfortunately cares only for the first (negative) word; and this in spite of the clear warning of Stolnitz that since the treatment cannot but be piecemeal, "the truth of [. . . his] account must be found in the total analysis and not in any single part of it."[64]

Feezell, who thinks that my approach to the issue ought to be different than it is, contends that though the aesthetic attitude may well be regarded as *distinctive,* "the comparative task" should follow "the phenomenological task."[65] Now, I readily accept this order of enquiry. But if "the phenomenological task" means a close scrutiny of the "states of affairs themselves," I must also add that my treatment of the subject has by no means been merely abstract. Yet, it may be that the way Feezell favours — that is, phenomenological

62. Saxena, "Reply to My Critics", p. 219.

63. J. Stolnitz, *Introductory Readings in Aesthetics*, p. 20.

64. Ibid., p. 19.

65. R.M. Feezell; "The Aesthetic Attitude Debate: Some Remarks on Saxena, Coleman, and a Phenomenological Approach to the Issue", *PEW*, January 1980. Hereafter, this article in *PEW* is referred to simply as *Remarks*.

analysis — is more revealing. So, I may ask, what (new) insights does his way deliver? Here is the answer, in Feezell's own words:

> . . . Through a phenomenological approach to the aesthetic attitude, we see that the attitude is distinctive insofar as (a) it *constitutes* its object as a candidate for appreciation, (b) *opens itself up* in an anticipatory and *discerning* manner, (c) expects to find intrinsic charateristics of the object which may be *appropriately encountered,* and (d) the initial constitution by consciousness is also a self-constitution, insofar as consciousness now tacitly understands itself as properly "attuned" for the possibility of further "aesthetic' experience, or for an appreciation of what Coleman calls "nuances of content and subtleties."[66]

Now, let me understand what all this means. Feezell, be it noted, here attempts "the comparative task" *after* doing the needful phenomenological preliminaries. But his very opening is here suspect. Does the aesthetic attitude in every case *constitute* its object as a candidate for appreciation? One can hardly answer, yes. Where it has to vivify the "zones of indeterminacy" in (say) a poem,[67] the aesthetic attitude may well be said to partly constitute its object. But when the poet's heart leaps up on seeing a rainbow in the sky, he does nothing to *make* the object admirable. It would be safer to say that the attitude in question constitutes *or* recognizes the object as a candidate for appreciation. Here, "recognizes" would cover simple cases of natural beauty, like the one I just cited, and "constitutes" would serve for (complex) works of art. Feezell himself is careful to make this enlargement, at least twice in

---

66. Saxena, "The Aesthetic Attitude Debate: Reply to Some New Criticisms", *PEW*, April, 1980, p. 265. The bracketed letters that list the points and the italics are here mine.

67. The reference here is to what Roman Ingraden calls concretion.

his "Remarks."[68] But if in *some* cases of the aesthetic attitude the object is only *recognized,* and in others *constituted* as being unique, neither of these words can by itself be taken to distinguish the aesthetic attitude. However, whether the object is constituted or merely recognized, that attitude is a concomitant which is always present here. Feezell puts it thus:

> . . . When this recognition occurs, there is movement from our natural everyday practical attitude to an attitude which now spontaneously begins a series of procedures by which the object might be appreciated.[69]

This movement away from our everyday concern with things is indeed there whenever our attitude is aesthetic; but is the point here made (in the extract cited) at all an improvement on the emphasis on "disinterestedness" as Stolnitz interprets it?[70]

The next point, "open itself up" (b) seems more acceptable, but I wonder if phenomenological analysis would bear out its *primacy* in all cases. For, sometimes it is *the object* that first elicits the aesthetic attitude which may then look forward to further experience. The object may achieve this by means of some striking regional quality or by virtue of its manifestly shapely form. A superb example of such form is provided by the Taj Mahal.[71] The very first look at it is, so to say, a shock of delight,

---

68. Thus, see the following:

> This constitution or recognition by consciousness of the unique status of its object is the very condition for aesthetic experience to occur. . . . Therefore, this initial recognition or constitution is an anticipation of further experience.

> Feezell's *Remarks,* p. 88.

69. Saxena, "The Aesthetic Attitude Debate: Reply to Some New Criticisms", p. 265.

70. J. Stolnitz, "The Aesthetic Attitude", *Introductory Readings in Aesthetics,* p. 20.

71. The best known architectural marvel of India.

transporting us into the contemplation of beauty; and it is only then that the eye is led to dwell on details of the architectural marvel.

Nor would it be proper to hold that the attitude in question necessarily opens itself in a "discerning manner." To discern is to distinguish. Now, where a work of art has an articulate structure, the right attitude to it would be doubtless discerning. But where, as in the experience of sublimity, the "object" overpowers us by its sheer might or immensity, without posing a real threat to life, the attitude may well be aesthetic without being discriminating or perceptive in respect of even slight differences. This is partly what Kant means by saying that the estimation is in such cases "aesthetic." What is more, if it be admitted that our attitude can be (or is) aesthetic even when we experience sublimity — and I see no reason to reject the possibility — Feezell's points that I have listed as (c) and (d) would at once appear questionable. Where the object seems to overwhelm us, we can neither say that its features are "appropriately encountered" nor speak of "an appreciation of subtleties of form." The word "form" signifies not only inner ordering, but (as Kant truly saw) also limitation. And it squares ill with "states of affairs themselves" to suppose that all aesthetic experience is merely a kind of *encounter*. At its best, I believe, it is seamless and *invasive*, like soulful prayer; and the attitude here is felt not as attunement for what is to come, but as surrender and indwelling.

So, I conclude, of all the features of the aesthetic attitude that Feezell arrives at as a result of phenomenological analysis, the only necessary ones are: isolating the object for attention, apartness from our everyday concerns, and openness to the object's own characteristics. How does this add to the view (of Stolnitz) I have defended in my essay?

The way I have built my argument around our experience

of the sublime is foreign to the essay of Stolnitz which Dickie criticizes.[72] But as for Feezell's emphases — that is, the object's being regarded "as a candidate for appreciation"; the "anticipatory and discerning manner" in which the aesthetic attitude opens up; looking forward to "the object's intrinsic characteristics"; and feeling "attuned" for "nuances of content and subtleties of form" — I wonder if any of these is left uncovered by the following unambiguous words of Stolnitz himself:

> Focusing upon the object . . . is not all that is meant by aesthetic "attention." *To savour fully the distinctive* value of the object, we must be attentive to the frequently *complex and subtle details.*
>
> Acute awareness of these details is *discrimination.* People . . . who . . . fail to "see" *all that is of significance in the work* . . . miss its *individuality.* . . . If we can *keep in mind* the chief themes in the movement of a symphony, *see how they are developed* and altered in the course of the movement . . . then there is a great gain in our experience.[73]

"Opening up" and "attuned" are the only words that appear to distinguish Feezell's account; but, here again, see the following from the essay of Stolnitz:

> As we develop discriminating attention, the work *comes alive to us.* . . . "Contemplation" . . . means that perception is directed to the object *in its own right* and that the spectator is not concerned to analyze it or to ask questions about it. Also, the word connotes *thoroughgoing absorption and interest,* as when we speak of being "lost in contemplation."[74]

---

72. The reference here is to: "The Aesthetic Attitude", by Stolnitz, and Dickie's "The Myth of the Aesthetic Attitude", in *Introductory Readings in Aesthetics,* pp. 17-44.

73. Stolniz: "The Aesthetic Attitude" *Introductory Readings in Aesthetics,* p. 23. Except the fourth one, all italics are here mine.

74. Ibid., pp. 23-24. Italics added.

Or again:

> We must make ourselves *receptive* to the object. . . . To maintain the aesthetic attitude, we must follow the lead of the object and respond *in concert with it.*[75]

In the light of all this, the instance of "the painting on my wall" which Feezell discusses by way of supporting his view can hardly be said to deliver any new truth; and the following, which may seem to make an additional point is, in my view, unclear:

> He has (when the aesthetic attitude has set in) . . . opened himself up to the object, and provisionally placed himself on the level of the object. A kind of spontaneous bracketing procedure has taken place. He has not implicitly posited the object as real or unreal.[76]

Whether the onlooker here posits the object as "real" would depend on what meaning we give to the word. If it be taken to mean "something out there," we will have to say that the object *is* here regarded as real; for, otherwise there would be no point in saying that the witness here opens himself up to — and places himself on the level of — the object. What is, in fact, here bracketed is the idea of being real as a thing *of utility*, and also of course *the question* (about) whether the thing is real or unreal. But all this, I repeat, is duly provided for when Stolnitz explains "disinterestedness' as follows:

> . . . Perception is directed to the object in its own right and . . . the spectator is not concerned to analyze it or to ask questions about it.[77]

---

75. Stolniz, op. cit., p. 21. Italics added.

76. Feezell, *Remarks*, p. 4.

77. Stolnitz, "The Aesthetic Attitude", *Introductory Readings in Aesthetics*, p. 24.

That the object is here seen as important in itself is, in Feezell's own "Remarks," a clear and recurring emphasis. But a part of what he says in this context seems no discovery when clarified. Consider, for instance, the following:

> I believe this feature is of the greatest importance . . . [that] the object as intended or meant is [here] constituted by consciousness as something *extraordinary,* something worthy of intrinsic appreciation . . . [yet?] there is a horizon of *familiarity* which surrounds our encounter with objects intended or meant in a distinctively aesthetic sense. And it is this horizon of familiarity or pre-acquaintanceship which provides the structural possibility for the constitution of the object as "aesthetic."[78]

If taken together, the words I have purposely italicized (in the extract just cited) involve a contradiction. But let us look at the passage closely. The aesthetic attitude "constitutes" its *object* as "extraordinary" in the sense that it here appears worthy of *intrinsic* appreciation, as against things of daily life which are of merely *instrumental* value. But, it is added, if its object is to be *so* "constituted," the aesthetic attitude also demands that our encounter with the object be surrounded by a horizon of "familiarity or pre-acquaintanceship." In other words, it is a (relatively) familiar thing that becomes the object of the aesthetic attitude by *somehow* coming to appear as a thing of intrinsic interest. Explaining this "somehow" is, for Feezell, unimportant from "the standpoint of phenomenological description."[79] But, I ask, if "the aesthetic" is held to be different from the commonplace, and if the familiar quality of the latter — the commonplace — is yet regarded as providing the very "structural possibility for the constitution of the object as 'aesthetic,'" does not a description of the transfiguration of the object become a necessary part of the phenomenological

78. Freezell, *Remarks,* p. 3. My italics.

79. Ibid.

task, and does not Bullough do it beautifully in his account of the way a fog at sea becomes an object of aesthetic contemplation?

Snoeyenbos makes three new protests.[80] I may put them thus, each along with my answer to it:

(a) Saxena maintains that "specific interests entail indifference to some aspects of an object"; and that, insofar as the aesthetic attitude is specific, "the utilitarian aspect of the object is here clearly ignored."[81] But consider an instance. The gracefulness of the blade of a knife is an aesthetic aspect. Its shape is, on the other hand, one of the object's utilitarian aspects. But, to be sure, one cannot notice the gracefulness without at once seeing the shape as well. So Saxena is wrong in saying that when we take an aesthetic interest in an object, its utilitarian aspect is ignored.

My answer, here, has to begin with some necessary distinguishing:

> In my words just cited I speak of the *aspects* of an object. These are not the same as its *parts.* A part is what goes to make up a whole. An aspect is a view, of a part or of the whole thing, from a particular angle or point of view. A part is, so to say, constitutive. An aspect is presentational as well; it implies some notice or regard. And therefore, though both "aspect" and "part" are in general opposed — and so related — to "whole," the relation to "whole" is not quite identical in the two cases. An aspect is better opposed to a whole *view* than to "whole" merely.

Let me now consider the word "aspect" first in relation to the complete object, and then in relation to a mere part. If I need a knife for chopping vegetables, I tend to regard it as merely a

80. *PEW*, January 1980, pp. 91-92.

81. Saxena, "Reply to My Critics", p. 219.

cutting instrument. In doing so I care only for its utilitarian aspect, not for its beauty of form. This aspect (of utility) here is not as such a given property or part of the knife. It is the thing as regarded in a particular way. So, where I speak of the object's utilitarian aspect being ignored, I mean simply that in the aesthetic attitude the object is not regarded as an object of utility.

Turn, now, to a part of the knife, say, its blade. Its shape is not *as such* a utilitarian *aspect*. It *becomes* so when it is regarded as good, say for piercing hard surfaces. And when we merely let our eye tarry at its streamlined quality, it (the same shape!) comes to appear graceful. Aesthetic interest does not — it cannot — mean that we blink the shape. It only means that we do not consider the shape from the point of view of utility.

(b) Saxena "owes us a more precise analysis of the distinction between the utilitarian and non-utilitarian aspects of an object."[82] He has not attempted the task. What is worse, some of his remarks make one suspect that he cannot do it without committing a circularity. "Aesthetic interest" and "non-utilitarian aspect" should be independently defined. But Saxena says, first, that "the point of view or attitude of the man who attends, and what features or meanings are, in consequence, revealed in the object are all actual parts[83] of the fact of attention"[84]; and secondly, that the interest (or attitude) of the person is not "independent of the aspect that is the focus of attention."[85] Here, he seems to imply that "a non-utilitarian aspect is any aspect that is the focus of attention controlled by

82. M.H. Snoeyenbos, *PEW*, January 1980, p. 91.

83. Snoeyenbos complains: "It is not clear how 'part' is used in this passage." Ibid. (I answer, in the sense: "that which constitutes or goes to make up a whole").

84. Ibid.

85. Ibid.

an aesthetic interest,"[86] and [that] an aesthetic interest is an interest in which attention focuses on the non-utilitarian aspects of an object; but then, "the circularity is (here) obvious."[87]

Now, before I set out to answer the above, let me see how Snoeyenbos himself separates the two kinds of aspects. He says:

> The hue, saturation, and brightness of the blade's colour would *ordinarily* be regarded as non-utilitarian aspects; they are irrelevant to the knife's function of cutting. . . . The size and shape of the blade would typically be considered to be utilitarian aspects; they are *standardly* relevant to the knife's use as a cutting instrument.[88]

Here, the words "ordinarily" and "standardly" provide a qualification which is necessary. For, though it is true that the shape (I leave out size) of the blade is more directly involved in the knife's function of cutting than, say, the brightness of its colour — and this makes us classify the shape as "utilitarian" in opposition to brightness — its being utilitarian or non-utilitarian is yet not as unchangeably fixed as, say, the blade's being merely a part of the knife. The shape may only be admired for its curvaceous quality; and one does sometimes regard the brightness as a sign of the newness of the knife, justifying a higher price. Here, in the first case, our way of looking would be non-utilitarian; and in the second case, utilitarian — just as clearly. To conclude, an aspect's appearing utilitarian or otherwise depends on how it is regarded.

This is the basis of the difference Snoeyenbos wants me to explicate, and I do it thus:

Aesthetic interest is concern for a thing or its parts because of their own intrinsic features, and not for the sake of their

86. M.H. Snoeyenbos, op. cit.

87. Ibid., pp. 2-3.

88. Ibid. Italics added.

usefulness. The aspects thus regarded *become* "aesthetic." The two are but concurrent poles, subjective and objective, of the same attitude; and the demand to define the one quite independently of the other is therefore improper. Be it noted that a difference here certainly holds. The attitude is an orientation *of the contemplator*, however brought about; and the aesthetic aspect is a feature (or the form) *of the object* as contemplated intransitively. All transitive attention is not utilitarian, as when I revel in the echo of my own experience that I may find in reading a play. Features become "utilitarian" when they are regarded from the point of view of their *usefulness as* ordinarily understood.

(c) Finally, even if Saxena is able to clarify the utilitarian-non-utilitarian distinction independently of the concept of aesthetic interest, it would not do. For then, aesthetic interest will become a matter of "attending to non-utilitarian aspects"; the utilitarian-non-utilitarian distinction will become primary; and aesthetic interest, secondary. This would, in turn, undercut the basic intent of the Bullough-Stolnitz theory; for "they regard their theory as a psychologically based theory in which the key terms are all defined via 'aesthetic interest.'"

To this, I have but two remarks to make. First, as already explained, if non-utilitarian be taken to mean "aesthetic," I would *not* wish to clarify the utilitarian-non-utilitarian distinction quite independently of the concept of aesthetic interest. Secondly, I do not quite see how Stolnitz could (in the end) be said to regard his theory as "psychologically *based.*"[89] The key terms are here the following: "disinterested, sympathetic, attention, and contemplation." The first term listed means that our interest comes to rest *upon the object alone;*[90] the

89. I leave out Bullough, for in my essay under review the emphasis was on Stolnitz.

90. Stolnitz, "The Aesthetic Attitude", in *Introductory Readings in Aesthetics*, p. 20.

second, that "we . . . follow *the lead of the object* and respond in concert with it";[91] the third, that "we want to make *the value of the object* come fully alive in our experience";[92] and the fourth, that "perception is directed *to the object in its own right.*" If we add to all this the final unmistakable words in the definition of Stolnitz: "for its (the object's) sake alone,"[93] would it still seem proper to regard his theory as "psychologically based?" Aesthetic interest itself is, for him, exclusive concern with *the object.*

Now that the debate has come to an end, I realize the need to say the following, largely from the viewpoint of phenomenology, about the view I have so far defended:

(a) Nowhere in his essay does Stolnitz speak of the *artist's own* attitude during creation as being or as capable of growing aesthetic. Yet we can hardly deny that when, as *during* art-making, one takes a shape from life to explore its creative possibilities or uses some material solely with an eye to creating beauty,[94] the attitude is aesthetic. The account of Stolnitz suggests, what is to me questionable, that the attitude in question is *confined to the external contemplation of a completed object.* The artist at work is absorbed in what he deals with here and now; so *his* indifference to ulterior ends and prefixed plans comes about easily; and hence his attitude is very freely aesthetic. I here see the value of the concept of *intentionality.*

(b) The same concept, I may add, by virtue of the provision it makes for openness to what the object itself suggests, could

---

91. Stolnitz, op. cit., 21. Italics added.

92. Ibid., 22. Italics added.

93. Ibid., 24. Italics added.

94. As when a note (or a beat in rhythm) is regarded not merely as a member of some series, but as the source or climax of diverse patterns.

make us see the truth that the aesthetic attitude can also be *elicited by the object*, and is not always *adopted by us*.[95] I am not sure if in the essay under review Stolnitz shows a due awareness of this truth, though he does at places speak as follows: "There are some objects which . . . 'catch our eye'."[96]

---

95. I may here point out that the very opening of the essay of Stolnitz warrants my suspicion: "Aesthetic perception will be explained in terms of the aesthetic *attitude*. It is the attitude *we take* which determines how we perceive the world."

    Stolnitz, "The Aesthetic Attitude", in *Introductory Readings in Aesthetics*, p. 17. Italics added.

    See again, ". . . The aesthetic attitude is not the attitude which people usually adopt." (Ibid., p. 18): or "The aesthetic attitude can be adopted towards 'any object of awareness whatever'." (Ibid., p. 24).

96. Ibid.

4

Aesthetic Theory and Hindustānī Rhythm[1]

THIS essay is, in part, a response to the call for internationalism in aesthetics. Two features of Hindustānī[2] music, *ālāpa* and *rhythm*, have not yet been given the notice they deserve. Sonant *ālāpa* is singing without words and rhythmic accompaniment. At its best, it seems an intense diffusion, a kind of atmosphere, rather than a form.[3] It can be the most deeply satisfying genre of Indian music. But attention to rhythm is of help in checking more ideas in our philosophic concern with art today. It is this that I here seek to argue.

But is rhythm one of the arts? Can it lay claim to independent status? My answer is, yes; but I know that many would disagree. Today, in India, rhythm is presented and admired mostly as accompaniment; and a lay listener would perhaps question the view that rhythm is autonomous. But, I may point out, it is also a fact that in our main music conferences

---

1. The present form of this article differs not only from the talk given on the subject to participants in the Aesthetics section of the World Philosophy Conference (University of Delhi, 2 January, 1976), but from the essay published, under the same title, by *The British Journal of Aesthetics* in its Summer 1976 issue, volume 16, no. 3.
2. *Hindustānī* here means "north Indian."
3. I say so because, as Kant pointed out long ago, the word *form* implies limitation.

even today, a *solo* rhythmic recital can well be the main draw of an entire session of music. In our country, in fact, it has ever been so. Sculpture, in the West, had to shake off subservience to architecture. Painting too had to win its freedom from representation. In the case of our rhythm, on the other hand, it is the heightened emphasis on *accompaniment* that seems to be of recent growth. The primal test of a drummer for us has ever been his capacity for *solo* playing.

The musicologist may protest by pointing to our well-known word *saṅgeet*. It certainly covers both music (vocal, instrumental) and dance, and *does not omit rhythm*. How then is rhythm independent? My reply here is that if the same word is used for many things, they are not thereby prevented from functioning severally. There is indeed no dancing with *ālāpa*; nor any vocal filigree with *tatkār*[4] or pure dance. It is true that, as is indeed quite manifest in our dancing today, the arts covered by the word *saṅgeet* can be interwoven easily. Further, there is in fact one element which is common to them all, that is, *laya* or pace as duly regulated. Further, *it* is not the necessary (or only) integrative principle where dance and music blend. In the case of an expressional dance item, for instance, they may both have to subserve, in the main, the demands of the text of the thematic number (or composition) rather than requirements of *laya*. Yet, the entire *nṛtta* (or purely rhythmic) part of Kathak dance, though it surely — and very importantly — builds on *laya*, enjoys an independent aesthetic status. It is in this context noteworthy that even Birju Maharaj, who represents the Lucknow Gharānā which is acclaimed for its expressiveness and grace, captivates audiences as much by his hold over *laya* as by the beauty of his *aṅg*.

However, apart from this evidence of fact, I can draw help from theory too. But to facilitate understanding, let me first

---

4. *Tatkār* is display of pure footwork in Kathak dance.

outline our rhythm quite simply. A rhythmic recital comprises a cycle and some patterns. The cycle is a whole of a specific number of beats moving at even speed. The first beat here is at once the focal beat or *sama*. From it we set out as we follow the rhythm; and to it we return, accurately, completing a round or *āvartan*.[5] The patterns that are woven across (or within) the cycle are infinitely various in respect of content and manner, but they must all in the end conform to the *sama* or heigthten it ideally.

The cyclic quality of our (basic) rhythm at once makes for the suggestion of wholeness. If the specific idiom of the cycle chosen has been truly "established";[6] if, further, the accents neither seem to tug, nor appear blurred in the flow; and if, finally, the playing has the requisite measure of euphonic charm, the rhythm may even *seem to move to a clear inner impetus*. All this conduces to concentration on the form and inside of the rhythmic whole itself. It is indeed quite easy for a duly played cycle to appear a miniature of what Dewey calls "an experience" — marked out and self-complete.[7]

But the independence of rhythm as an art can be argued in a much fuller way. Langer suggests that an art is autonomous if it can be said to have its own materials, its "peculiar primary creation," and its own creative principles.[8] So, I may now set out to show how rhythm meets all these requirements, and one or two more; and also, in passing and subsequently, its value for aesthetics.

---

5. How, even *aesthetically*, the *sama* is both the source and destiny of rhythm will be brought out later.
6. This is the English word for our: *quāyem karnā*.
7. A much better illustration of the point in question would, however, be a *quāyedā* because it has a far richer structure than a mere cycle.
8. S.K. Langer, *Problems of Art*, London: Routledge and Kegan Paul, 1957, pp. 78-79.

Rhythm as an Art

A. *The material of rhythm* is doubtless distinctive. It is mnemonic syllables (or *bol*s) that aim at seizing the look of sounds produced by striking the drum(s) in specific ways.[9] They are mere letters or meaningless bunches of letters, like *tā, dhā, tin, dhin* (ता, धा, तिन, धिन); but in every case they seek to be approximate formal analogues of actual sounds. They are not unmusical, but they mark but one or two notes of the scale. Their function is to make us identify the actual sounds drummed, and their beauty arises from the way of their segmentation and clear execution.

Now, it is possible to hold with some show of reason that *because of this uniqueness of its material,* rhythm is not only distinctive but *important* among the arts. One may here build upon Herbert Read's way of arguing for the pre-eminence of *music*:

> . . . almost in music alone, it is possible for the artist to appeal to his audience directly, without the intervention of a medium of communication in common use for other purposes. The architect must express himself in buildings which have [some] utilitarian purpose. The poet must use words which are bandied about in the daily give-and-take of conversation.[10]

Now *if*, as here, the rank of an art is made to depend on the requirement that its medium is *not* used for "other (non-aesthetic) purposes," rhythm could well claim to be superior to music. For, whereas musical notes are in fact sweetly

9. I do not here speak of *mātrā*s or beats, because a *mātrā*, by virtue of its very meaning as a word, is a *measure*; so related to what it is a measure of; and therefore a unit of rhythm's artistic *content*, and not its mere material. The word *bol*, on the other hand, if it is taken wholly by itself, does not imply relation.

10. Herbert Read's essay, "A Definition of Art", included in *Aesthetics and the Arts*, ed. L.A. Jacobus, McGraw Hill Book Co., 1968, p. 4. Bracketed word added.

employed — say, by some hawkers in their typical cries, or by some bells to chime the hour pleasantly, purposes which are both clearly utilitarian — the mnemonic syllables (or *bol*s) of rhythm are never employed for any non-aesthetic purpose.

Nor do they refer to anything external. A good rhythmic recital is quite non-representational. Yet, because of the excellence of its own inner organization (and clarity), it can be so absorbing that it may induce in knowledgeable listeners a state of self-forgetfulness and attune them in *tādātmya*[11] with the winged variform beauty of rhythm. Of course, if he so decides, the drummer *can* produce syllables that *resemble* everyday sounds and familiar happenings, such as the movement and noise of a train as it steams out and gathers speed; but whenever such imitation is attempted, those who know what rhythm *as an art* is only feel amused. Our rhythm is indeed very true to the ideal of "pure" art.

Here, I may add, it would be clearly wrong to contend that rhythm *as played* represents or imitates *bols as recited* or thought; and that rhythm is therefore not free from representation. Why I say so is easy to put. Merely as it occurs in speech, writing or thought, a *bol* is nothing self-complete. It is *meant to be played*; it only receives the supplement it itself demands when it is played out at the drums; and *as played*, the *bols* are not imitated by, but only incorporated in rhythm, like words in poetry.

B. *The primary creation of rhythm* is, in my view, *the automotive and articulate symmetry of pure pace*. The keywords here may be explained as follows:

By "symmetry" I mean beauty of form. Everything in the region of rhythm is indeed required to look well ordered and shapely. This is true of both the basic rhythm-cycle and the

11. *Tādātmya* is one's imaginative self-identification with the essence of the other.

patterns which are woven across it and never stray from its focal beat randomly.

As for the epithet *articulate*, I think it is truer of our rhythm than of any other art. Langer emphasizes it in the context of music. "A composition," she says, "is not merely produced by mixture like a new colour made by mixing paints but is articulated, i.e. its internal structure is given to our perception." The parts here, it is added, "maintain some degree of separate existence."[12] But I do not think this is entirely true of musical form. To speak quite generally, where harmony dominates the music it is difficult to distinguish the notes as appearing to have a "separate existence." Further, in Hindustānī music *meeṇḍ*s or glides, if suitably employed, are always found to make for, rather than to weaken the form of music; yet it is impossible to say that the notes in a *meeṇḍ* retain "some degree of *separate* existence." Such existence is here neither present nor desired. In fact, what distinguishes a *meeṇḍ* as a formal device is the quite opposite fact that the notes it comprises seem to *flow into one another*.

Nor is articulation, as Langer interprets it, indispensable to painting. The structure or the organization of details is not here mainfest in the case of every work. Consider, for instance, the masterpieces of Turner, the famous English painter of seascapes and landscapes. Take his well-known work *Snowstorm*. Turner himself feared its details would not be easily clear to the onlooker. That is indeed why he had to exhibit the work with the following elaborate rubric: "Snowstorm: steamboat off a harbour's mouth making signals in shallow water, and going by the lead." Yet the work *is* a masterpiece, "one of the vastest representations," as Ruskin said, "of the

---

12. S.K. Langer, *Feeling and Form*, London: Routledge and Kegan Paul Ltd., 1963, Third Impression, p. 31.

sea in motion, and of clouds and light."[13]

In respect of rhythm, on the other hand, articulation is always a key requirement. Here, even in the case of such patterns as *relā* or a *rau* which are meant to be presented at a very quick pace, we insist on the clarity of syllables, without of course a sacrifice of fluency for the sake of inner clarity. Generally, the *bol*s are required to be "cut out." This detail of manner is called *bol kātnā*; and playing which meets this requirement admirably is called *khushkhat* (ख़ुशख़त). The syllable *dir, dir,* in quick playing, may seem an exception to this general rule; but even here, we may note, the effect sought is one of *tremulous* fluency, *and the palpitation must not be quite eclipsed in the flow*. It should now be easy to see why the old masters would, as a rule, be averse to playing at hectic speed[14] where the syllables are bedimmed and seem to become a mere flowing lump.

Its *automotive* character is another main feature of rhythm. The meaning is not that rhythm *somehow* seems self-propelling, but that the length or brevity of the very first syllable or beat as played or rather as recited[15] — *or* its own temporal character — directly determines whether the entire subsequent playing is to be leisurely or brisk. In *paṛhant* (or recitation of *bol*s) it is in fact quite easy to see the point that if one utters the first *bol* (tied to the opening beat) slowly — say, in the manner of a drawl — the entire subsequent counting has to be just as

---

13. Giuseppe Gatt, *Turner*, A Dolphin Art Book, Thames and Hudson, 1968, p. 37.

14. An oft quoted example of such masters is the Late Ustad Natthu Khan of Delhi.

15. In the case of Indian rhythm, most of the sounds that the drummer produces while playing can be recited by him, as syllables or *bol*s, the playing and the speaking being related by similarity of mere manner. Proper recitation of the rhythmic syllables is for us an important aspect of the drummer's art.

leisurely; and if the same *bol* is then spoken sharply and briefly, the following beats too are required to be quickened correspondingly. I wonder if we can anywhere find a *more obvious* instance of determination of the whole-form by the character of a part. And this is, I may add, a more definite pointer to the "autonomous form" of rhythm than Langer's following remark on some records of African music in which the constructive power of the drum is (in her view) paramount:

> . . . Anyone familiar with many works of that sort would probably feel their structure and mood almost from the opening beat.[16]

The automotive symmetry of rhythm is, however, not uniform. It has three main expressions:

- a pattern flitting across, and variegating the basic rhythm (cycle);
- or making for, and (so to speak) efflorescing at the *sama*; or, much less commonly,
- deviating, on purpose, from the focal beat, and yet not losing sight of it.

The first is the common effect of patterns after the basic rhythm (cycle) has been established. The second and the third may be called, respectively, the rhythms of orientation *and* intentional deviance. *These* have been missed by those who have written on rhythm.[17] So I may comment on them at some length.

---

16. S.K. Langer, *Feeling and Form*, p. 125.

17. As by Frye, where he speaks of the various kinds of rhythm. See his *Anatomy of Criticism*, Princeton University Press, 1957, (PB), pp. 251-81.

    Langer too speaks *only* of the setting up and release of tensions, and continuity and repetition where she discusses rhythm. See her *Feeling and Form*, pp. 125-32.

THE RHYTHM OF ORIENTATION

When a well-designed integration of *bol*s is being played by the drummer, it often happens that from a particular point within its run, the pattern, so to say, gathers and activates itself perceptibly and tends towards, and finally blooms forth at the *sama* in delightful self-completion of form. The *sama* here appears as the destiny — and not the mere terminus — of a clearly oriented rhythmic flow. Such flow is of help like a clear direction line in a painting; and form is here heightened as a *passage, not mere process* of efflorescence. Perhaps in no other art is the precise point or region of organization, or the dominant motif or movement, so clearly identifiable as in our rhythm.

It may also be noted, in passing, that — as seems requisite for any art that claims to be independent — in respect of rhythm too we have some criteria that apply to it uniquely. One of these is the drummer's capacity for a "blended" employment of the two drums. The reference here is obviously to *tablā* which comprises two drums; but the point needs clearing. The thing is that each drum has its own share in the fabric of playing. The "left" drum is meant to work up effects of a certain breathing continuity (called *sāns*) and of depth and inwardness; and the "right" one contributes crispness, discreteness, sweetness, fluency and clarity. The requirement is that (at least) in playing the basic rhythm-cycle the use of the two drums should be duly co-ordinated, so that the playing may seem neither a mere succession of disconnected sounds, due to undue dominance of "the right one," nor a mere booming loudness due to tyranny on the left, but a mellow, flowing sound wherein the details occur daintily, without being blurred in, or marring the resonance produced by "the left" one. Another requirement which relates to rhythm alone is the drummer's ability to arrive at the *sama* with split second accuracy.[18]

---

18. And in a well-designed way.

Now, this second criterion, I insist, is a more clearly usable requirement than the criteria which govern evaluation in the field of other arts. Two critics, equally competent, honest and watchful, may find it difficult to decide whether an item of music is or is not properly structured *or* expressive. But two listeners who have but a fair knowledge of rhythm are almost bound to agree as to whether or not the drummer has reached the first beat accurately. For them it is as easy a matter as our judging, in daily life, that a man has arrived sharply on time.

The Rhythm of Intentional Deviance

Some patterns are so knit and played that they end a little after or before the *sama*. The deviation is here willed; and is demanded by the very economy or ebullience of structure. The *sama* is overstepped or just not touched; but it is heightened in idea by the very design of refusing to comply. A *part* of this artifice may not seem new to those who are familiar with poetry. It is indeed common knowledge that inspired poetic content may well spill, so to say, the bounds of prefixed extent, and thereby vivify *form* as internal structure. See, for instance, the following from Stephen Spender:

> Form does not lie simply in the correct observance of rules. It lies in the struggle of certain living material to achieve itself within a pattern. The very refusal of a poet to sacrifice what he means to a perfectly correct rhyme, for example, can more powerfully suggest the rhyme than correctness itself would.[19]

But, I believe, it is not *so* easy to realize the other half of the matter, that is, the truth that our awareness of "form" may be heightened even by the act of ending a little *short* of the normal stretch, in response to the immanent needs of design. Yet this exactly is what is done by our patterns that are made

---

19. Stephen Spender, *World within World*, London: Hamilton, pp. 313-14.

to terminate a little before the *sama.*[20] (In the region of sculpture a parallel is perhaps provided by a detail of Rodin's way of working. Once he had succeeded in finding the exact movement or expression in a figure or bust, he would often stop and leave, say, the hands and feet unfinished — without detracting from the seeming self-completeness of the work as contemplated.)

The Rhythm of Simultaneity

But a better known rhythm — and easier to follow — is that of simultaneity. I have here in mind the kind of rhythm that *distinguishes* the drummer's art of providing "accompaniment" to the main performer — say, a sitārist — namely, the rhythm not only of structural sameness and confluence, but of co-extension and unitive completion. I refer here to a consummate kind of *saṅgat*[21] and may put it as follows. When the musician sets out to play a pattern that is frolicsome in rhythm, the drummer may promptly seize the former's very manner (*andāz*); and without ever slackening his hold over the cycle, may so adapt his own playing to that of the main performer that the two flowing forms may appear to be a quite free confluence, and also end at the *sama* in perfect similutaneity. Here, *what* syllables the drummer plays is not the basic thing; and what counts, I repeat, is only his unerring grasp and replication of the *manner* of music. The instant of jointly reaching the *sama* satisfies not in detachedness, but largely because it consummates a flowing *design*; and the net effect, because of confluent and very similar forms and rhythmic turns, is one of

---

20. Such rhythmic patterns are called *anāgat*.

21. The other kind, which is easier and more current today, is quite different. Here, the drummer reproduces the rhythmic parallel *after* the sitārist has begun playing the basic *gat* (composition) again. But this, I protest, is closer to *solo* playing than *saṅgat* which literally means "accompaniment," and not mere following or reproduction.

intertwining.[22]

C. Rhythm also has its own "*principles of constructing* its final creations."[23] Some of these resemble poetic craft, such as the artifice of *quāfiyā radeef* (in the case of a *quāyedā*)[24] which is similar to end-rhymes; and there is also, in the making of rhythm, a free use of the Gestalt laws of perception such as those of figure ground and common destiny. I may here dwell on only one constructional device which is at once basic to and distinctive of rhythm. This is the act of so filling a stretch of some beats, or the duration *between* two separate beats (where the pace is leisurely), with orderly bunches of *bol*s that rhythm gets invested with the *spatial suggestions of teeming, being crowded, or even overflowing* with them. A single syllable so inserted may also come to look like a wedge holding the neighbouring ones apart. The richer and the more orderly the filling of *bol*s within a narrow time-length, the greater is the title of the drummer to acclaim. From the viewpoint of this artifice, rhythm may well be regarded as an aesthetic demonstration of the divisibility of time.

But the *form and content* of its filling (of *bol*s) at once distinguish rhythm from actual or "lived" time. This, however, is not the only reason for regarding rhythmic time as "virtual." Indeed there are quite a few other details of winsome appearance that mark the run of a rhythmic recital uniquely.

---

22. The Hindustānī word, here, is *lipatnā*.

23. S.K. Langer, *Problems of Art*, p. 79.

24. A *quāyedā* is an impressive, elaborate and methodically organized pattern. The terminal syllables of its two sections have to be similar in sound, though not identical in content, such as: *tīnākinā, dhīnāginā*. For a fuller account of what a *quāyedā* is, see pp. 47-48 of Sudhir Kumar Saxena's *The Art of Tabla Rhythm: Essentials, Tradition and Creativity*, Sangeet Natak Akademi and D.K. Printworld (P.) Ltd., 2nd Impression, 2008.

The following ones of these are well known to those who love *tablā*-playing.

Whether as the matrix of a solo recital, or as providing "accompaniment," how exactly a *cycle* affects us, on the whole, turns (also) on its relation to the patterns which it initiates, supervenes or sustains. Thus, when in a solo recital the drummer lapses back to the cycle steadily after executing a *tukṛā*[25] of extra fluent pace, the *ṭhekā* may *seem to be* slower than it really is. And if, while providing simple[26] "accompaniment" to (say) the singer's filigree of *svaras*, the drummer goes on playing the *cycle* steadily, the rhythm may be felt as just a *moveless* background, not as being occurrent or flowing, though some actual process is obviously there. Here, the question of *drut*[27] or *vilambit*[28] is not raised at all, and what we admire is only the the *ṭhekā*'s seeming fixedness.[29]

Again, any rhythmic pattern can be made to look a little more fleet than it actually is by just playing it emphatically. But real time may be more sweetly surpassed when the playing makes the *sama* appear as the climax of a shapely rhythmic upsurge. Here, as we follow the flowing form approaching its terminus, we only *think of the sama*; and *as thus apprehended*, it cannot seem extended. The unfoldment that we watch is that of the pattern, and when it ends at the *sama* immaculately, we just nod at the fusion in instant approval instead of estimating *how long the sama-bol lasts*. It does in fact occupy a measurable time, but it *appears* to be over without *occupying* any time.

25. A *tukṛā* is a small rhythmic pattern, not exceeding two *āvṛttis* of the cycle.

26. By *simple* accompaniment I here mean the steady playing of the *ṭhekā* alone, not imitating the manner of the vocalist's patterns.

27. *Drut* means allegro.

28. *Vilambit* is adagio.

29. *Our* words of acclaim here are: "कैसा ठेका गाढ़ा है.

Calculative following as a quiet *counting* of beats — to which our awareness of lived time — say, in some moments of anxiety — may be similar, is here quite suspended. Assuredly, we do not measure the single moment when a tension is relieved, or a target just attained in daily life. What is more, if during the course of making a pattern move designedly towards the *sama*, the drummer also gradually increases the intensity of the constituent *bols*, the additional suggestion of an *ascent* — not of mere reaching, but of an *upflow* — will be clearly worked up.

Rhythm and Aesthetic Theory

We may finally make some explicit comments on the relevance of Hindustānī rhythm to modern aesthetic theory, — to the following concepts, in particular: *living form*,[30] *embodiment*, *symbol* and *expression*.

a. The concept of *living form*, I believe, gets a new meaning in the light of those patterns which (for a brief while) abandon the basic rhythm in movements of diverse design, without really going astray. Such "wanton heed" is also a kind of drummer's self-testing, a testing of the firmness of his hold over *laya*, which is at once a kind of creative self-possession.

b. In the light of this fact, it hardly seems proper to speak of rhythm as *embodiment*, because this word suggests inertness. Rhythm is an occurrent art. It happens. We see it being made. What is more, in playing any pattern the drummer may — with guarded abandon and distinct aesthetic gain — shorten or momentarily withhold one syllable, or tarry at or displace another against its set speed and location, without of course

30. Say, as used by Susanne Langer in *Mind: An Essay on Human Feeling*, vol. I. Baltimore and London: The John Hopkins University Press, Second printing (paper) 1975, pp. 199-244, 324, 331.

failing to mark (or suggest) the *sama*. And this can make for an effect that is wholly new. Thus, quite apart from the design of the patterns he chooses to play, the drummer may invest the *sama* with some extra incisiveness by playing the penultimate *bol* just a little later than its grammatically set moment. This ever-present room for creative variations is not at all provided for when we speak of rhythm as embodiment.[31] Above all, with regard to drumming which is extremely fluent, and may seem to have the rapidity of a torrent, it would be as improper to use the word "embodiment" as to say that a waterfall *embodies* a flow.

c. Can (an exposition of) rhythm be said to be a *symbol*? My answer is here in the negative. Whatever is a symbol permits and calls for the question; "what does it symbolize?" But this is exactly what cannot be asked in respect of rhythm. At different moments it just *looks* lively, ebullient or torrential, steadfast, intricate and involute. If however we *have* to regard it as being in some sense a symbol, it would be proper to call it a presentational one, in Langer's sense. Indeed, as we listen to good drumming, it is just not possible to detach what it "says" from its syllabic material.

d. Nor is *expressiveness* any truer to rhythm. I have yet to see a drummer or a critic saying that rhythm is expressive of something. The commonest words of critical acclaim here are: fluent, effortless, methodical, sparkling, brilliant; and the key features of rhythm, I repeat, are clarity and organization of syllables.

(However, I here visualize a possible objection. If

31. For similar (and other) objections to the view that *embodiment* is the key aesthetic concept, see essay no. 2 in this book.

rhythm neither represents nor expresses life-content, how is it at all significant? *My* ready answer is that it charms us by its very "look," like beautiful objects of nature which are not ordinarily said to symbolize, express or embody anything.)

e. But, perhaps the clearest way in which Hindustānī rhythm is relevant to aesthetic theory is the infinite ground it provides for analysis. Analytic writing on its basic concepts has only begun,[32] and the whole rhythmic discourse of our unlettered *ustāds*,[33] often quite obscure but never *sans* insight, is waiting to be analysed.

---

32. The first step here, I believe, is my essay on *laya* which appeared in *Indian Philosophical Quarterly*, Pune, vol. I. no. 2, January 1974, under the title: "The Concept of *Laya* in Hindustānī Music".

33. *Ustād* here means a professional Muslim musician or teacher of music or rhythm. Here, I must add that, if not exhaustively, the analysis referred to has now been duty attempted in my book *Hindustani Music and Aesthetics Today*, brought out jointly by Sangeet Natak Akademi and Hope India Publications early this year.

5

Music and Silence[1]

It is not generally realized that the actual, ultimate impact of music, be it vocal or instrumental, is inseparable not only from the uniquely trained sensibility and imagination of the *rasika*, but even from his (or her) general sense of values. There is, however, yet another relation to which music itself is necessarily subject, but which has rarely been made an object of study. This is the relation of music to *silence*. Very few aestheticians have reflected on this subject; and, to the best of my knowledge, perhaps no one has so far addressed the question how *Hindustānī* music relates to silence. The only generally relevant essay that I have come across is the one by Gisele Brelet which appeared in the twenty-second volume of *La Revue Musicale* more than half a century ago.[2] It is doubtless a thoughtful essay written, at places, in a markedly phenomenological vein; but it does not clearly bring out how silence relates to the three distinct ways in which music concerns us, that is, as composition, performance, and listening; and, of course, it could not be expected to have any direct bearing on north Indian music with which alone I can truly claim to be familiar.

---

1. This is a slightly modified repeat of the essay as it appeared under the same head in the *Journal of Indian Council of Philosophical Research*, vol. XX, no. 3, July–September 2003, pp. 224-34.

2. This essay appears in *Reflections on Art*, ed. by Susanne K. Langer, Baltimore: The Johns Hopkins Press, 2nd printing 1960, pp. 102-21.

However, before I proceed further I must face a possible question. Does the subject I have chosen deserve philosophic reflection at all? Is it not quite apparent that, as privation of sound, silence is just *opposed to* music which must build upon *svaras* that are all meant to be *heard*, and discriminatingly? The point of such sceptical questions, however, dissovles the moment we look at two simple facts. First, for listening to music properly we need a measure of quiet in the auditorium; and secondly, moments of quiet are not only *inevitable* within the very run of music itself, but even *desirable* because music is essentially a contemplative, not a dramatic art. It *can* appear dramatic as when a singer becomes flamboyantly emotional or tries to cover up lack of intrinsic quality in his music with frequent and exaggerated gestures. But where it is of the highest class, our classical music needs contemplation in ample measure; and, what is more, the need is equal for the performer *and* his audience. How this very need calls for recurring moments of silence would become clear if we gave some thought to what contemplation itself is. Here, the following from Harold Osborne should be of help:

> Aesthetic contemplation . . . [is a special] form of absorption . . . [Here] . . . the field of attention is narrowed; our usual practical concerns are put in abeyance. . . . When aesthetic contemplation is successful and absorption is achieved there is a loss of subjective time-sense, a loss of the sense of place and a loss of bodily consciousness.[3]

What is here said is perfectly true, but it does not go far enough. As engrossment, contemplation is not an instantaneous peck of attention, however focused it may be. It needs time to settle itself and to take over the mind. This is why the *vilambit* idiom is essential for music.[4] Now, it is obvious, leisurely or reposeful

3. Harold Osborne, *The Art of Appreciation*, OUP, 1970, pp. 34-35.

4. See, here, the following ". . . Is not speed normally *opposed to* →

singing just cannot be unremitting; it has to let in some moments of silence. Even generally, no one can sing absolutely without any break; and if one somehow could, it would be an aesthetic disaster. It would just leave no time for the singer and the listener to internalize the ongoing music; the course of singing will have no depth or inwardness about it; and the heard sounds would only tickle the ear. The experience, in either case, would be merely perceptual.

Contemplation, however, is not the only key term that relates to our present purpose. We will also be using, pretty freely, words like music, silence, composition, and performance. These are all familiar words, to be sure; but a little close thinking on what they really mean in the context of practice *and* understanding of art in general may yet be found to help. *Music* is of course commonly taken to be pre-eminent among the arts, but its inseparability from *laya* (or aesthetic pace) and rhythm is not generally seen quite clearly. For those who are wedded to Hindustānī (or north Indian) music it should be easy to see why it is essential to distinguish *laya* from rhythm. Here, in the kind of music which is all along the context of my thinking in this essay (that is, Hindustānī Music) *rhythm* or *tāla* is an extent of temporal flow measured by means of *mātrās* (or beats); made internally articulate with the additional help of *bols* which are meaningless letters (or their bunches which are equally non-semantic) and segments (or *vibhāgs*), all conjoining to make a cycle with a focal point (called the *sama*); and meant, in the main, to be *played* at some drum.

All this is just not there along with *ālāpa* of the *dhruvapad* genre where the duration of *sustainment* of individual notes — and the pace of tonal *passages* — are both determined by the singer's own creative ability to produce different effects. So

→ contemplation? . . . Incidentally, the Oxford Dictionary . . . *pace* Winterbourne . . . gives 'contemplation' as *opposed* to active." David Best's essay, "Reply to My Critics" in *The British Journal of Aesthetics*, vol. 23, no. 2, Spring 1983, p. 158.

the temporal element in *ālāpa* can only be said to be *laya* or aesthetic pace, that is, tempo as determined essentially by the vocalist's own ability to evoke varying effects, consistently of course with the character of the *rāga* chosen. Now, bearing all this in mind, and as demanded by the subject we are dealing with, two points may be made here. First, intervals of silence in *ālāpa* cannot easily be so *long* as in *khayāl*-singing where the gaps in vocal utterance can easily appear filled up by listeners' attention to the ongoing *ṭhekā*. Secondly, there are some specific and *brief*, but intentional and aesthetically significant bits of quiet which just cannot be there in *ālāpa* because it is devoid of *tāla*. My reference here is to such moments of silence as the ones that may (be made to) separate the three segments of a *taan* modelled as a *tiyā*, or the dainty and adroit bit of quiet which is sometimes brought about by the vocalist when he intentionally completes a predetermined *taan* or phrase just a little before the *sama*, inducing us, the listeners, to visualize the focal beat and to bridge the vacant little interval imaginatively and happily.

The way I have taken *rhythm* so far is, however, relevant only to our music. Aestheticians, on the other hand, have given a wider meaning to the word, with a view to covering all art quite generally, say, as follows:

> Rhythm not only dominates music and poetry, but also, in a wider sense, architecture, sculpture, and painting: the bigger part of a space is heavier than the smaller; one spatial form, whether linear or plane, weightier, more striking, or stronger in character than another; colours, also, are distinguished from various points of view by their greatly varied impressiveness. . . . If, therefore, we want to define rhythm in general, we have to say: rhythm is the alternation between heavy (stressed) and light (unstressed or less stressed) parts, in so far as it follows certain rules.[5]

5. *Reflections on Art*, p. 26 of the essay, "Art and Feeling" by Otto Baensch.

The view given above is quite relevant to our rhythm too. I say so because our rhythm-cycles have off beats as well — beats which may be said to be unstressed because they are not marked on the *tablā*. However, the noteworthy point here is that the *temporal flow between the beats,* which is naturally unheard because not marked on the drums, has got to be held on to by the listener *imaginatively*. In fact, it is this fact which throws a tissue of ideality over our listening to music and prevents it, along with some other factors, from being a merely sensuous experience.

To turn now to *silence,* its commonest meaning is absence of sound or speech. But here two points may be made at once. First, if we take silence as sheer absence of sound in the outer world, a very faint sound may serve to heighten the feel of enveloping silence. This truth can even be seized imaginatively. Thus, when in the very opening of Shakespeare's *Hamlet,* we come across talk like the following:

> Bernardo: Have you had *quiet* guard?
> Francisco: Not a mouse stirring,—[6]

we lose no time in imagining that the quiet of the night is very deep indeed.

This, however, is not the only way in which sound relates to silence. Nor is absence of outer sound or speech the only meaning of *silence*. The word is also freely taken to mean a *period* of such absence, stillness, refusal or failure to speak or communicate, and oblivion or obscurity. The last of these meanings is irrelevant to the making and contemplation of music. Of all the other meanings *stillness* perhaps needs a little extra attention because it means privation not only of sound or speech, but of motion or activity as well. This activity may be the inner tumult of thought, desire or anxiety as is implied

6. Shakespeare's *Hamlet*, Act I, Speeches 10, 11.

by the Biblical maxim: "Be still and know that I am God." But when a philosopher (Profesor Whitehead, if I remember correctly) characterizes *silence* as "the medium in which great things fashion themselves," the word has to be taken in a fuller sense, that is, to signify not only a period of utter quiet on the outside, but of intense and undisturbed concentration. On the other hand, where we speak of "the still waters" of a lake we mean that the lake is free from motion and noise, *both* alike features of the *outer* world.

Such a concern with the terms' mere meanings, however, only distinguishes and juxtaposes the inner and the outer. It hardly takes due notice of how the two overlap or interpenetrate in actual experience; in other words, the phenomenology of sound and silence remains quite untouched. In real life we have *many* sounds and *many* silences, not just one sound and one silence; and their individual character is determined not only by the way they interrelate, but also by their context of situations and happenings, our attitudes and experience, and even by our state in the present which may be one of sheer vacancy or of intense absorption in some thought or activity. Now, it is easy to see how sounds in the outer world differ not only because of their intrinsic character, but also because of the different ways in which they relate to silence. A pop and a thud are of course both pretty quickly accomplished; but only the second one of these looks like making a passing dent in the quiet around. Likewise, a splash seems to do what a plop clearly does not, that is, appearing to scatter the frame of silence for a while. Sounds emanating from human beings are also easily distinguishable. To sob is clearly not the same thing as to wail. With its own intermittent gulps for breath, the act of sobbing only lets in some moments of nervous calm; it cannot look like tearing the quiet air apart as wailing can easily appear to do.

The way is now paved to see how the distinguishing we have done above can help us see why actual musical utterance strikes us variously. To speak quite generally, how exactly the voice is made to enter immediate quiet, gently and contemplatively or abruptly and full blown; how long a stretch of silence it overlays; and how exactly it re-enters the calm it has covered, as a taper or as an emphatic cut — all this determines the look and impact of singing. Such thinking has a bearing also on the sonant variety of the very basic material of music, namely, the *svara*s as they have been named (or note names) — that is, as *sa, re, ga, ma,* and so on. Of all these *svara*s of the musical scale *re* alone (as a note-name duly sung) seems to enter silence as an incline. All other *svara*s up to (and including) *dhā* appear to rest on silence horizontally and open. The note *ni* is the only other note which appears a little singular by virtue of making a closed linear entry into silence. It seems to me that precisely because of this singularity a sustained singing of *ni* (as such) is perhaps better able to evoke a semblance of engrossment than a resting of voice at one of the "open" *svara*s. As for *re* (as such), specially where it is *komal* or nearer to *shadj* (than its "pure" colleague), its little incline which does not (as a rule) appear to cleave silence, makes it admirably suited to produce a suggestion of gentle emergence of sound from within its melodic neighbour, *shadj*. This is probably the reason why quite a few morning *rāga*s build on the *komal rishabh* to make the music chime with the image of sunrise.

Here, however, a question may well be put. Am I justified in giving so much attention to note-names, and incidentally to *sargam*s (or patterns of note-names)? Have they actually distinguished the singing of any eminent vocalist? Yes, I can straight away refer to at least two vocalists of repute: first, the late Ustad Aman Ali Khan of Bhendi Bazar, and Ustad Ali Bux Khan (Bade Ghulam Ali's father) who specialized "in singing intricate *sargams*."[7] Further, a devoted practice of *merkhand paltās* (patterns of varying disposition of *note-names*) is generally thought to make an essential part of a classical vocalist's initial training. Some *paltās* can be of such vital importance that they may have to be practised assiduously for one whole year.[8] *Note-names*, we may note, enable us to *identify* the sonant character of a *svara* (even as names assist us in identifying people) *and* its location in the scale. And this is extremely important. Note-names as such are of course not the same thing as *taans*; but unless their places in the scale are identified and held on to through long and devoted *riyaz* (or practice), their occurrence in the run of *taans* is bound to become a little off-key and so to lose colour.

However, yet another doubt may disturb us. Why do I speak of the *sound* (of note-names) entering into silence, implying that silence is the matrix of sound? Why shouldn't one speak rather of silence creeping into the region of sound? To questions such as these my ready answer is that I realize the validity of the alternative suggested; that, later in the article, I myself will have to argue that without the entry of quiet moments into actual or visualized sounds we can have neither the composition or performance, nor even the contemplation of music as art; and that silence must *yet* be regarded as the matrix of sounds. The reason why I insist on the primacy of silence simply is that whereas we can surely have fair periods of silence quite without sounds, we just cannot have sound without some silence (as recurrent or simultaneous environment). Sound is an event; it happens; it emerges as a passing overlay of silence; acquires its character, as already illustrated, partly because of how it appears against the

7. Malti Gilani and Quratulain Hyder (eds.), *Ustād Bade Ghulam Ali Khan: His Life and Music*, New Delhi: Harman Publishing House, 2003, p. 7.

8. Ibid., p. 29.

background of silence; and obviously re-enters the region of quiet when it ends.

However, before we proceed further one more question, arising from what has been said about *sargams*, may be put and discussed. If the singing of the very basic material of vocal music — that is, the note-names — includes two sounds, *re* and *ni*, (which are not really open), how can the norm of *shuddh akāra*, by which we generally mean that the musical use of voice should appear natural or uncontrived and *quite unconstricted* besides being sweet, be said to be essential to, or preservable in, actual singing? By common consent, it was the *akāra* of Ustad Ghulam Ali Khan (besides that of some others whom I cannot recall at the moment) which could be said to be a model; it indeed was sweet, luminous, without any creases within or rough edges at the periphery. What is more, he would even revel in singing *taar svaras* majestically in a perfectly open *akāra*. But did not the *text* of some of his songs contain words including ओ, ए, and ई sounds? Consider, for instance, his following composition in *rāga Āsāvrī*:

> अब भई भोर नहीं आए लालन
> मैं तो सगरी रैन जागी[9]

Therefore, a *consistent openness* cannot be said to be demanded by the norm of *shuddḥ akāra*. Take, again, the criterion of *naturalness*. Did our maestros like Ustad Faiyaz Khan and Pandit Kumar Gandharva use their voices in really as natural a way as an average and untutored man, yet with a flair for sweet singing, does? Is sheer naturalness of manner unquestionably preferable to an aesthetically cultivated way of musical utterance? Can it ever be binding on a painter to keep his colouring continually bright and every detail of his works perfectly open to perception? Does any material or element

9. Malti Gilani and Quratulain Hyder, op. cit., p. 188.

quite retain its own independent character in the organic form of a complete work of art? To all such questions our genuine *rasika*s may be expected to say *no*. I therefore suggest that the only meaning which can be fairly given to the norm of *shuddh akāra* in classical singing is that the vocalist's utterance should be all along pleasing to the ear, and that *akāra* has to be cultivated to this overriding end, without letting it *appear* merely contrived and so a source of displeasure. In the wholeness of singing and listening, indeed, even the involvement of silence is far from being uniform. This should become clear as we turn to consider the place of silence in the creation (as composition), performance, inner run, and appreciation of music.

Take *creation* (as composition) to begin with. The details of the ways in which composers create music are, in principle, infinite; and all that we may do (as required by our present purpose) is to make the following simple points. First, a more or less quiet environment is generally quite as necessary for *composing* music as for intense thinking. But, secondly, for proper pursuance of the task in hand one has also to put aside all such thought and concerns as are likely to disturb the act of creation. See, here, the following from Beethoven:

> All genuine [musical] invention . . . [requires one] to submit to its inscrutable laws, . . . to overcome and control one's own mind, so that it shall set forth the revelation that is the isolating principle of art.[10]

In respect of this extract two distinct points may be made. First, though as an outer fact silence may well be taken as mere absence of noise, there is an inner calm too which issues from a kind of self-gathering, a positive control of irrelevant thoughts and impulses; and which seems to be an essential prerequisite for focusing duly on the creative activity at hand. It may not

10. Cited by Susanne K. Langer in her book, *Feeling and Form*, Routledge and Kegan Paul, 3rd Impression, 1963, p. 31.

be quite serene, because it is at once ripe with the readiness to begin what one is so keen about; but at the same time, as disengagement from one's practical concerns, it is positive enough to steady one for the work ahead; and so is felt as a calm, if short-lived and not really absolute. I think it is more or less similar to the state of a vocalist who finds himself seated on the stage and is all set to begin singing the moment the compere finishes his (or her) work of introducing the artist and the music to come.

Second, a distinction may be made between the determinants and the *process* of creation. The generative forces of art creation are various. Any powerful impression in the present or poignant reminiscence can trigger off the act of creation; and there is much to support Beethoven's view that the laws of creation are "inscrutable" or hard to determine. Even Wagner, who is perhaps the most verbal of all the great composers, "wrote about everything under the sun . . . except composition," probably because "the music rose to his pen [for notation] from levels deeper than anything that even he could verbalize."[11] Yet, in respect of the process, as distinguished from the determinants of creation, one remark may be made with certainty. As Coleridge pointed out long ago, the creative process is an alternation of two impulses, the impulse to create and the impulse to contemplate. Indeed, cases where the process of creation is literally continuous are extremely rare; and in most cases there are frequent intervals, at times covering a lapse of two or three years (as happened at least once in the case of Kumar Gandharva),[12] when the artist just quietly mulls over the part which has been completed with a view to determining what it itself demands as the next step. And this

---

11. Peter Kivy, *Music Alone*, Cornell University Press, 1st printing, Cornell Paperbacks, 1991, pp. 103-4.

12. Ashok Vajpeyi (ed.), *Kumar Gandharva*, New Delhi: Rajkamal Prakashan, 1st edn., 1982, p. 196.

aesthetic demand may be quite unforeseen. This happened, for instance, with Tagore when he found that the very marks and lines with which he sought to correct and improve the running text of his poems admitted of being turned into aesthetically significant designs. Be that as it may, the noteworthy point here is that the moments of contemplation which intermit the creative process may well be regarded as silences in the sense of intervals in active making.

However, it is only in the actual run of *music* that the role of intervening silence is perfectly clear. When we witness a good play of the traditional kind, absorption (*tanmayī bhāvanā*) is secured, as Bharata would say, by an integration of many factors, of which *abhinaya*, specially as *vāchika* and *āṅgika*, is importantly one. Such aesthetic resources are not available to music. To elicit absorption it has to rely on some quite different factors, such as sweetness of tone, the recurring cycle of rhythm, and the organized and distinct melodic character of the *rāga* being sung. But whereas, as notated, a *rāga* simply leaves a little empty space between the different *svara*s, when it assumes the living form of singing the space which separates — and interlinks — the different *svara*s or *svara-samooha*s (tonal phrases) has to be filled either with the help of glides (*meeṇḍ*s) or regulated *silences*. In actual singing, we may note, these privations of sound are no mere vacuity; they are effective invitations to both the singer and the listener to *ideally hold on to the* flow of *rhythm* — even as it runs *unmarked* on the drums *between* the different *mātrā*s — as also to the form of the *rāga* where it is not audibly manifest (or actually heard), exemplifying what phenomenology speaks of as "constitution" by the contemplator. This ideal holding on to the music (and rhythm) is contemplation and what not only allows but invites it to rise and run as a confluence is deft interposition of silence, besides of course the charm that is intrinsic to melody and rhythm. How these quiet intervals relate to the singer and the listener *differently* has, however, to be brought out.

The performing vocalist gets a little time not only to tune himself anew to the ongoing rhythm as marked by the drummer, but to visualize and even visibly cherish the next melodic step. This indeed is why a classical singer is occasionally seen swaying his head serenely even where there is no actual singing. Even generally, the very logic of creation in art (as performance) makes such silences necessary. On the one hand, we may note, the act of art-making is not the directed pursuit of a clearly *pre*determined (ultimate) end. Yet, on the other hand, it is not a random activity either, because every onward step in the creative process *is determined* by (what appears to the singer as) the aesthetic demand of what has just been accomplished. This is precisely what distinguishes such activity from indulgence in a mere reverie where the subject just lets himself float over fanciful images or ideas as *they* suggest each other without any attempt on *his* part to actively subject their run to norms of consistency or probability. Now, the performing musician's contemplation of what he has just completed with an eye to determine its aesthetic lead is (here too) a momentary suspension of active singing and so an interval of silence, if a little tense and uneasy, because of the implicit urge to proceed.

Here, before we turn our attention to how the subject of this article relates to *listeners* at a concert, let us see how silences in fact vary according to situations we find ourselves in. Where we are stunned momentarily into silence by the quite *unexpected* news of a dear one's death, everything around seems to come to a halt; our impulses too appear to freeze; and it is only a little later that open grieving may animate us into feeling alive once again. On the other hand, the silence that fills the act of getting set — say, at the blocks — to face the competitive challenge of a race is at once a felt, tight focusing on the task ahead. Yet another kind of silence — falling, so to say, midway between the two we have just distinguished — is provided by a poet's quiet communion with a beautiful object of nature. As a *wise* passiveness it is quite ready to register impulses "from a vernal wood" (Wordsworth), and so is by no means numb; at the same time it is quite without any uneasy feeling of tenseness. It is this last kind of silence which comes pretty close to the *rasika*'s state as he just waits, after the compere's prefatory remarks, for the singer to open the *rāga* "announced." But though this has to be the pervasive tenor of his silence throughout the recital, it may well be relieved at times by impressions of different kinds. A meteoric, yet well beaded (दानेदार) *taan* from Bade Ghulam Ali Khan may just *dazzle* the listener's contemplative calm with sonority; a pattern of yearning effulgence from Kumar Gandharva may make our silence swell with a sense of high seriousness, and so provide an illustration in music of what may perhaps be called (following Kant) a "look of dynamical sublimity," or of what Plotinus meant when he spoke of art as a kind of "metaphysical homesickness"; and the recurring melodic moments of quintessential fineness in Rahimuddin Khan Dagar's *ālāpa* may just deepen the listener's quiet into a felt tranquillity of spirit which is finer than the charms of mere outer ornament.

6

Hindustānī Rhythm and an Aesthetical Issue[1]

In this essay I propose to discuss, in brief, just one question of aesthetic theory. Is the time (or its semblance) that we find in Hindustānī (or north Indian) rhythm[2] similar to or different from time as we experience it in daily life? I cannot, however, proceed without first giving an account of what the rhythm that I speak of is and what it does. My reference, I may add, will be throughout to rhythm as an independent art, and not to rhythm as a mere component of music. The question, if it is at all proper to regard rhythm as an autonomous art, has been already discussed by me earlier;[3] and here it should suffice if I simply drew attention to the fact that, in India, a solo exposition of rhythm by a competent drummer — be it on a single drum or on a pair of drums[4] — has always been regarded as a work of intrinsic aesthetic value.

---

1. This essay is a very slightly modified version of the way it appeared in *Sangeet Natak*, nos. 129-130, 1998, pp. 34-37.
2. I may add that a good deal of what I have said in this essay is true of south Indian rhythm as well.
3. In Ch. 4 of this book; and much earlier in my essay "Aesthetic Theory and Hindustani Rhythm", which appeared in *The British Journal of Aesthetics*, Summer 1976, vol. 16, no. 3; was reprinted in my book *The Winged Form: Aesthetical Essays on Hindustani Rhythm*, Sangeet Natak Akademi, Delhi, 1979, pp. 1-17.
4. The single (or one-piece) drums I am here thinking of are the →

Now, to the question, what is Hindustānī rhythm, I may straight away give the following succinct answer:

The essential purpose of Hindustānī rhythm (as an independent art) is to establish a basic *cycle* of steadfast pace, and to create patterns of infinite variety within its bounds, both with the help of beats and *bol*s (or mnemonic syllables[5]) which not only christen the beats, so to say, but provide a decorative filling between and across them, yet never in such a way that *the regulative and formative character of the focal beat* (of the cycle) may be wantonly disregarded, they (or the syllables) themselves — and also the patterns which they go to make — being quite capable of being memorized and recited agreeably.

Let me now bring out the key ideas implicit in this summary characterization of rhythm:

a. To begin with, we may note that the matrix of all trellis-work in Hindustānī rhythm is a cycle. It comprises a specific number of beats. But these beats are not alone here. Tied to everyone of them, and often spread over them, there is a letter or a bunch of letters — such as *kā, dhiṭ, tirkiṭ, dhā, ā* — which are all without verbal meaning, and which only resemble, more or less, the sounds of the beats (as played[6]). It is this linkage of

---

→ *pakhāwaj* and *mṛdaṅgam;* and the two-piece drum referred to North Indian classical music is the *tablā*.

5. A *bol* is a single letter *or* a small group of letters, quite without verbal meaning. Every *bol* is not strictly a syllable, for it may not be utterable by a single effort of the voice. But I cannot think of a better English word for what is called *bol* in Indian rhythm. Further, as a verb, "syllable" means to utter articulately; and the utterance (or rather *recitation*) of *bol*s in Indian rhythm is also required to be articulate. "Mnemonic" means "helpful to memory"; and this is an admitted quality of *bol*s. They enable us to memorize and repeat the (corresponding) sounds produced (as patterns) in drumming.

6. What the Indian (classical) drummer plays is not mere beats, but →

beats with specific letters[7] which makes it easy for us to recognize and remember the different sounds which the playing of the cycle (and the patterns) produces. Even the offbeat, which is not actually sounded on the drum, but only gently hinted or visualized, carries a syllable as its indicator.

b. It is important to see how exactly the matrix of Hindustānī rhythm is *cyclic*, and how this character determines all creation in the region of this art. In following the rhythm which the matrix in question embodies and projects we not only set out from the first beat, but return to it, completing a round, so to say, and (I repeat) making the first beat appear focal. This beat is, indeed, of special value here. The cycle, and the patterns that may be woven across it — and ultimately within it — have all to attain to the focal beat (called *sama*) with split-second accuracy. This is something which the drummer has to bear in mind all along, as a basic requirement. Further, the *sama* is the beat where the cycle and the patterns all attain completion of their individual forms.

c. Above all, a pattern owes its excellence as such also to the *general shapeliness* of the way in which it realizes the *sama*. Every pattern is a configuration, an organized whole. In some cases, however, it is distinguished by a specific *terminal segment*[8] where, because of *its*

→ *bols* which are tied to, and spread over, beats. So an ensemble which presents both Westerm and Indian rhythm is not really conducive to a proper appreciation of Indian rhythm, for it generally highlights only the parity of *beats* — in respect of number and disposition.

7. Mere letters, I repeat, not (meaningful) words.

8. Corresponding to what is called *āmad* in Hindustānī music, meaning a segment which strikes the discerning listener as an orderly approach to the focal beat.

orientation, the pattern appears (so to say) to gather its beauty, and to proceed to deliver it at the *sama*. Yet the *sama* is not only the target of patterns, but their apex where they themselves appear to flower. This suggestion of (what may be called) efflorescence[9] is irresistible where the pattern's overall shapeliness is capped with such a playing of the *sama* beat that the sound produced may seem to accomplish itself instantly. The beauty here arises, so to say, from an electric chipping of the *sama*-instant (or stroke) itself. No other art, I believe, provides a *better* instance of the aesthetic divisibility of minimal time, or of the power of a mere point to lend both beauty and wholeness to what paves the way to it.

d. A very interesting feature of *bol*s is their sonant character. It is so rich in variety that it can easily hold discriminating attention for long. Some *bol*s, indeed, appear to sparkle like a star, and others engage the ear with their wedge-like sharpness in saving (as it seems) two adjacent syllables from collision. Coupled with due accentuation of some syllables and regulated variation of the pace of the segments that they generally go to make, this fascinating diversity of their character as sheer sounds makes Indian rhythm[10] a quite uncommon object of aesthetic contemplation. Its content is neither meaningful speech nor a mere medley of indistinct sounds, such as may be produced by the jostling of utensils in a big bag, but series of differently ordered, but all identifiable alphabets of our native languages. *Form*, I believe, is *more manifestly* articulate in Indian rhythm than in the other arts.

---

9. The Hindi/Urdu word, here, is *khilnā* meaning "to flower."

10. Not merely north Indian rhythm.

e. Further, what shapes the essential features of form — that is, the run and inner knitting of patterns — is a necessary orientation. As a rule, patterns have to terminate in a clear and accurate show of the *sama*. Further, it is desirable that before they actually hit the target, they may appear to be *making for* it. The critic judges their quality as patterns largely by checking if these two requirements are met. Conjointly, they make a very clear criterion indeed.[11] But, I hasten to add, some patterns — that is, those which represent the *ateet* and *anāgat* kinds — are so *designed* that they end expressly — and, therefore, not wantonly — a little *after or before* the focal beat. In such cases, the beat in question is, of course, not played at its grammatically set moment; but in so far as the drummer's adroit avoidance of it is intentional, it is duly kept in mind. Such "giddy cunning,"[12] in fact, only heightens our awareness of the form of both the cycle and the pattern,[13] assuming of course that we are able to follow, in due accordance, the course of the pattern — which can sometimes be pretty intricate — *without* losing our

---

11. Clear, however, only to those who can follow the extent and distinctive idiom of the cycle.

12. I have here in mind the following lines in Milton's poem, *L'Allegro:*

    In notes with many a winding bout
    Of linked sweetness long drawn out
    With wanton heed and giddy cunning

    Douglas Bush (ed.), *Milton: Poetical Works*, London: OUP, 1968, p. 91.

13. Cf. "Form does not lie simply in the correct observance of rules. It lies in the struggle of certain living material to achieve itself within a pattern. The very refusal of a poet to sacrifice what he means to a perfectly correct rhyme, for example, can more powerfully suggest the rhythm than correctness itself would." Stephen Spender, *World within World*, London: Hamilton pp. 313-14.

hold on the basic pace as embodied in the cycle.[14]

The onward flow of the pattern, brisk or leisurely, is of course not the same thing as the felt passage of life as lived. Quite unlike the latter, the former (or rhythmic *time*) is a decorative run directed towards a mere moment — the moment of the focal beat. Yet it is as common to speak of *time* in music (as rhythm) as of time that we experience as the very course of life. Now, the question is: are the two appearances of time *essentially* similar?

We cannot at once say *no*. Patterns in rhythm are not only serial, but occurrent. They comprise beats (and *bol*s) that we see running as a series. Yet successiveness, or the before-after order, is not the only feature of lived time that the art of rhythm builds on. Simultaneousness is another. As a rule, the terminal syllable of a pattern is also a moment of perfect *coincidence* with the *sama*-instant. Further, when it has been perfectly established,[15] the cycle appears to *endure* as a stable frame of reference in relation to which the quality of patterns is largely discerned. But if the formal features of time *as ordinarily experienced* all serve as the material of time *as it appears in rhythm*, is there no *essential* difference between the two?

Aestheticians are divided on this issue. Thus, whereas Langer,[16] M. Sauvage,[17] and Basil de Selincourt[18] take pains to

14. Because of this dual engagement of attention, contemplation of patterns in rhythm may be said to be *bifocal*, in a way.

15. After a few rounds of proper playing, a cycle comes to look firmly set or unwavering. "Establish" is the right word for what is called *quāyem karnā* in Urdu.

16. S.K. Langer, *Feeling and Form*, New York: Routledge and Kegan Paul, Third Impression, 1963, pp. 109-10.

17. M. Sauvage's essay "Notes on the Superposition of the Temporal Modes in Works of Art", in *Reflections on Art*, ed. S.K. Langer, Baltimore: The John Hopkins Press, 2nd printing, 1960, p. 162.

18. Selincourt's essay "Music and Duration", in *Reflections on Art*, p. 153.

distinguish time *in music* (or rhythm[19]) as "virtual" and "special," or as an "ideal substitute" of ordinary time, Philip Alperson sees no essential difference between the two. He admits that music gives rise to a specific class of tensions. But, he continues, what is there to prevent us from saying that the build-up and release of musical tensions is experienced *in the same way* as the rise and ebb of life-tensions, that is, in a before-after order? And if the two kinds of tensions are experienced *in the same way*, how is it warranted to say (as Susanne Langer does) that music creates a distinct of order of *virtual* time? Generally, it is as an important element of music that rhythm makes its presence and power felt; and in so far as the same "mental functions of attention, memory, and expectation which are characterstic of musical perception seem to apply to the perception of noise" too in daily life,[20] it seems improper to hold that the experience of the temporality of specifically musical phenomena . . . [is] *sui generis*[21] or unique?

This argument, however, is not likely to convince one who takes rhythm as it is freely regarded in India, that is, as an autonomous art too, with its own unique material, creative devices, and criteria of evaluation. And he could argue his dissent quite simply, say, as follows:

Suppose two essentially dissimilar orders *of time* are really there. Where could the difference lie? Not in the (alleged) absence, in one of them, of the formal features we have distinguished, like continuance and successiveness; for, without these features, time would be a mere word. Nor could we say that one of them is quite without content. Such a time too would

19. Not as an autonomous art.

20. Philip Alperson's essay "Musical Time and Music as an 'Art of Time'", in the *Journal of Aesthetics and Art Criticism*, Summer 1980, p. 411.

21. Ibid., p. 412.

be a sheer abstraction. Even our moments of vacancy have a filling of some tension, ennui, reminiscence or looking for. Therefore, the difference we are seeking could only lie in the *specific* character — and some inner arrangements — of the *content* of the two temporal orders. But if this conclusion is accepted — and I do not see how it can be avoided — the time that we find in rhythm must be said to be quite different from the temporality that makes the fabric of our daily living; for whereas the content of the former is provided (we have seen) by beats, *bol*s, and varying pace, that of lived time comprises sequences of events in the outer world and one's own doing and suffering. As for the argument that the two temporal orders, rhythmic and everyday, cannot be regarded as being quite *dissimilar* because the *same* mental acts or attitudes are involved in our experiencing them, it is, in my view, quite unavailing. Would it make sense to deny the distinctness of sweet from salted food on the ground that they are both known by tasting? It is, I repeat, not *how* we experience them, but *what* exactly we experience *in* them that makes the two orders of time quite different from each other.

Indeed, the time that we experience as rhythm forms a world of its own, with features that are not to be found anywhere else. A *tablā* maestro dwells in the world of rhythm — comprising beats, *bol*s and regular patterns — with as perfect a sense of encompassment as a scientist in his world of symbols and formulae. And "happenings" in the drummer's world can be quite out of the ordinary. Where, for instance, in the everyday world do we create beauty, as we may easily do in the region of rhythm, by just deviating (for a while) designedly from a set course, *with meaningless letter*s *alone as our* material *of creation*? Even generally, the time that *we* regulate and beautify purposely cannot be the same as the time which is only *given to us* and is so often the locus of unforeseen, unhappy events.

7

Attenborough's *Gandhi*: An Essay in Understanding[1]

SIR Richard Attenborough's film *Gandhi* has elicited various reactions. Some have admired the "pathos and poignancy of its sensitive portrayal of Gandhi's basic philosophy of life," and its ability to bring out his relevance to our times. Attenborough, they add, "has made Gandhi dynamic."[2] Others have complained that some major personalities of the Indian struggle for Independence appear but puny men in the film.[3] Most of the critics however agree that it is a great film. I seek in this essay to merely unfold the fabric of this film as an art-work; and, in passing, to throw some light on the reactions just cited.

I may begin by stating what I regard as necessary equipment for a task of this kind. One needs a fair knowledge of the following: the ancient Indian view of the good life; classical (north) Indian music;[4] the basic faiths of Gandhi; and

1. This essay is a reprint of my article, "Richard Attenborough's 'Gandhi': An Essay in Understanding"; as it appeared in *Journal of Comparative Literature and Aesthetics*, Orissa, vol. V, nos. 1-2, 1982, pp. 75-85.
2. Arun Gandhi on Attenborough's *Gandhi* in *Imprint* (Bombay), December 1982, p. 7.
3. Abu Abraham in his essay "Unsupporting Cast" in *The Hindustan Times* (New Delhi), 20 February 1983.
4. The music is by Pandit Ravi Shankar; and one feels impelled to →

his social and individual objectives. It would be of help if I quickly explained the last two of these.

There are quite a few set beliefs that determine a large part of Gandhi's life. The most important of these is his faith in God and prayer;[5] and in *ahiṁsā* as the best way to oppose evil and to realize God or (the ultimate) Truth. But he is also convinced of: the superiority of ideals over merely individual life; equality of religions in respect of their life-giving value; and the intrinsic dignity of every human individual and of all (permissible) work. Further, like all orthodox Hindus, he regards vows (or *yama*s or *niyama*s)[6] as essential to goodness of being and behaviour, and accepts the theory of *karma*, if only in so far as it posits an inexorable link between the moral quality of an act and its consequences. As for the goals he seeks to realize, those that relate to society are: Hindu-Muslim unity; removal of both untouchability and oppression of women; and, of course, the political independence of India. Gandhi's personal objectives are not all well known. Some of these crystallize in his closing years. He now longs to fill himself evermore with faith; and — as attestation of his faith in both God and *non-violence* — to meet, if necessary, the assassin's

---

→ refer to the very effective employment of what seemed to be snatches of *rāga*s (melody-types) like *Jog, Gurjarī Toḍī* and *Tilak Kāmod*.

5. Though mammoth gatherings at Gandhi's prayers are nowhere shown, there are at least three references in the film to prayer and his faith in it: his "invitation" to pray for all those who are killed for (and in) derailing an arms train; his utterance, during the fast unto death, that he will regard his prayer as answered only when rioting totally ends; and the asassination scene which (twice) shows Gandhi breathing his last with the name of the Lord (Rama) upon his lips.

6. The five *yama*s are: truth, non-violence, non-stealing, non-acquisitiveness and celibacy; and *niyama*s are: purity, contentment, self-study, fortitude and surrender to God.

bullet with nothing but love in his heart and God's name on his lips.[7]

Almost all these shapers of Gandhi's life are in my view projected in the film,[8] sometimes as mere hints, yet always intelligibly. But the viewer has to know not merely what Gandhi's faiths are, but how he *interprets* them. Consider an instance. In the scene which shows Kasturba in deathbed, Gandhi says: "It is my time for a walk, but I will soon return." Why is this utterance permitted? After all, Gandhi does not actually leave for a walk; and what impresses the average beholder here is his appearing visibly moved, and shedding *a* tear[9] in spite of his customary poise. What then, I repeat, is the value of the words in question? Are they only the index of a habit? No; they are not so for those who are aware of the subtler details of Gandhi's thought. To them, the utterance is a sign of his living faith in God; and this because of his following way of thinking:

> He alone can claim to have faith . . . who in life ceaselessly endeavours to observe the law of God. For . . . He and His law are one.[10]

> God [Himself] is continuously in action. I claim to have faith in God . . . [and so] keep my routine with clock-like regularity.[11]

---

7. Pyarelal, *The Last Phase*, Ahmedabad: Navajivan Publishing House, 1958, p. 766.

8. Gandhi's penchant for vows is manifest where he rehearses his marriage with Kasturba; and the value of ideals, as against the life of a mere individual, is openly affirmed by Gandhi during his Calcutta fast.

9. The *singleness* of the tear is here an index of Attenborough's consummate concern for truth. I can clearly recall that when Kasturba actually died the caption of the news item (with a photo) in a leading daily was: "Even the great shed *a* tear."

10. *The Last Phase*, p. 242.

11. *In Search of the Supreme*, by M.K. Gandhi, compiled and edited by →

At many a place indeed the film articulates by *distilling* what it is about. This is here unavoidable. Where only a small part of historical reality can be incorporated in a work, every detail picked must be somehow made multiple in meaning. Such *is*, I believe, the moment when (in the film) Gandhi suddenly leaves off serious parley with his colleagues to treat a limping goat with a mud-pack.[12] It signifies, on the one hand, his faith in nature-cure to which there is no other reference in the film; and, on the other, his well-known view that, in so far as a good way to worship God is to serve his creatures, every act which gives relief to any one of them is of positive value. The second of these may seem odd to many. But it explains an impressive aspect of Gandhi's personality. He could lavish attention on, and imbue with significance what seems trivial to the average man. This must be foreknown to us. Otherwise, the scene where Gandhi initiates Margaret[13] in the art of spinning would appear, *because of its manifest leisureliness,* quite discordant with the situation; for Gandhi is here confessedly *oppressed* with the very serious matter of the Muslims' growing fear of Hindu domination after Independence, a factor which Jinnah turned into an argument for Partition, and which therefore shattered Gandhi's dream of freedom for an *undivided* India. Attenborough seems anxious to ensure that we mark Gandhi's equitable concern for all necessary activity; and so, during his very last meal before assassination, we find Gandhi making two such remarks, both with *visible* relish,[14] as appear disconnected and inequal in value: the one proclaiming his

---

→ V.B. Kher, Ahmedabad: Navajivan Publishing House, 1961, vol. II, p. 127.

12. *The Last Phase*, pp. 242-43.

13. Margaret Bourke-White of *Life* magazine. Here, I may add, Attenborough also projects Gandhi's emphasis on constructive programme and village handicrafts.

14. Visible, yet inequal.

heroic resolve to go to Pakistan to assuage communal passion, and to show that "Satan resides only in the hearts of men"; and the other drawing notice to the right way of eating a radish. In another context Gandhi declares his intention, with perfect equipoise, to dwell in the same speech on both the evils of war and the place of goat's milk in human diet. Such a coupling of what appears trite with the clearly momentous is likely to bewilder us unless we remember that, for Gandhi, alertness in respect of every due concern is a mark of the man of faith.[15]

If what the film builds on is thus an abstraction from a very rich fabric of faith, incident and action,[16] it must surely have been difficult to make the projection appear self-complete. How does the film manage to secure this requisite semblance? My answer is: by the use of a device which is quite rare in the region of films, but is commonly employed in our classical *sangeet*.[17] Attenborough makes the work emanate from and upgather itself in the selfsame focus. This is how I interpret the feature that the film both begins from and ends with the assassination scene. Is such a practice necessarily outlandish for art? I must answer in the negative. A clear source of self-completeness in north Indian music is the cyclic quality of its rhythm. The music freely begins from and flows back to the first beat which thereby appears as a focus. And a presentation of the *Bharata Nāṭyam* style of our classical dance commonly begins with the number called *alārippu* which is both begun and rounded off by showing an identical disposition of the

15. Thus see: "The mark of a man of faith is that he is always awake and alert in every little thing," *The Last Phase*, p. 242.

16. This the film clearly is, on the maker's own admission. It opens with a screen projection of the notice that it is but a modest attempt to gain some insight into Gandhi's mind and soul, and into "the essence of his life-current." So it is unfair to criticize the work for its inadequacy to the *wholeness* of what it is about.

17. *Sangeet* is the Indian word for vocal-instrumental music and dance.

two hands (over the head) known as *añjali hastakam.*[18]

I refuse to accept the suggestion (made by some critics) that the film's *similar* beginning and ending signify predestination. I am aware of the view, fairly common in India, that the whole course of a man's life may be regarded as but the unfoldment of a prefixed plan. But this is surely not the net import of the film under review. Its dominant look is one of resolute, ceaseless action;[19] and, I suggest, it is not without purpose that the work is made to open and end with the sight of a movement — that is, of *gathering* for prayer in the one case and of flowers stil *afloat* in the other. In this context, however, I attach greater value to some other features. The opening assassination scene, for instance, is followed directly — *and with an apt little suddenness* — by a firm, if fleeting projection of many feet marching *solidly* as one before the whole funeral procession is shown at a distance. I see in this detail the hint of an attitude that distinguished the real Gandhi in crises: resorting to action *with a will* instead of mere sorrowing.[20] Further, in the second close projection of the funeral march, only one or two feeble wails are allowed to ruffle the ear.

Throughout the film indeed, action seems to overrun — and outdo — spells of quiet thinking, leisurely reminiscence or immediate discomfiture. Thus, as we see him lit up by some

18. *Bharata Nāṭyam* is the well-known classical dance of south India. For knowledge of the detail I here speak of I am indebted to Smt. Tara Balagopal.

19. Which is only proper, for Gandhi's philosophy "was essentially a philosophy in action." Pyarelal, *The Last Phase*, Preface, v.

20. Thus, even when (quite against his explicit wishes), partition of the country was about to be accepted, Gandhi "was not the one to waste a single word in futile sorrow. Resilient, wondrously more now than ever, he began teaching the people to start thinking in terms of their future and particularly their own immediate duty." *The Last Phase*, p. 215.

happy, unhurrying recollections[21] on the seaside in Porbandar, Gandhi suddenly arises with a *visible jerk*, sets out so nimbly towards his *āshram*,[22] and voices an intent of such resoluteness[23] that the suggestion of leisurely recall is utterly cancelled. Gandhi's *silences*, we may note, are no mere pauses between sounds, as in music;[24] they either teem with self-searching, or release an impulse to heroic action. In the case I just referred to, what issues is the resolve to undertake the famous Dāṇḍī March; and, what is more, even in the interval that here separates resolution from overt action — I mean where he is shown as resting, with Ba[25] massaging his head — Gandhi does not appear to *be truly at rest*. He promptly "appoints" successive commanders of the historic march; speaks with assurance of his ability to walk for full five hundred miles; and voices his faith in the success of the venture by *repeating*: "Time will tell."

The resolution is by no means a commonplace one, and I should soon be able to show that its emergence is not quite explainable in human terms alone. But at the same time, (I may add) with a view to keeping Gandhi look human all along, Attenborough duly takes care to make the seaside reminiscence follow a quite natural linkage of ideas: the sea with its openness — the city itself, quite as open to men of various faiths who freely inhabit it — the open-minded priest whom Gandhi knew

21. Gandhi is here talking to Hugh Walker. As it ends such talk by Gandhi, we may note, does nothing to bedim his awareness of God as the indwelling spirit (*antaryāmin*).

22. An *āshram* is a place of rest *cum* moral and spiritual training, *The Last Phase*, p. 215.

23. The utterance here is: "I shall first go to the *āshram* and then give a proof of the fact that the British government is not going to last."

24. It is true that the pauses here make for the build-up of effect, and enable the listener to, so to say, get into the music; but they are not in themselves the locus of any self-critical activity.

25. Or Kasturba, Gandhi's wife.

as a child, and who would recite, with equitable reverence, texts from scriptures of different religions — and, sea-brine-salt law (to be broken). *In fine, a passage of easy recall delivers a granitic resolve.*

Turn now to a shot that shows Gandhi moveless, listening intently to a harrowing account of the riots searing Calcutta, as a result of Partition. Here too, as the next step dawns on his inner eye, he gets up suddenly — but *sans* nimbleness now, because he is ageing; and appears a little bent as he makes for the door. Intrepid in Calcutta, he begins a heroic fast. The end is Herculean, but is at last realized: the rioting ends.[26]

But, be it marked, the two situations I have just cited are alike indicators of a feature of Gandhi's faith. To him God is always "a very present help in trouble." This is hinted adroitly in the film, by opposing Gandhi's manner to that of Charlie (Andrews). The latter speaks of God but twice[27] in the whole film; and in either case he appears to think of God as merely transcendent. In the first situation, where they both manage to pass by three menacing lads (on the pavement) unharmed, Charlie thanks his *stars*, and Gandhi is made to appear a little surprised, saying that he had so far regarded Charlie as a believer (in God as an immediate presence). Gandhi's own emphasis is on God as an indwelling Spirit on which he feels "stayed,"[28] and which is at once an impulse to moral endeavour

---

26. When this happens, and before Gandhi ends the (successful) fast, a serene sunrise is made to herald the ultimate victory of peaceful endeavour. I owe this notice to Mr Shailendra Singh, a well-known playback singer in his younger days.

27. In one case Charlie's remark is: "Why should I disturb the peace of the One *up there* for my sake"; and in the other, where Kasturba wonders what he has in mind as he struggles to climb to the *top* of the train, he says: "I am going closer to God."

28. *In Search of the Supreme*, vol. I, p. 213.

and a norm of its quality. It is faith as continual awareness of God *so regarded* that imbues his silences and even retrospective talk with a power to energize action. The following from his writings may here be cited:

> Faith is nothing but a living wide-awake consciousness of God within.[29] There is not a moment when I do not feel the presence of a witness whose eye misses nothing and with whom I strive to keep in tune.[30]

But even if it be admitted that the film rightly projects Gandhi as (in the main) a man of action, a question remains. How is the assassination scene (as I have said) focal in value? As follows, I may argue:

The kind of death Gandhi actually meets is in truth the attainment of his *personal* destiny. A day before his death, we are told, he (yet again) longs "to demonstrate by one perfect act the faith that filled him and which he had struggled through his life to express."[31] His own words here are:

> Note that if someone were to end my life by putting a bullet through me . . . and I met his bullet without a groan, and breathed my last taking God's name, then alone would I have made good my claim (to be a man of God).[32]

The mainspring of Gandhi's dynamic life is his well-known dual faith — in God (or Truth) and *ahiṁsā* as loving but resolute opposition to evil; and this faith is clearly aglow in the manner of his death. If it is so taken in respect of its significance, the

---

29. *The Mind of Mahatma Gandhi*, compiled and edited by R.K. Prabhu and U.R. Rao, Ahmedabad: Navajivan Publishing House, 1967, p. 63.
30. *Prayer*, edited and compiled by C. Kaji, Navajivan, 1977, p. 35.
31. *The Last Phase*, pp. 765-66.
32. Ibid., p. 766.

death scene would appear as a focus of the film as well. For what follows the opening scene — say, depiction of Gandhi's struggles in South Africa and of his trials in India, be they in courts of law or in the thick of public life — all teems with a display of the same resoluteness. And this is clearly also the effect of such dramatic situations in the film as the Dāṇḍī March and the Calcutta fast. Indeed, if the opening projection of "the end" and the film's evolution towards it be taken as one, the whole work would seem to be the story of a life that is self-fulfilling, *though not self-enclosed*.

I add the qualifier because of what I *see* in the film as it ultimately ends: the flowers that *keep afloat* when events and persons have all disappeared. Gandhi's *disembodied* words that here meet the ear reinforce the suggestion. Providing the only utterance that occurs twice in the film,[33] they deepen the visual meaning; they firmly, if gently, declare that Truth and justice outlive tyranny. At this point, however, one may sense a discordance. Does not Gandhi himself disappear from the scene? How exactly then does Truth abide? The answer may be had, I suggest, by recalling a detail of the opening: I mean, what the three commentators say about Gandhi as the funeral procession moves on. "Here was a man who, without any specialized training in art or science, put tyranny to rout by force of mere humility and truth." On the other hand, the finale and the way it is attained conjoin to bear out the opening tributes. If therefore the film's two ends — its opening and close — are taken along with the content of effort and attainment they bracket, Gandhi would appear to pass away not without leaving a rack behind, but as blazing a trail of glory. In attaining to its close the film not only appears self-completing but releases value for contemplation; and the viewer is not merely deeply moved, but feels edified.

---

33. Once during the fast unto death; and next towards the end, as accompaniment to the carriage of ashes.

Another question may now be taken up. How is the film made to appear undivided on the inside? I say, by means of many details. There is first (I repeat) a single thread running through the whole film: the attitude of resolute but non-violent opposition to evil. Further, if a dialogue is used to make a point or project a principle, accordant action follows forthwith. The film is replete with instances of such balance. But here, of course, Attenborough is helped by the subject's own quality. Parity of practice and principle was a key feature of Gandhi's life. Besides, such deft use is made at times of contrast and likeness that sequences easily bring about a mutual heightening of effect. Thus, when the scene opens up for Gandhi's entry into the state of Porbandar after he has shown (as a votary of Truth) singular *steadfastness* in a legal trial, what meets the viewer's eye is not only the landscape, but a *boulder*[34] so jutting and close to vision that one does not miss it. Again, where the Dāṇḍī March is shown, Gandhi's frequent — and, at places, a little protrusive — *namaskāras* (salutations with *conjoint* palms) along with his nimble pressing forward (on the one hand), and the concave convergence of two rows of marchers from opposite sides (on the other), unite to project the powerful sight of a popular, though peaceful uprising for a *common* goal.

As an instance of the use of contrast, I attach very great value to Attenborough's placement of the scene where General O'Dyer is tried for the Jalliāṅwālā Bāgh massacre. The bloodshed and the trial are in one way alike: I mean their *calculated* quality which many little details, of words[35] and behaviour, clearly project. But, the *poise and the slow,* incisive

34. Towards the left upper corner of the screen.

35. In the massacre scene, I recall, O'Dyer expressly commands: "Shoot accurately"; and the shooters themselves lose no time in obeying the command when some men seek to escape by climbing the wall on the onlooker's left.

accents in which the jury phrases its questions heighten by contrast the *tumult* of the preceding scene — the wanton killing; and the *threadbare* quality of judicial enquiry heigtens by contrast the *intense* pensiveness, the blow-up of a mood which is made to appear through the figure of Gandhi, as it fills a very large part of the screen, and which the *sāraṅgī* music — a passage in *rāga Gurjarī Toḍī* — makes beautifully manifest.[36]

Take, again, the two visuals that bring out the immediate joy *and agony* of the way Independence dawns (as attenuated). In callous disregard of Gandhi's clear stand, Partition is accepted; and the rival camps cheer as the flags are unfurled, of a newly born Pakistan and a sovereign India. As the cheering dies down we see an adroit use of the film-maker's distinctive ability to make an object *appear completing itself before the eye.* A pole erect but bare, *unlike the gay flagstaffs of the two new nations,* slowly ekes itself towards the ground, revealing Gandhi in poor light literally,[37] and as poring over the *charkhā* (or the spinning wheel) which now hums to him, we may say, "the still sad music of humanity." There is no sound here, of music or spoken word. Yet the pathos is writ large, though it is made to issue very gently by means of the touching suggestion that the daughter by commitment — Mira Behn, here with her back

36. Another effective employment of *Sāraṅgī* music occurs where mass migration is seen to follow the country's partition. *Sāraṅgī* is a musical instrument which most Indians regard as eminently capable of reproducing the subtleties of classical vocal music even where they aim at expressing human emotions.

37. I wonder if the same purpose, of highlighting Gandhi's isolation — arising from the very singularity of his exalted sense of values — is served if we couple (in imagination) the only two scenes projecting a downpour: the one which follows Gandhi's release without bail in Champaran where *a huge crowd* ovates his *lone* presence; and the other when he leaves the abortive Round Table Conference and is shown with just two escorts, all huddled under a *single* umbrella.

towards Gandhi — cannot bear to look at her crestfallen Bapu![38] It is a consummate speaking through silence; and in my view the most moving scene. But its impact, I repeat, will be feeble on one who is not aware of Gandhi's following confession:

> My life seems to be over . . . I hope God will spare me further humiliation. . . . Today I find myself all alone . . . (the others all believe) that peace is sure to return if Partition is agreed upon. . . . But I can clearly see that the future of independence gained at this price is going to be dark.[39]

And if it is taken by itself — or as wholly apart from its context in the film and real life — the scene in question would seem to be what it literally is: quite without colour.

On the other hand, there are quite a few shots which, in respect of their ability to move us,[40] are relatively independent of their context. Such a one, for instance, is the Ba death scene. And when I say so I have in mind not the detail which bespeaks Attenborough's amazing eye for truth of fact — that is, the *one* whole tear that comes to nestle in Gandhi's eye — but *the quiet build-up of heartfelt pain as it wells up to, and for a moment dishevels and overruns a visage that is generally serene.*

In most other cases, however, we must consider the context to see what a projected incident means. Or the detail may strike us as merely amusing, if not quite unnecessary. I have here in mind Charlie's ascent to the roof of the moving train. His being pulled out in two opposite ways — by men sitting atop who are quick to befriend him, and by Kasturba (in the train) who does not want him to incur the risk — seems a little overdrawn and at best amusing. But the moment we take into account all that goes along with it, the doubt disappears. It is now seen as

38. "Bapu" is a simple Hindi word of reverential love for "father."

39. *The Last Phase*, pp. 210-11.

40. If not in that of being quite intelligible.

an index, on the one hand, of Kasturba's motherly concern for Charlie; and, on the other, of the fact that the average Indian of those days certainly did not hate Englishmen as such. The latter suggestion is itself needful to see the true character of what follows:[41] the sight of many corpses of Indians (on the railway track) killed as a reprisal for the derailment of an arms train by revolutionaries. The overall meaning is that *un*provoked violence is not (yet) the creed of the average Indian. Above all, if taken along with Gandhi's remark that there is anyway *no room in the compartment, and also with the sight of many* passengers sitting at its top, the visual reinforces what the prior cloth-wafting scene[42] projects so poignantly, namely, the fact that Gandhi's self-identification with the masses in their plight has truly begun.

A yet more embracive look is required to see how the characters appear to *grow* in the film. From a hubby who has to coerce his own wife into discipline, Gandhi soon matures into a father-figure for many, for the inmates of his *āshram* in particular, so that even the daughter by commitment (Mira Behn) quietly obeys his forthright orders;[43] and lastly, he mellows (in his fasts) into a symbol of self-effacing love. Correspondingly, he rises also in the eyes of his opponents. During his first imprisonment, an officer calls for Gandhi "the

---

41. Though not immediately, a brief glimpse of Jinnah-Nehru-Patel preceding the gory sight I here speak of.

42. The reference is to Gandhi's letting his shawl float towards a lady who is very scantily dressed. This is the only occasion in the entire film where Gandhi helps someone with a *thing*. Henceforward, *because he reduces his own possessions to a minimum*, he can serve others only by *self-giving*, or by trying to get their grievances redressed with utmost devotion.

43. I have here in mind Gandhi's following order to Mira Behn, when she wishes to participate in a movement: "You first spin: let others join the *morchā*."

goat"; later, he is "Gandhi, Sir" for those who come to arrest him; again, when he is tried for inciting people to rise against authority, once the whole court (following the chief judge), arises in respect as he enters; and ultimately, by virtue of his surpassing goodness culminating in martyrdom, he becomes truly eligible to receive the superlative eulogy that Einstein has crowned him with.

I wonder if the other arts permit such an *easy-to-follow growth* of character, as against mere consistency of its portrayal.[44] Attenborough makes the most of this power of his medium. It is *not* true of the way Patel is projected in the film. But Ba, to be sure matures noticeably; and Nehru's meteoric moods could not have occurred earlier than where they do in the film. Finally, if the work's focus is professedly on Gandhi, is it fair to expect that just because his colleagues seem great *to us*, they should so appear also as seen in relation *to him*?

---

44. My emphasis, here, is on the italicized words, "easy-to-follow." It is true that the portrayal of characters in Shakespeare's plays is, as a rule, admirably consistent. But whereas such consistency is followed by *understanding* (and imagining) what the verbal medium has to say, in watching a film the task is much easier because the spectator is helped not only by the meaning of dialogic words, but can *hear* them, register differences in tone which may bespeak changes in temper — say, from overweening confidence to mellowness and humility; and also *see* the corresponding shifts in bodily bearing. The aesthetic response is here easier and fuller. It is not for nothing that Bharata chose to characterize only the ear and the eye as aesthetic senses.

8

The Rasa Theory: Its Meaning and Relevance[1]

THE Rasa theory of Bharata Muni has evoked at least as much scholarly debate as the Aristotelian theory of tragedy. What is more, its run as a determinative force of actual artistic practice has perhaps been longer that of the Greek theory. The more systematic classical dances of India still take pride in keeping to Bharata's injunctions in respect of the details and basic function of artistic creation. It is true that both Aristotle and Bharata seek to ground the charm of the art-forms of their choice in some inborn tendencies of humanity as a whole. But whereas Aristotle, in this context, focuses only on our natural proneness to pity and fear, Bharata chooses many more original propensities as bases for his account of the way of evoking *rasa* which is his word for how the impact of a proper presentation *and* contemplation of plays, dance and music actually feels. Bharata's account is also distinguished by the fact that it gives meticulous attention to the details of experience *and* expression of subjective states in respect of both actors who actually create the stage presentation *and* those who follow it knowledgeably, that is, those who make the audience. He is also careful not only to list the various factors that prevent us from adopting the right aesthetic attitude, but to relate variations in aesthetic response to differences in age, sex, and temperamental

1. This chapter only reproduces what has already appeared, under the same title, in *Sangeet Natak*, vol. XXXVII, no. 2, pp. 3-39.

characterstics. Above all, our systems of philosophy, Vedānta and Sāṁkhya in particular, have been more actively concerned with the *rasa* theory than the Western philosophies with Aristotle's view of tragedy.

My purpose in this eassy is essentially interpretative. But it is also exploratory in the sense that it seeks to consider if Bharata's theory is applicable also to some such art-forms as non-dramatic poetry and Kathak dance, to which it has not been convincingly related so far. If other art-forms have to be left out, as is indeed unavoidable, it is due to two main factors: first, my own limitations; and, second, the fact that Kathak is perhaps the only one of our major dance-forms in respect of which no one has tried *to show in detail* and plausibly the relevance of the *rasa* theory. But even generally I have to proceed very carefully for, as has been pointed out by Harold Osborne, one of our top aestheticians today, the theory in question is an extremely intricate one.

So I have to reflect on it piecemeal, say, by trying to answer some key questions, if not exactly in the same order in which they are listed below:

1. What exactly is *rasa*?

   (The answer, to begin with, may be given as a quick listing of the main emphases of the *rasa* theory.)

2. How is the evocation of *rasa* brought about?

   (This will require us to distinguish and explain the various objective and subjective factors that make for the eventual emergence of *rasa*.)

3. How does *rasa* really feel to one who actually experiences it?

   (Here, the answer will call for attention to some of the more important ways in which *rasa* has been spoken of by our traditional theorists *in a way which is today the well known idiom of phenomenology.*)

4. Finally, can the relevance of the *rasa* theory be fairly extended to cover arts *other than* drama say, non-dramatic poetry and *sangeet* or music and dance?

I. To turn now to the first question, we may begin by noting that *rasa* is not exactly the same thing as aesthetic experience taken quite generally. We often grow ecstatic at the beauty of nature. *Rasa*, on the other hand, is (said to be) produced by contemplation of *art* alone, specially of drama, dance and poetry; and the *what* and *how* of it may be put, quite briefly, as follows:

> *Rasa* is the aesthetically sublimated, yet direct and deeply satisfying experience of *a basic determinative mode of our emotional life* (*sthāyībhāva*). The process of sublimation here consists in so treating this mode with a configuration of some essential factors — namely, *vibhāva*, *anubhāva*, and *vyabhichārī bhāva*s — that the resulting emotional experience appears in utter freedom from those factors that tend to delimit, bedim, and disturb our experience of emotions in daily life; and may therefore be said to be quite otherworldly, nay, even a close approximation to the bliss of realizing ultimate Reality.

Almost all the major emphases of Bharata's view of *rasa* have been noted above, if rather tightly. They may now be brought out at some length. However, before we set out to do so some immediate comment is needed in respect of the way *rasa* has been commonly spoken of, that is, as an exalted emotion. The word *exalted* not only means noble, but *exaggerated*. On the other hand, the word we have chosen, *sublimated*, can only be taken to mean *purified* or refined.[2] Even generally, it does not carry

---

2. The psychoanalytic meaning of sublimation — that is, the channelling of a morally or socially unacceptable impulse, especially a sexual one, towards something creative and more →

any derogatory sense. Positively, *rasa*-experience has indeed been regarded as pure and refined because the emotion here sensed is utterly free from linkages with particualr individuals, places or occasions in real life. Yet, in spite of its being quite different from our mundane emotional experiences, it feels as a very personal experience; and is, what is more, deeply satisfying not only because the process of its evocation involves a good deal that fascinates the ear and the eye, both aesthetic senses according to Bharata, but because it presents to us, for vivid contemplation, the primal determinants of our emotional life and behaviour. Nor is it difficult to see why we have thought it necessary to qualify *sublimated* with *aesthetically*. It is easy for a poet to invest his poems with a sublime look by just packing them with words of profound ethical impart. The bulk of our saint poetry is a case in point. Indeed, who can deny the exalted look of *bhajan*s like that well-known one of Narsi Mehta which fixes the essential marks of Vaiṣṇava jana?[3] Bharata, on the other hand, looks on *śṛṅgāra* as the pre-eminent *rasa*[4] and entertainment as the essential function of *drama*. So, from his point of view, the sublimation of a *sthāyībhāva* (into *rasa*) is to be secured aesthetically, that is, through the principal artistic

---

→ appropriate — is here irrelevant, for even the *sthāyībhāva* of *rati* is (for Bharata) only our natural liking for delight or enjoyment (R. Gnoli, *The Aesthetic Experience According to Abhinavagupta*, Varanasi: Chowkhamba Sanskrit Series Office, 2nd edition, 1968, p. xv), and not the sexual impulse.

3. The reference here is to the *bhajan* which opens thus: "वैष्णव जन तो तेने कहिए (*vaiṣṇava jana to tene kahiye*)."

4. Thus, the 16th *sūtra* of Chapter VI of Babu Lal Śukla's *Nāṭyaśāstra*, 2nd edn., Saṁvat 2040 (Hereafter referred to simply as *NŚ* 2nd, part I) as given on p. 218 which lists the eight *rasa*s (that relate to the art of drama) opens with a mention of *śṛṅgāra* and the reason why this *rasa* has been regarded as pre-eminent is simply that it appeals to the generality of mankind. Ibid., p. 220, f.n.

device of so integrating the constituent elements (*saṁyoga*) that they may all help each other in making the whole work significant. In respect of the *rasa* theory, indeed, it only means such an interlacement of the various *bhāva*s that the resulting complex or the dramatic presentation as a whole may, so to say, liberate the onlookers from all such factors as delimit experience to individual concerns or specific time-place settings, and so provide them with an exalted *or purified* emotional experience.

As for the total meaning of the way we have distinguished, in brief, the main ideas implicit in the *theory* of *rasa*, it will emerge by degrees as we proceed. But the word *rasa* itself provides some clues to what the *theory* may be taken to say. Traditionally, this word has been commonly translated as *taste*, not in the sense of cultivated or poor taste — say, in respect of clothing or the arts — but in that of relish of what we eat or drink. Even in this everyday sense, however, the word "taste" may be taken as a noun *or* as a verb: that is, as what is tasted (*rasyate iti rasaḥ*) — namely, *something* edible as it feels to the tongue — or as the *act* of taking the taste of the edible in question (*rasānām rasaḥ*). As that which is tasted, *rasa* may well be the juice of a fruit. *Juice* is also, as we know, a commonly acknowledged meaning of *rasa*. Taken in this sense *and* as an aesthetic concept, the word *rasa* would mean that just as its juice is the very essence of (the value of) a fruit, so *rasa* is the secret of the charm of a work of art as contemplated. The analogy, however, should not be pressed too far, for whereas the pulp of a fruit is commonly thrown away after its juice has been extracted, a work of art — say, a good poem — remains a single, undivided object of relish even after many careful readings.[5]

We have also to remember that every act of tasting is not

5. T. Gnoli, *The Aesthetic Experience According to Abhinavagupta*, I[st] edn., Rome, 1956, pp. 60f.

welcome to the palate. Very few, for example, relish the taste of bitter gourd. *Rasa*, on the other hand, is said to be always a felicitous experience. Partly because of this one consideration, *relish* would probably be a better word for *rasa* (taken as a verb) than *taste*. What is more, *relish* does not only mean "to enjoy something greatly," but "with discrimination"; and this again makes the word *relish* more accordant with Bharata's real view than *taste*. What justifies our saying so is an analogy which he expressly uses and which may be put as follows. Just as a dish, in the making of which various spices have been used, must be tasted *by a connoisseur* of food if its distinctive taste is to be rightly perceived, so, because it is no simple property of any given object — but is rather a kind of rich and elevated delight which arises from the interplay of various factors — *rasa* too is an object of relish only for those who can contemplate works of art knowledgeably.

But even when it is so interpreted the sensuous analogy is open to a question. If, as the theorists insist, in experiencing *rasa* we do not *severally* identify the various factors which have gone into its evocation, how are training and discrimination necessary (as they are emphatically said to be) for those who expect to experience *rasa*? An answer is however possible, and we may put it thus. What is demanded and exercised in the case of *rasa*-experience is *intuitive* discrimination, and no explicit analysis. Yet such discrimination, though it here *works* instantly, is the *product* of a long course of discipline of our apprehending powers. It would not be proper to doubt if discrimination can ever be *intuitive*,[6] for differences can certainly be felt as such without being blown up into clear distinctions. It is, in fact, an

6. See, here, the following statement by Susanne K. Langer in *Problems of Art*, London: Routledge & Kegan Paul, 1957 (p. 166): "There are certain relational factors in experience which are either intuitively recognized or not at all, for example, distinctness, similarity, congruence, relevance. These are formal characteristics which are protological in that they must be seen to be appreciated."

everyday experience for a gourmet to sense the various condiments that have gone into the making of a dish *without* letting his overall relish suffer for a moment because of abidance of attention at a particular condiment.

At the same time, as sensitiveness to a relish, *tasting* is not mere *eating*. The latter can be done absent-mindedly; the former, never.[7] There is yet another way in which the metaphor of tasting is of help to us in the present context. Just as the experience of tasting is so immediate that the truth of what is tasted, along with that of the experience itself, is quietly admitted in the very act, so *rasa*, as a kind of tasting, is itself a witness to its own truth.[8] *This* tasting, however, is no mere isolated act of *momentary* relish (or चखना). It is the *course* or process of enjoying an experience. In spite of the charm that may be there in the aesthetic presentation itself, the person involved has to put in some effort, though he is also impelled to hold on to the act. This is why the dual ability to concentrate on, and to adopt an impartial attitude towards the aesthetic object is regarded as one of the essential preconditions for experiencing *rasa*. But, of course, once *rasa* has come into being as the experience of a relish, the *rasika*'s effort operates as just a quiet impulse to keep himself open or available to the bliss. It is because of this (partly deliberate) attitude of effortless attention and *self-surrender* (of a sort) that when the experience is over, the *rasika* is often able to *recall* it all as his, not with any self-conscious sense of having been its agent, but as one who was, so to say, just blessed with, and enlivened by the experience — a fact which explains why we cannot be prompted by a play to take recourse to righteous actions that make for felicity if it could *not* evoke *rasa*,[9] and so has failed to impress us deeply.

7. R. Gnoli, *Aesthetic Experience According to Abhinavgupta*, 1st edn., p. 66, 4th footnote.
8. Ibid., p. 38, 2nd footnote.
9. Babu Lal Śukla, *NŚ*, 2nd, part I, 3rd footnote on p. 228.

In other words, in the act of "tasting" *rasa* the ego is only submerged, *not utterly undone* as it is in mystical experience. It may seem odd to speak thus, but we cannot dismiss the suggestion outright; for if the *object* can be perceived with varying degrees of distinctness, why should we find it difficult to believe that in having an experience the *ego* can be more or less self-conscious? The truth indeed is that, in the experience of *rasa*, one's own self is neither quite eclipsed (*tiraskr̥ta*) nor in a state of tending to cut into (*ullikh*) the felt unruffledness. Were the self here wholly eclipsed, the cognition would be not merely aesthetic, but mystical or utterly free from distinct apprehensions (*vikalpa*); and were it to remain a distinct, self-conscious ego, the experience in question will tend to take the form of subject-object relatedness, or be merely discursive, like the bulk of everyday experience, dissipating *tādātmya* without which *rasa* can neither arise or continue. Here, as a fair analogy, we could point to the possibility of an intensely devout man's *regarding himself as a mere channel of His Will.* Here his *ego-sense* is not wholly rubbed out, for he truly feels both humbled and nourished by the attitude, and so happily lets himself be imbued with it ever deeper; but, on the other hand, the sense of being the bearer of an experience does not obtrude upon the feeling of surrender, and so keeps up the beatitude.

We may not here wonder if our recourse to an instance of *non*-sensuous experience is not a mere leap, for Bharata is quite explicit on the point that, though he surely uses the analogy of tasting food, *rasāsvādana*, in his view, is *mānasāsvādana*[10] in reality, and that the analogy in question is meant only to heighten the immediacy, or the self-certifying, presentational character of *rasa*-experience.

All this has been repeatedly pointed out by learned writers on *rasa*, both in the past and in our own day. What has, however, perhaps not been quite clearly seen is *the relation* between

---

10. Babu Lal Śukla, op. cit., p. 287.

Bharata's recourse to the metaphor of tasting and the other emphases of his theory of drama. The point is that what is tasted is not only directly sensed but directly *presented*. It is this which explains Bharata's unremitting and extremely detailed emphasis on the presentational side, and not merely on the inner details of the art of drama; and so necessarily on *overt* physical changes that make for effective *abhinaya*. This is also what makes the *rasa* theory pre-eminently relevant to drama (as staged) and dance. In both these arts what directly meets the eye is of paramount importance, and the ideal content or what is expressed never looks disembodied. It is this which can easily make our experience here *sākṣātkarātmaka*, or of the nature of encountering a *presence* (as Marcel uses the word).[11] Phenomenologically, there is no gap here for *rasika*s between sensing and the seizure of expressiveness. Yet, we may note, it would be wrong to assume that Bharata is indifferent to the actors' need to be watchful in respect of the subjective aspect of *abhinaya*. What he speaks of as *sāttvika abhinaya* is impossible without the actors' intense imaginative oneness with the ideal content being expressed.[12] It would here be pertinent to note that even today our better known directors and writers of plays regard intensity as a key requirement of effective acting.[13]

Nor can we say that Bharata's emphasis on the paramount need to train actors in the art of making the requisite *gestures and movements* is wholly irrelevant today. Our classical dancers educate themselves in both; and some of our directors of plays

11. That is, something which is not only directly encountered, but is at once a benign influence.

12. Śukla, *NŚ*, 2nd, part I, p. 84 of editor's own Preface, and p. 222.

13. The reference here is specially to the following words of Utpal Dutt: "Intensity is the most important thing. Actors cannot act [effectively] if they don't find joy in the acting. The moment acting in a rehearsal or a performance feels like a torture, one has to stop it." *Contemporary India Theatre: Interviews with Playwrights and Directors*, New Delhi: Sangeet Natak Akademi, 1989, p. 17.

today have thought it necessary to subject their actors to a regular course in body discipline. See here the following emphasis of Kavalam Narayana Panikkar in respect of his presentation of (a part of) *Śākuntalam*:

> The body is of paramount importance to an actor. So we chose the Kalaripayattu system as the basic method of training. Kalari is the martial art of Kerala. . . . In our process of training, we try to combine body movements with the *bhāva*, the inner state of being.[14]

Our main concern, however, is with Bharata's own formulation of his *rasa* theory and not with the measure in which it still holds good today. So we may now turn to what we have listed as the second question relating to our task.

II. How is the experience of *rasa*, which is said to be otherworldly, actually evoked? To be sure, it does not arise on its own, and quite as definitely it is very different from our everyday emotions. The joys and sorrows of our daily life occur quite easily; they do not need that happy, yet controlled interplay of subjective and objective factors without which *rasa* cannot arise. Now, the factors that make for the emergence of *rasa* are put thus in the famous *rasa sūtra*:[15]

vibhāvanubhāvavyabhichārīsaṁyogādrasaniṣpattiḥ.[16]

---

14. *Contemporary India Theatre: Interviews with Playwrights and Directors*, New Delhi: Sangeet Natak Akademi, 1989, p. 62.

15. The common belief that this *sūtra* is an utterance of Bharata has, however, been challenged. Thus, see the following statement in Dr Radhavallabh Tripathi's review of Prof. Kapil Kapoor's book, *Literary Theory — Indian Conceptual Framework*, in the *Journal of Indian Council of Philosophical Research*, Special Issue ("Life-Worlds"), March 2002, p. 160. "The fact is that the theory of *rasa* does not originate with Bharata's *Nāṭyaśāstra*. The famous *rasa sūtra* . . . was not given by Bharata, it was handed over to him by the tradition of earlier *ācāryas*."

16. 32nd Sūtra of ch. VI on p. 228 of Sukla's *NŚ* 2nd, part I.

According to this *sūtra*, *rasa* results from the *saṁyoga* of three factors, namely, *vibhāva*, *anubhāva* and *vyabhichārī bhāva*s. *Sthāyībhāva* does not here figure in this list, though it is undoubtedly regarded as the basis of the whole aesthetic configuration. But, then, how are we to account for its omission in the *sūtra* itself? Some answer to this question may perhaps be had by considering the very order in which Bharata proceeds in the sixth chapter of his *Nāṭyaśāstra*, and by reflecting on it expressly in relation to some key questions, say, as follows:

> What is the ultimate objective of the artist's (or dramatist's) creative effort?
>
> It is evocation of some *rasa*. So, in the 16th *sūtra* Bharata lists all the eight *rasa*s.[17]
>
> As against the ultimate *aim*, what is the basic, fundamental *ground* on which art creation is to proceed?
>
> It is (in Bharata's view) some *sthāyībhāva*. So, in the 17th *sūtra*, Bharata lists the eight *sthāyībhāva*s.[18] *What* exactly he means by making *sthāyībhāva* the very anchor of the creative process, and *why* he does so can be brought out quite simply. Is the dramatist to begin by choosing any subject straight away? No; if he wishes to make his work acceptable to *rasika*s at large (as he surely does), and not to any highbrow penchant of some people who may choose to affect a cultural stance superior to the common man's attitude, he has to begin by picking a subject which admits of a particular *sthāyībhāva* for artistic treatment, because these *bhāva*s are integral to our being, and are already familiar to us as common determinants of our emotional life. Everything else that is needed to make a good play has to follow subsidiarily, — that is, in such a way that the *sthāyībhāva*'s aesthetical potential, or its openness to be exalted into a super-personal and deeply

---

17. Sukla's *NŚ* 2nd, part I, p. 218.

18. *Sūtra* 18, Ibid., p. 221.

unified (*niravacchinna*) emotion may be duly realized. This is *the essential logic* of artistic creation, as distinguished from its *devices of construction*.

Finally, after the ultimate goal and the regulative principle of artistic creation have both been fixed, how is one to proceed? What are the elements to be built upon or the creative devices one may use?

These are, we are told, *vibhāva*, *vyabhichārībhāvas* (*sūtras* 19-22), *sāttvika-bhāvas* (23), and *abhinaya* of four kinds (24).[19]

As components of the creative process (which integrates them) they may be called *elements;* but in so far as they have all to be *created* — that is, projected or performed by actors or provided by the stage manager — they may also be called devices of construction. None of these elements can work in a kind of philosophical vacuum. Like emotional reactions in our daily lives, they become meaningful *only* as related to some *specific* situation or pre-existing factors, essentially objective or subjective, or both at once (*vibhāva*). Yet, they are to be creatively visualized (in writing a play) or actively presented on the stage, *and* integrated in either case, for the sake of exalting a *sthāyībhāva* (which is already there is us as human beings) into *rasa*. This is why where (as in the *rasa-sūtra*) Bharata speaks of elements which are to be brought together for the purpose of evoking *rasa*, *sthāyībhāva* is not included. The omission cannot be taken to suggest that he here undervalues *sthāyībhāva*. In fact, in the two *sūtras* (33, 34) which naturally follow the *rasa sūtra* (32) pretty quickly,[20] we are told that just as those who have expert knowledge of the *rasas* found in food can relish the delicacies made out of various ingredients, so *sahṛdaya jana* (non-sensuously or mentally) taste the *sthāyībhāvas* as *rasa* in dramatic compositions. Here, it is obvious, the primacy of *sthāyībhāva* is reaffirmed.

19. Sukla's *NŚ* 2nd, part I, pp. 222-3.

20. Ibid., pp. 286-7.

It is, in this context, noteworthy that Bharata relates (the individual emotive character of) every *rasa* to a specific *sthāyībhāva*, and not to any particular *vibhāva* or detail of *anubhāva*. However various be the factors that go into the rise of, say, *sṛṅgāra rasa*, it must have the feel of *rati* (sheer delight or amorous enjoyment); and, similarly, the *rasa* known as *karuṇa*, though of course it is not our immediate response to any actual tragic news or event, must induce in us a serious and symphathetic mood, as can easily happen when we actually find someone in a sorry state. For abstract understanding it may suffice to think of *rasa* in terms of its *general* attributes, such as tranquillity or repose and freedom from desire or from thoughts of reality and utility; but when we experience *rasa*, it is always a *specific rasa*, and its distinctness arises from, and retains and evokes the unique feel of the particular *sthāyībhāva* which it builds on. This is a vital part of Bharata's meaning when he fixes specific *sthāyībhāva*s (s.b.) as the bases of different *rasa*s as follows:

> s.b. *rati* (desire for happiness, amorous or general) — *rasa, śṛṅgāra; hāsa* (innate love of mirth or laughter) — *rasa, hāsya; śoka* (tendency to grieve) — *rasa, karuṇa; krodha* (tendency to get angry) — *rasa, raudra; utsāha* (impulse to feel enthused) — *rasa, vīra; bhaya* (propensity to feel afraid) — *rasa, bhayānaka; jugupsā* (tendency to dislike, abhor) *rasa, bībhatsa;* and *vismaya* (proneness to wonder) — *rasa, adbhuta*.

But what exactly is a *sthāyībhāva*? It is obvious that whatever be the way we put it in English, it should go well with the literal meaning of the Sanskrit word. Now, the word *sthāyī* means *permanent* or *abiding*; and as for *bhāva*, we have to go by the way Bharata interprets the word at the very start of the seventh chapter of his treatise.[21] Derived from the causative of *bhu*, to be, it is also intended to mean *to cause to be, create, or*

21. Sukla's *NŚ* 2nd, part I, pp. 368-9.

bring about. So, taking the two meanings together, *bhāva* may be taken to signify something which (already) is and which also brings about something, say, the projection of dramatic meaning through speech, bodily limbs and *sāttvikabhāvas*. The complete word *sthāyībhāva* therefore comes to mean an original or already present tendency or disposition in the mind which makes for the *experience and expression* of some ideal content.[22] So to understand the *concept* of *sthāyībhāva* is however not the same thing as an *actual sthāyībhāva*. The latter always bears a specific character. This is why Bharata takes pains to distinguish the different *sthāyībhāvas*. The *sthāyībhāva* of *rati* inclines us to rejoice and seek happiness generally; that of *śoka*, to commiserate with others; and so on. Words *we* have chosen for *bhāva* — that is, *tendency, disposition* — are both open-ended in the sense that they alike mean the supplement *to do* or *bring about*. So they may both be taken to facilitate Bharata's passage from a *sthāyībhāva* to its corresponding *rasa*. Even apart from this semantic consideration, actual experience bears out the way Bharata here speaks. Relating the *sthāyībhāvas* of *śoka* and *utsāha*, for example, to *karuṇa* and *vīra rasas* (respectively) is obviously proper. The sight of someone sorrowing may easily make us feel moved; and how can anyone be a hero without being enthused for the pursuit of some definite objective? Further, in so far as the *sthāyībhāvas*, regarded as dispositions, are here taken to *operate* as tendencies that (can) *produce* emotional experiences of different kinds, instead of merely *being* this or that, their full meaning may be put thus: dispositional *modes* of emotional experience.[23]

At this point, however, a question may be put. Emotion is also an acknowledged meaning of *bhāva*. So why can't *sthāyībhāva*

22. I also here follow, in part, what Gnoli says about *bhāva* in the first footnote on p. xv of his *The Aesthetic Experience According to Abhinavagupta*, 2nd edn., op. cit.

23. Harold Osborne, *The Art of Appreciation*, OUP, 1970, p. 116.

be translated as "permanent or fixed *emotion*"[24] rather than as "permanent *disposition*"? To this our answer would readily be that the word *emotion*, as commonly understood, stands for something that is merely occurrent, something which comes and goes; and that therefore it cannot go with the word *sthāyī*. Precisely for the same reason it is difficult to accept the suggestion, put forth by both Ananda Coomaraswamy[25] and S.K. De,[26] that *sthāyībhāva* may be taken to mean "permanent mood." A mood is always *felt*, however dimly.[27] A *sthāyībhāva*, on the other hand, is said to abide in us as a *latent* disposition.[28] Further, whereas any stray object can quicken a mood (say, a gloomy one) into re-awakening its parent emotion (say, grief) *quite easily* — as when a bereaved parent, still close to the loss, starts crying at once on recovering a dress which the toddler used to wear — a specific *sthāyībhāva* is *made to* bloom into its corresponding *rasa* through a close, skilful and creative mixing of diverse elements. Finally, a mood is often the gradual way in which an emotion is seen to taper. So it does not abide, or is *asthāyī*. Surely, the irritable mood which comes in the wake of violent anger, and the blues which may follow intense grieving, both generally pass off quickly. Nor can a *sthāyībhāva* be

24. "Fixed emotion" is S.K. De's translation of *sthāyībhāva*. See his *Sanskrit Poetics as a Study of Aesthetic*, OUP, 1963, p. 103. (From now on this work is referred to simply as *Sanskrit Poetics*). Yet, as we have just suggested, it does seem proper to translate *sthāyībhāva* as "permanent or dispositional mode of emotion." Cf. K. Krishnamoorthy's essay, "Traditional Indian Aesthetics in Theory and Practice" in *Indian Aesthetics and Art Activity*, Shimla: Indian Institute of Advanced Study, 1968, p. 44.

25. Ananda Coomaraswamy, *The Dance of Śiva*, Asia Publishing House, 3rd printing, 1956, p. 53.

26. Cf. S.K. De: *Sanskrit Poetics*, 1963, p. 53.

27. This is obviously implied when we say, as we freely do, "Please do not disturb me; *I am not* in a good mood."

28. Or, as a *vāsanā*.

identified with *sentiment*. *Sentiment* is of course an admitted meaning of *bhāva*. What is more, sentiments like friendship and patriotism work as fairly *stable* determinants of our attitudes and behaviour. However, they cannot be said to be a part of the *original* equipment of our minds. We *develop* sentiments. Two men become friends by experiencing, say, joy, sorrow, or anxiety with regard to each other in different situations. Nor can anyone be said to be born with the patriotic sentiment. A *sthāyībhāva*, on the other hand, is (for Bharata, and quite rightly) a part of our mental make-up from the very beginning of our lives. This is borne out by the way in which he posits the reality of *sthāyībhāva*s. All human beings, he argues, desire the company of those whom they love, enjoy making fun of others, and are saddened when their loved ones depart. So it would only be proper to believe in the universal (if uneven)[29] presence of *sthāyībhāva*s like *rati*, *hāsa* and *śoka*, and also of the other ones, following the same line of argument. It would here be relevant to add that the deeply satisfying character of actual *rasa*-experience — distinguished by the feeling that though it is (in the main) objectively evoked, the experience strikes a chord in our hearts, instead of appearing as an imposition from outside — is better explained on the assumption that *sthāyībhāva*s are inborn. So, because of their being original, they cannot be regarded as being identical with sentiments. In case it is protested that *sentiment* can also be taken in senses other than the one we have focused on — say, as refined feelings expressed in art or literature — our answer would be the same as we have already given in respect of taking *sthāyībhāva* as (permanent or fixed) emotion.

Nor can we equate *sthāyībhāva* with instinct. The difference is, in fact, easy to see. As a native capacity to *deal with* a situation in terms of some overt and relatively determinate action, an

29. Śukla, *NŚ* 2nd, part I, p. 266.

instinct is essentially conative in character.[30] A *sthāyībhāva*, on the other hand, is essentially an original tendency to *feel*. To speak of a *sthāyībhāva*, as being original to human nature is simply to mean that we have an inborn tendency to become sad, angry or happy in appropriate situations. On the other hand, where we act out of (what have been regarded as) the instincts of sex, pugnacity or self-preservation, the resulting feeling is one of having been able *to do* what we wanted to do. The aesthetic evocation of a *sthāyībhāva* in terms of *rasa* just gives one the *feeling* of emotional exaltation,[31] or *sublimation* (as we have interpreted the word); and so long as it is not evoked, it may be said to remain in a state of latent abidance, or as *vāsanā*.

At this point too, a sceptical question is possible. Can we not produce a good play without relating it to any specific *sthāyībhāva* or *rasa*? A negative answer cannot be given here at once, especially if we take care to go by contemporary evidence. On December 31, 1959, under the banner of Little Theatre Group, Utpal Dutt produced *Angār* "the immediate provocation" of which was simply the occurrence of some coal-mine disasters, and which was yet a definite commercial success.[32] Again, *Ādhe Adhūre*, a well-known play of Mohan Rakesh, has been successfully produced more than once. In 1970, it was directed by Shyamanand Jalan;[33] in 1976, by Amal Allama from the National School of Drama;[34] and yet again on 8 September 1989, by Jalan, in connection with the Nehru

30. The commonly acknowledged meanings of "instinct," we may note, are an involuntary prompting to *action*, and the natural impulse by which animals are guided *in their behaviour* apparently without the help of reason or experience.

31. M. Hiriyanna, *Art Experience*, Mysore: Kavyalaya Publishers, 1954, p. 38.

32. *Contemporary Indian Theatre*, p. 14.

33. Ibid., p. 69.

34. Ibid., p. 68.

Shatābdi Nāṭya Samāroha. But the underrunning theme of this play, as of all the other plays of Mohan Rakesh, from *Āṣāḍh kā ek Din* onwards, does not conduce to evocation of any definite *rasa*, but is simply the contemporary

> breakdown of communication in human relations and the consequent tragedy . . . observed and experienced at its direct and most delicate in man-woman relations.[35]

Are we then to say that the *rasa* theory has now utterly lost the value it has been so widely attributed to it?

A fair answer here would simply be that though a play can surely be good in itself and also as a stage presentation without owing allegiance to the *rasa* theory, it is doubtful if such works can have as *wide and abiding an appeal*, as distinguished from merely contemporary acclaim, as (say) *Śākuntalam* of Kālidāsa or Shakespeare's *Romeo and Juliet*.[36]

On the other hand, it would be wrong to believe than an element of merely contemporary interest is necessarily a barrier to the evocation of *rasa* by a work of art. Consider, in this context, the widely (and rightly) acclaimed film *Lagaan*. The *rasa* theory seems to be quite applicable to it. Even generally, it would be odd to hold that a theory which holds good for drama and dance is necessarily irrelevant to films. It is true that drama and film differ in some quite clear ways. In the former we look at a stage; in the latter, at a screen; and the diverse visual effects produced by the actual entry and exit of actors, or by their living movements across the stage, are obviously missing for those who watch a film. Further, it is only in the presentation of a play that an actor may seem to be addressing the audience

---

35. *Contemporary Indian Theatre*, p. 67.

36. If I do not here mention the great Shakespearan tragedies like *King Lear*, *Hamlet and Macbeth*, it is simply because (in my present state of understanding) I find it difficult to relate them to the *rasa* theory.

directly. But, on the other hand, the two arts of drama and film also share a great deal. Both are instances of occurrent art. Stability is not the dominant character of what here meets the eye. Again, there is plenty of *abhinaya*, even of the *sāttvika* kind, in both. Music and dance, included by Bharata in *āhārya abhinaya*, are perhaps even more pronounced in the majority of our films today than in contemporary theatre. Again, in respect of films like *Ānand* one could even speak of a continual undercurrent of the *sthāyībhāva* of *śoka*, say, because of a manifest all-round apprehensiveness at the thought of what is imminent for the sick and overly cheerful hero; and so also of an effective evocation, finally, of *karuṇa rasa*. In respect of *Lagaan*, perhaps even more convincingly, one could speak of the *sthāyībhāva* of *utsāha* and of the corresponding *rasa*, *vīra*. Violence, we may note, is *not* one of the essential *vibhāva*s that make for the evocation of this *rasa*. According to Bharata, these *vibhāva*s are rather the following:

> highly exalted and enthusiastic nature; freedom from confusion, insensibility, and ignorance (*a-sammoha*); mental effort (*adhyavasāya*); *bala* (strength, power); *parākrama* (enterprise, courage); *śakti* (capability); *pratāp* (reputation); *sthairya* (steadfastness, perseverance, tranquillity); *dhairya* (patience): *śaurya* (heroism, valour); *tyāga* (giving up, resigning, sacrificing one's life, liberality); and *vaiśāradya* (expertness, wisdom).[37]

None of these means physical violence. It is true that at least one commentator has translated *bala* as an army which comprises horses, elephants, and soldiers.[38] But this is not one

37. Sūtra 68 in Śukla's *NŚ* 2nd, vol. I pp. 336-37. Bracketed English equivalents of listed words have been taken from *A Sanskrit–English Dictionary* by M. Monier Williams (hereafter referred to as *MW*), Motilal Banarsidass, Corrected edition, 2002.

38. The reference here is to Śukla's own footnote on p. 337 of vol. I., *NŚ* 2nd.

of the acknowledged meanings of the word;[39] and to insist on this meaning is just being driven by our chronic, but mistaken, tendency to take the word in question in a merely physical sense. Do we not speak of the strength of will quite as freely (and as justifiably) as of a strong body? Indeed, anyone who pursues or struggles for a noble objective persistently and patiently, without being discouraged by opposition, criticism, or difficulties like lack of resources, deserves to be regarded as *vīra*.

Now, to turn again to the film in question, right from its beginning to the very end what strikes the onlooker is the determined and perfectly fair opposition to the imposition of a quite unfair tax (*lagaan*), spearheaded by the hero Bhuvan, and gradually taken up by most of the villagers. They may all be said to be acting *nobly* not only because of the manifest rightness of the cause they are fighting for, but because of their recourse to fervent collective prayer — rather than to any devious means or sheer abdication of the fight — in a life-and-death situation. The hero, Bhuvan — highlighted not only as the target of the British army officer's venomous challenge, but as the central rallying force that galvanizes almost the whole village into action — is here the *ālambana vibhāva*; and the ominous situation created by the challenge, and the thought of the ruinous consequences that are bound to follow the failure to meet it, are *uddīpana vibhāva*, because it is these factors that quicken and intensify the hero's resolve. The cricket match, where the challenge comes to a head, is of course an element of contemporary interest for urban Indians, most of whom are cricket crazy; but the way it is fought out against some very heavy odds and machinations of the opponents, overriding occasional moments of despair, is so manifestly courageous that the finale is not the mere winning of a game, but the very

39. I say so on the basis of the way the word has been interpreted in *MW*, p. 722.

climax of a fight for justice which we *all* hail happily, because of our innate propensity to get enthused for a noble cause;[40] and so experience *vīra rasa*.

In thus reflecting on the film in question, however, we have used some terms, such as *vibhāva* (*ālambana* and *uddīpana*) and *āhārya abhinaya*, the precise significance of which is yet to be brought out. It is this defect which we may now try to remedy. Like our everyday experience of emotions, *rasa*-evocation needs appropriate pre-conditions or *vibhāva*. Generally, *vibhāva* is taken to mean an objective situation[41] which is more or less lifelike by virtue of having a distinct emotive character, yet without representing a real, living individual. It is lifelike also in the sense that it comprises a human focus (*ālambana*) and a context which is commonly known as *uddīpana* because it is favourable for the self-revelation of (a particular *sthāyībhāva* in terms of) an emotion. Thus, where (a semblance of) the *sthāyībhāva* of *rati* is to be evoked, the togetherness of the *nāyak* and the *nāyika* can easily appear as the focus (or *ālambana*) of the situation, and details like a moonlit night and a bower in the garden may be said to serve as *uddīpana* or stimulus to love-making. To make the point clearer, an example may here be taken from the well-known classic of Kālidāsa, *Abhijñāna Śākuntalam*. At a particular juncture in the course of the play, King Dushyanta, as he moves about the hermitage of Kaṇva Ṛṣi, gets his first glimpse of the lovely Śakuntalā watering the plants of the garden, accompanied by her two close friends. When she casually asks one of them to slightly loosen her improvized bra of bark which, she complains, has been tied a

---

40. See here the following relevant remark of Śukla: "उत्तम वर्णों का उत्साह सर्वत्र आस्वाद्य होता है।" *NŚ* 2nd, part I, p. 336, footnote.

41. Thus, in his *Sanskrit Poetics*, De is seen to explain *vibhāva* as follows: "Conditions appropriate to the emotion to be evoked, as a garden or a beautiful woman" (p. 88). The word is explained similarly on p. 104 as well.

bit too tightly by the other friend, the latter retorts: "Why do you pick me for blame? It is rather the blooming of your own youth which is at fault."[42] Now, here Śakuntalā may be said to be the *ālambana vibhāva* because she has been brought to a focus by the pleasantry; and the beautiful natural surroundings of the hermitage and the amiable friends, the *uddīpana vibhāva*, because they conjoin to bestir the king's ardent love for Śakuntalā.

However, if we stop here, as has indeed been done by some scholars,[43] our account of *vibhāva* will be incomplete and even misleading. In Bharata's total view *vibhāva* is not always merely objective. As already pointed out, he includes the following *essentially subjective* qualities or attitudes in the list of *vibhāva*s that make for the quickening of *utsāha* which is the *sthāyībhāva* of *vīra rasa: adhyavasāya* (mental effort, apprehension) and *asammoha* (freedom not only from confusion but also from insensibility, ignorance, folly, and bewilderment).[44] So, *vibhāva* has to be taken to mean all those factors — subjective or objective, or both at once — which serve as essential *pre-conditions* of the very start of the creative process whereby a *sthāyībhāva* is made to bloom into its corresponding *rasa*. Both the points here made in respect of *vibhāva* have to be borne in mind, that is, not only its being essential as a pre-condition, but its being related to our subjective attitudes. A pre-condition is simply a condition to be satisfied in advance, like just getting properly set at the blocks for running a race. *Vibhāva* too does not itself evoke *rasa* directly, but only facilitates or prepares

42. This example has been taken from K.C. Pandey's *Comparative Aesthetics*, vol. I (Indian Aesthetics), 2nd edn. 1959, Varanasi: Chowkhamba Sanskrit Series Office, p. 25. The way I have put it, however, differs from the way it appears in the work referred to.

43. Śukla, for instance, interprets *vibhāva* as simply the situation or occasion which makes for the awareness of *sthāyībhāva* in the *nāyak*. *NŚ* 2nd, part I, p. 67.

44. In translating *asammoha* into English I have followed *MW*, p. 118.

the ground for evocation of the experience. So, as compared to the manifestly active character of *abhinaya* (acting and dialogue, in particular) included in *anubhāva*, the due value of *vibhāva* is likely to be missed. But a simple example should suffice to make us see that the effectiveness of *abhinaya* itself depends on *vibhāva*, if but partly. A mere class-room lecture (by a danseuse) on *abhinaya* relating to *śṛṅgāra rasa* may be accompanied by the most accurate "illustrations" in terms of actual bodily postures, gestures, and movements; but because the only figure present here is that of the danseuse herself, and further because what here surrounds her — say, the barren walls of the room — is not at all suggestive of *rati bhāva*, the impact of the entire exercise will be much less than that of similar *abhinaya*, say, during the course of an actual dance involving a (male-female) couple of performers, and supported by appropriate singing and stage decoration.

On the other hand, *vibhāva* itself needs the supplement of *anubhāva*, specially as movement and speech. Even in the case of the instance we cited from *Śākuntalam*, what appears to put life into the visualized setting of man and nature is the sweet little bout of words between Śakuntalā and her friends, the gestures which naturally go along with such talk, and the act of watering.

It is indeed quite easy to see the value of the second factor listed in the *rasa sūtra*, that is, *anubhāva* which comprises *abhinaya* of different kinds, say, the following: *āṅgika* (or bodily, as movement, gesture, and posturing); *vāchika* (relating to utterance, dialogue); *sāttvika* (or involuntary) comprising those bodily changes which serve as unmistakable signs of some actual emotion; and *āhārya*, or those super-added things which are not really a part of the psycho-physical being of the actors, namely, costumes, lighting arrangements and *sangeet* (that is, vocal and instrumental music, and dance). It is noteworthy that *āhārya* can add substantially to the effect of stage presentation. This is borne out by the practice of both dance and drama even today. Thus, where a Kathak danseuse begins the dancing of a *trivat* composition which, we may say, opens with the syllable *kṛān* (क्ड़ान) after a flourish of some prefatory music, the sonant suddenness of the syllable would be greatly enhanced if, exactly when it is uttered (by the vocal accompanist), the stage lights are also switched on promptly. And, to turn to contemporary ways of presenting *plays*, directors have been seen to use.

> the proscenium stage itself, the apron, the ramp . . . [extending] from the stage down to the middle of the auditorium, allowing for . . . [actors'] entrances and exits, from one of the side doors of the auditorium. . . .[45]

What is perhaps not quite heeded today in the presentation of plays is Bharata's emphasis on *sāttvikabhāva*s which have been put as follows: stupefaction, loss of consciousness, horripilation, sweating, loss of lustre or colour, tremor, tears, and changes of tone. The neglect may be due to the consideration that some of these *bhāva*s can be noticed only by those who are seated in the first one or two rows in today's large halls, and are therefore not relevant to the bulk of the audience.

Here, however, a question may be put. The last three of the *sāttvikabhāva*s we have just listed — namely tremor, tears, and tonal changes — can also be simulated or projected without the actual presence of related emotions on the inside. How, then, is it proper to regard these three *bhāva*s as *sāttvika* or truthful expressions of actual feelings? To this our answer may be that Bharata is all along keen on genuineness, as against mere manifestness of expression, which is exactly why he justifies the practice of enlisting *actresses* to play such roles as involve portraying typically feminine reactions;[46] and that,

45. *Contemporary Indian Theatre*, p. 14.

46. K.C. Pandey, op. cit., p. 34.

therefore, though they can *also* be simulated, Bharata would like the *sāttvikabhāvas* in question to be genuine indices of what is actually felt, and so to invest *abhinaya* with a (more) natural and convincing look. What we truly feel easily spills into identifiable gestures; and so from Bharata's point of view, we may note, it would not be right to hold (as Susanne K. Langer seems to do) that all artistic expression is wilfully controlled. At the same time, with a view to lending some balance to what we have just said about Bharata's view, it is necessary to add that, in the 24th chapter of his *Nāṭyaśāstra*, Bharata not only details how the different kinds of *nāyikās* have to act (positively), but what they may *not* be allowed to show on the stage, such as bathing and robing themselves. In other words, decorum is not to be sacrificed for the sake of representational accuracy.

Yet, by and large, Bharata's emphasis on such fidelity is unremitting; and he takes care to add that the convincing quality of *abhinaya* also needs *vyabhichārībhāvas* (33 in all) which are so called because, as opposed to *sthāyībhāvas* that form an *abiding* part of our mental equipment, they just flit across the run of an emotional experience, adding to its true-to-life look. These fickle *bhāvas* include the following: self-disparagement, apprehension of encountering what is (nonetheless) desired, depression due to poverty and pain, perplexity, shrinking from censure, agitation caused by pleasant happenings, and drowsiness.

Now, it is common to speak of all these as *sañchāribhāvas* too. However, a close look at what the word *sañchāra* means does not allow us to identify the two *bhāvas*, *vyabhichārī* and *sañchārī* straight away. *Sañchāra* does not only mean transition or passage, but transference and transmission as well. The last of these (or sending-out) is indeed the meaning of this word when, for instance, we speak of *dūrsanchāra*. This, again, is the meaning of that segment of *dhruvapad*-singing which is called *sañchārī* as distinguished from the other three segments, namely, *sthāyī, antarā* and *ābhog. Sañchārī* here is the more or less free unfoldment of the aesthetic range of a *rāga*, as against the mere indication of its basic, grammatical character. So the word *sañchārībhāva* may be said to point to the disseminating or expressive, as distinguished from the merely fleeting character of *vyabhichārī bhāvas*.

Some thought may now be given to the two remaining terms in the *rasa sūtra*, namely, *saṁyoga* and *nishpatti*, the meanings of which have perhaps not been quite clearly brought out anywhere in the *Nāṭyaśāstra*.[47] Now, as for *saṁyoga*, some of its acknowledged meanings are: conjunction, connection, combination, and absorption-in. The first three meanings[48] make obvious sense in the light of what the *rasa sūtra* as a whole may be taken to say quite generally. If, as is evident, *rasa* is not said to arise from any *one* of the factors listed in the *sūtra*, it would only look proper to hold that they all *conjointly* evoke *rasa*. But, we may note, to indicate *what* goes into the evocation of *rasa* is not the same thing as to explain *how* it is evoked in the presentation of a play. The latter, or the "how" of evocation, has got to take into account the work of the actors too; and from this viewpoint of actual stage presentation, to which Bharata is all along very clearly alive, it is (what we have listed as) the fourth meaning of *saṁyoga* — that is, *saṁyoga* as absorption-in — which seems preferable. A good actor does not merely find himself in, *or* conjoin himself with a specific situation (or *vibhāva*), but is sensitized by it; and the way he reacts is importantly determined by his imaginative attunement with what the situation (or *vibhāva*) does not merely show but

47. Śukla, *NŚ* 2nd, part I, p. 229, 1st footnote.

48. Which are not quite identical. In fact, they can be distinguished easily. In "I am no longer connected with that company," *connected* cannot be replaced with "in conjunction with"; and words like *and, but, if* and *because* are neither combinations nor connections, but conjunctions.

suggests. *Sāttvika abhinaya* would otherwise be impossible.[49] Even apart from this specific consideration, it is easy to see that the *vibhāva* which a good actor finds himself in, inspires, or at least prompts him to act appropriately.

A simple example from the region of musical practice should make the point clear. The right setting (or *vibhāva*) for a classical vocalist as he gets set to begin singing is an attentive, expectant audience and a well-tuned *tānpūrā*. But this prefatory getting-set is not merely to get conjoined with the sounding *tānpūrā*; the latter rather inspires him, or puts him in the right mood to sing; and the vocalist, in turn, remains so continually open to the impact of the sound that its slightest deviation from the correct tone disturbs him instantly. In other words, the insturmental sound and the singer here interact. Hence, from the actors' point of view, it is by no means odd to interpret *saṁyoga* as absorption of the different *bhāva*s into each other. This may be said to be the dramatic parallel of what is called *form* in the region of other arts. But, quite differently from the interplay of elements in arts like painting, architecture, sculpture, and literature — where the locus of integration of elements is canvas, stone, wood, or language — here, in the presentation of a play, it is the sensitiveness and imaginative powers of living actors which serve as the efficient cause of integration, and so we have to speak of their getting imbued with, and activated by what *vibhāva* as outer situation demands or suggests, and what the language of dialogues means and is expected to convey. It is because of this close integration of utterance, meaning, accordant movement, music and spectacle (*āhārya abhinaya*); and, above all, because of the *presentational* character of the entire complex that the *rasa* thereby evoked acquires a *prismatic* look which is not to be found in any one of the *bhāva*s taken individually or even in their mere aggregation. This is what Bharata means where he likens the aesthetic

49. Śukla, *NŚ* 2nd, part I, pp. 84, 222.

configuration which makes for *rasa* to a dish emitting a new flavour which is not to be found in any one of the condiments used;[50] and what *we* have said here about the integration in question should provide a clue to why Bharata speaks of *rasānubhūti* as *ujjavalveṣātmakaḥ* and as *sākṣātkarātmaka.*

Saṁyoga, however, calls for three more comments. First, it is not a blending of the various constituents *in equal measure;* for, with an eye to evoking the specific *rasa* aimed at, any one of them may be emphasized. Consider, for instance, the following verbal stimulant of *śṛṅgāra rasa:*

> O lovely damsel! your body is the locus of the honey that love-making exudes; the shapely arch of your eyebrows is the bow of the love-god, Kāmadeva, with its striking bend; and the wine that oozes from your lotus-face quickens desire by its very aroma — that is, without being drunk. In all the three worlds, indeed, you remain unmatched as a specially beautiful creation of Brahmā.

Here, obviously, the word-bound images and the overall meaning both alike heighten the charm of the *nāyikā* who is the *ālambana of the vibhāva. Vyabhichārī bhāva*s may be projected as follows:

> This lady, possessed of liquid eyes, is repeatedly impelled to throw away the water cupped in her hands; for, though she is impatient to bedew her lover with it, she is disturbed by the presence of fish in the water as it mirrors the shape of her own eyes.

Here, it is clear, the emphasis is on *vyabhichārī bhāva*s. Liquidity of eyes at the passing thought of a mischief, impatience, and agitation are obviously all transitory states. So *saṁyoga* admits of uneven emphasis on the factors that make for the evocation of *rasa*.

---

50. Śukla, *NŚ* 2nd, part I, p. 83.

Second, the way we have interpreted *saṁyoga* — that is, as an interplay, and not merely as a putting together of the various *bhāvas* — is favoured by the basic consideration that all the details of the creative process have to aim at sublimating the *sthāyībhāva*. It is this common, underrunning reference which determines what these details are going to be. Thus, where the *rasa* aimed at is *śṛṅgāra* and the *sthāyībhāva* is *rati*, a moonlit garden alone cannot serve as *vibhāva*, for such a garden may well be used also for an after-dinner leisurely stroll. A pair of lovers too have to be shown; and they have to *appear* to register (mainly through *mukhaj* or facial *abhinaya*) the charm of the setting, and to be stimulated by it. The greater their attunement with the precise suggestiveness of the *vibhāva* the more effortless and convincing will their *abhinaya* be, aided of course by the import of dialogues and the due measure of *vyabhichārī* and *sāttvikabhāvas*.

Thirdly, to turn now to those who are watching the play, their self-identification with what they see on the stage goes on waxing as they follow the *intense knitwork of bhāvas*, essentially because it is perceptibly true to their common experience of how the *sthāyībhāva* being built on (in the dramatic presentation) actually determines the inner run and expression of emotions in their own actual lives. The result is that the deepening of this attunement (or *tādātmya*) is at once an experience of the *ekaghanatā* (or intense unity) of the *rasa* ultimately evoked. This word, *ekaghanatā* has to be taken with care. Derived from the root *ghana* (to strike) it simply means unity of impact. Some scholars, like Coomaraswamy and Gnoli, ignore this derivative meaning and prefer to translate *ghana* as "a condensation of multiple factors without extension in space;"[51] and *ekaghanata* as the quality of being "dense, compact,

---

51. A.K. Coomarasway, *The Transformation of Nature in Art*, Harvard, 1934, p. 209.

uniform," or as the character of "a state of consciousness which does not allow the interference of obstacles"[52] (or *vighnas*). But the prefix *eka* makes better sense when related to *ghana* in the sense of *impact* than as conjoined with *ghana* taken as *condensation*. Moreover, whereas the negative remark that, as an experience, *rasa* is not discursive or analytical (or is *niravacchinna*) — or not separated by distinctions — seems perfectly warranted, the positive insistence that the experience in question is utterly dense or compact would tend to make *rasa* appear as a static something, and to merely ignore the flow that *rasa* as experience necessarily is, as also its quickening and illuminative effect on the audience.

It is indeed important to realize how *what the rasikas* see on the stage relates to *how* they see it. Generally, of course, care has to be taken to ensure that *vibhāva* is so structured that it may appeal to the generality of *sāmājikas*,[53] and not to any particular person. To illustrate, whereas in a man's personal life even the passing thought (say) of how his wife reacted happily when he teased her endearingly on her last birthday may excite the *rati bhāva*, on the stage the *vibhāva* — that is, a setting which is expected to be duly evocative — must be typical of lovers in general, for otherwise it would fail to engage the attention of the majority of onlookers. Yet, however true it be to our general experience, *vibhāva* in itself is by no means enough to have the requisite effect. The audience too has to be of the right age and attitudes. No amount of effort to make the *vibhāva* in question meaningful — say, emblematic of *rati bhāva* — would succeed where the audience is of young children only. In other words, the perception of *vibhāvas* (as significant) is not merely objective. It draws upon or awakens the latent traces — *saṁskāras* or *vāsanās* — already present in the

---

52. R. Gnoli, *Aesthetic Experience According to Abhinavagupta*, 1st edn., p. 71. 2nd footnote.

53. A *sāmājika* is "One of the assembly." De, *Sanskrit Poetics*, p. 99.

spectators. A young male member of the audience will not perceive the representation of a young woman quite impersonally, or in the way of *tāṭasthya* or *neutrality* which is the exact opposite of *anupraveśa* that is, intimate and active participation. The truth rather is that the very description of a beautiful woman easily arouses the pre-existing sexual interest in male readers. But, on the other hand, the (knowledgeable) *rasika* surely does not *behave* erotically in this context, as he might in his personal life, but is only led *to comprehend and follow the growth of a specific kind of emotive situation*, so that, instead of experiencing *rati* in the everyday manner, he is drawn out to contemplate how *rati* feels.

The other term *nishpatti* too calls for some critical attention. Its more important meanings are: (a) going forth or out; (b) being brought about or effected; (c) completion; and (d) consummation. Now, from the viewpoint of stage presentation as such, *rasa*-evocation may well be said to crown the creative effort of actors with success, and not merely to bring it is a close. Or the terminus here may be called a climax. But *for the audience,* the evocation of *rasa* is no mere culmination of an outer process. It comes to pass not only because of proper integration of the different *bhāva*s on the stage, but because, as *sāmājika*s (spectators), they have been following the presentation in question all along, attentively and knowledgeably; *and* because the *sthāyībhāva* which the entire play builds upon is already there in them as an inherent emotional disposition. This is why, in spite of the rich and elaborate outer process that goes into its evocation, the actual experience of *rasa* or *rasānubhūti* is felt by the spectators not as an imposition from outside, but as a deep and delighted expansion of their own sensibilities, a creative quickening of the very springs of their emotional nature. It is partly in this sense too that *rasa*-experience is a *nishpatti*, a going-forth or a welling-up. Even in our daily lives there is no dearth of situations where experience does not seem to be produced only by what is external to us, but is at once felt by us as inner enlivenment. The poet's heart leaps up when he beholds a rainbow in the sky and we too often *pine for*, and not merely think of *what is not*.

Yet, it is important to note that the way in which the *sthāyībhāvas* are made to conduce to the evocation of *rasa* is different from their working in real life. In the everyday world a person feels angry or sad generally in accordance with his *uniquely* developed attitudes. To illustrate, whereas the man who has meticulously trained himself to put everything always at its proper place may at once grow a little angry or sad at the sight of even a slight displacement of books from their proper positions on his study table, his friend who believes, let us say, that some disorder serves only to lend an informal or lived-in appearance to the place of work — and so is likely to make him feel relaxed — would remain quite unaffected by the displacement in question. Further, when we experience an emotion in real life, which always happens in a specific situation, our emphasis (as a rule) is on *behaving* in a particular way, so as to deal with the situation properly, not on *contemplating* how the emotion itself feels. Thus, if a man feels afraid at the sight of a snake, he will either run away from the place or try to kill the reptile somehow. Here the urgent need for personal safety demands quick action, and just does not give him time to attend to his feeling of fear. In other words, the emotions of real life remain tied down to individual persons; and though they are certainly felt, and even quite intensely at times, our awareness of their own inner character is only incidental to, and so is bedimmed by the demands of personal adjustment.

But, one may ask, is the complex dovetailing of various elements, which we have taken pains to explain and justify, really necessary? Why can't we say that *rasa* is our more or less direct response to a theme or subject of a specific emotional hue? Now, questions such as these may be answered as follows:

An emotive subject is not by itself enough to generate *rasa*, for the way it is dealt with may be just philosophical, that is, the way of serious, meaningful statement or reasoning which is only to be understood and accepted as true or rejected as false. This is the case, for instance, where a Shakespearean sonnet speaks of love as "an ever-fixed mark," and asserts that

> . . . Love is not love
> Which alters when it alteration finds . . .[54]

Here the subject is love; yet the whole sonnet only induces us to *think* of love, instead of enabling us to experience *Śṛṅgāra rasa.* The same may be said of (Urdu) poet Jigar's famous poem on love which opens even more philosophically than the sonnet from which we have just cited. Here, in one daring sweep the poet professes to sum up the whole story (*fasānā*) of love as follows: quintessentially, it appears in the heart of a lover; and should it decide to unfurl itself, it can cover the whole wide world — as love of humanity.[55]

Nor is a poem on a *sad* subject necessarily evocative of *karuṇa rasa*. Tennyson's poem: *Tears, Idle Tears*[56] is also only *about* the commonest expression of acute sadness; and though, in both its first and closing stanzas, it bemoans with "idle tears . . . the days that are no more," it gives us at the most a fitful feeling of sadness at what has ceased to be, which is quite different from the *bhogīkaraṇa* (or enlivening, making available for relish)[57]

54. Sonnet No. 116 in *Master Poems of the English Language*, ed. Oscar Williams, New York: Trident Press, 1966, p. 55. Hereafter, this work is referred to simply as *Master Poems*.

55. The reference is to the following opening lines of the poem:
इक लफ्ज़े मोहब्बत का अदना ये फ़साना है।
सिमटे तो दिले आशिक़ फैले तो ज़माना है।।

56. *Master Poems*, p. 658.

57. De, *Sanskrit Poetics*, p. 103.

of *karuṇa rasa* which is a single, undivided run of emotional experience. This is so also because, like the sonnet already referred to, this poem is pretty short in length. Tennyson's lament comprises only twenty lines; and Shakespeare's poem, being a sonnet, even less, just fourteen. So, though the sentiments they express are true and even noble, their reading fails to make us feel that we are being led over the build-up of an emotion, instead of being merely provided with some readymade statements of truth or images of longing or reminiscence.

This does not, however, warrant the view that *all poetry other than its dramatic genre* is necessarily incapable of evoking *rasa*; and we must duly heed Viswanath's account of how poetry *can* well evoke *rasa*, if not the sweeping way he *appear*s to decree that *rasa* is the soul of poetry.[58] This is how he himself explains (a part of) his view in brief:

> When *sthāyībhāva*s like *rati* (which are already there in us as *vāsanā*s) become manifest (as transformed) for the blissful, immediate relish of *sahṛdaya jana* through the poet's depiction of *vibhāva*, *anubhāva*, and *sañchārībhāva*, they are said to be *rasa*.[59]

How exactly this can happen in our concern with (*non*-dramatic) poetry may now be brought out by considering two well-known English poems: Keats' *The Eve of St. Agnes* (for *śṛṅgāra rasa*) and Shelley's *Adonais* (for *karuṇa rasa*). The former tickles

58. That Vishvanath actually does so is the view of S.K. De. See his *Sanskrit Poetics*, p. 90. If I have yet thought it necessary to italicize the word "*appears*," it is simply because it has been suggested (and I think quite rightly) by at least one eminent scholar that the utterance in question should be taken as an eulogy of the poetic art *rather than as an assertion of its essential character*. The reference here is to p. 11 of Vishvanatha Kaviraja's *Sāhityadarpaṇa*, ed. Dr. Satyavrata Singh, Varanasi: Chowkhamba Vidya Bhawan, New edn., 1992.

59. Ibid., p. 69.

the *sthāyībhāva* of *rati* repeatedly and all along, through images and thoughts of love, longing, and beauty, such as the following:

a. . . . These let us wish away
And turn, sole-thoughted, to one Lady there,
Whose heart *had brooded, all that wintry day,*
On love . . .[60]

b. They told her how, upon St. Agnes' Eve
Young virgins might have visions of delight
Upon the honey'd middle of the night
If ceremonies due they did aright;
As, supperless to bed they must retire
And couch supine their beauties, lily white;[61]
. . . .

c. *Full of this whim* was thoughtful Madeline
The music, *yearning* like a God in pain,
She scarcely heard . . .
. . . her heart was otherwhere:
She *sigh'd* for Agnes' dreams, the sweetest of the year[62]

d. . . . Meantime, across the moors.
Had come young Porphyro, *with heart on fire*
For Madeline . . .[63]

It is easy to see that, along with making a quiet appeal to the *sthāyībhāva* of *rati* (as desire for amorous bliss), the lines cited above also at once make for the needed *vibhāva* by inducing us to visualize situations and happenings relating to *rati*. As for

60. *Master Poems*, p. 60.
61. Ibid.
62. Ibid.
63. Ibid.

anubhāva, we are not of course expected to see any actual acting here, as we do in witnessing a play; but, on the other hand, there is no dearth of word-bound images which prompt us to visualize movements, action, postures, and even such details (of stage management, basically) as disposition of things and figures in space. Thus, see the following:

> . . . *Beside* the portal doors,
> Buttress'd from moonlight, *stands* he, and implores
> All saints to give him sight of Madeline,
> But for one moment . . .
> That he might *gaze* and worship all unseen;
> Perchance *speak, kneel, touch, kiss* — in sooth such things have been,[64]

Or again:

> Ah, happy chance! the aged creature *came,*
> *Shuffling along* with ivory-headed wand,
> To where he *stood, hid from the torch's flame,*
> *Behind* a broad hall-pillar, far *beyond*[65]

What is more, even *vyabhichārī bhāva*s are traceable in some such lines of the poem as the following:

> a. She danc'd along with *vague, regardless eyes,*
> *Anxious her lips, her breathing quick and short*:
> . . . : she *sighs*[66]
>
> b. . . .; with aged *eyes aghast*
> *From fright of dim espial.*[67]

---

64. *Master Poems*, p. 601. In the second quote, here, the words italicized are obviously such as signify positioning in space.
65. Ibid.
66. Ibid., p. 601.
67. Ibid., p. 604.

c. She clos'd the door, . . .
No uttered syllable, or, woe betide!
But to her heart, her heart was voluble
Paining with eloquence her balmy side;
As though a tongueless nightingale should swell
Her throat in vain, and die, heart-stifled, in her dell.[68]

The *regardless eyes* which (*a*) speaks of are *śūnya dr̥ṣṭi*, and "*eyes aghast*" (in *b*) are *śaṅkitā dr̥ṣṭi* in Bharata's account of how eyes can be made to express *bhāva* and *rasa*; and both are meant to express *sañchārībhāvas*.[69] Further, the *pain* of having to hold searing longings of love which press for fulfilment is a deeply subjective *vyabhichārī bhāva* in the course of being in love. It may not last long, but it feels excruciating. On the stage it may well be expressed through some subtle bodily signs of felt inner discomfort through *mukhaj* (or facial) *abhinaya*.[70] But *āngika abhinaya* is clearly not a part of poesy's resources; and so, in the lines just cited, the poet has to use an endearing image of anguish — that is, the *nightingale* image, with such specificity that the reader can easily visualize the *vyabhichārī bhāva* in question, and so quietly do without the prop of actual *abhinaya*.

This, however, is not all that may be said to support our view that the poem makes for evocation of *śr̥ṅgāra rasa*. Two more points can be made. First, quite in accordance with one of Bharata's basic emphases, the locus of *rasa* in question is here kept free from sensuality; nay, it is even made to look ethereal, both at its core, that is, in the heart, *love*'s *fevrous citadel*,[71] and in respect of its overall setting. Secondly, care has been taken to ensure that our relish of the poem is almost as immediate an experience as that of witnessing a play. The

---

68. *Master Poems*, pp. 604-05.
69. *Sūtras* 40, 41, 42 in ch. VIII of Śukla's *NŚ* 2nd, part II, p. 11 *of the text*.
70. *Sūtra* 11. Ibid., p. 5 *of the text*.
71. 84th line of the poem in *Master Poems*, p. 62.

former end is secured, first, by providing the poem with a very chilly (or passion-free!) and devout opening:

> St. Agnes' Eve — Ah, bitter chill it was!
> . . .
> Numb were the Beadsman's fingers while he told
> His rosary, and while his frosted breath,
> Like pious incense from a censer old,
> Seem'd taking flight for heaven without a death,[72]

and, secondly, through some express projections of purity directly in relation to those who are yet indissolubly in love:

> a. "I will not harm her, by all saints I swear,"
> Quoth Porphyro: Or may I ne'er find grace
> . . .
> If one of her soft ringlets I displace,
> *Or look with ruffian passion in her face*[73]
> . . .
>
> b. Full on this casement shone the wintry moon
> . . .
> As down she knelt for heaven's grace and boon;
> . . .
> And on her hair a glory, like a saint:
> She seem'd a splendid angel, newly drest,
> Save wings, for heaven:- Porphyro grew faint:
> She knelt, so pure a thing, so free from mortal taint.[74]

The past tense of the second quote (b) balances Porphyro's solemn swearing in the present (Quote a). Such balancing is in fact a recurring device which the poet uses all along. Further, whichever be the temporal mode of what the poem says, past or present, pinpointing of details that make our real life experience is all along immaculate:

---

72. *Master Poems*, p. 600.

73. Ibid., p. 603.

74. Ibid., p. 605.

a. Her falt'ring hand upon the balustrade,
Old Angela was feeling for the stair,[75]
. . .

b. Out went the taper as she hurried in;
Its little smoke, in pallied moonshine, died:[76]

It is precisely these two poetic devices, present-past equipoise and fidelity to detail, that lend to the whole poem an air of presentational immediacy, in spite of the fact that it is meant to be "a dream, in olden times."[77] Indeed, "the power of language to overcome distance . . . looms throughout the poem";[78] and this is how a poet provides a parallel of our direct attention to what is shown on the stage. The two are in fact by no means disparate. We should not forget that, as we have already said earlier, what Bharata speaks of as *rasāsvādana* by *sahṛdaya jana* (or persons of responsive sensibility) is not a physical, but essentially a mental act (*mānas-asvādana*).

In respect of Shelley's *Adonais* too it is not difficult to show how the interplay of different *bhāva*s makes for the evocation of *karuṇa rasa*. What makes our task here easy is the fact that, in dealing with this *rasa*, Bharata includes separation from a loved one and death importantly in the list of requisite *vibhāva*s; weeping and lamentation in *anubhāva*s that make for proper *abhinaya* of the *rasa* on the stage; and attachment (*moha*) and dying (*maraṇa*) among the relevant *sañchārī* and *sāttvikabhāva*s.

Now, all this is traceable in *Adonais*, as follows:

The very title of the poem is significant. It opens with the word *Adonai*s — "a name that partakes of Adonis, the youth *slain* by a wild boar and hence a sacrificed seasonal god, and

75. *Master Poems*, p. 604.

76. Ibid.

77. Ibid., p. 612.

78. Ibid., p. 610.

Adonai, the Hebrew name for Supreme Being";[79] and quickly follows it up with a sub-title which says that the poem is an elegy on the death of John Keats, author of *Endymion, Hyperion,* etc. Now, the slaying of a youth and death taken generally are both common causes of making us commiserate. But such moments of compassion produced by isolated thoughts are fickle and merely personal; and it is important to see how our everyday experiences not only of pity for others but of our own grieving differ from *karuṇa rasa*. This *rasa* is no mere prolongation of sorrow. One may keep wallowing in grief because of the death of a child for days on end, but it would not be nameable as an experience of *karuṇa rasa;* for such an actual experience is not only personal, but painful. The feeling of compassion has to be released from concern with those who matter in one's merely individual life — and sustained through a pleasing organization of such factors as are common to all — before it can truly claim the status of *karuṇa rasa;* and this is precisely what the elegy in question does. Our innate propensity to grieve (*sthāyībhāva* of *śoka*) over the death of a loved one (*vibhāva*) is repeatedly quickened by verbal invitations to mourn — in ways which we are *all* familiar with, and which are therefore trans-individual or *sādhāraṇa* (general). Phenomenologically, the course of actual sorrowing is never uniform; it runs in waves, so to say, which surge up and subside; and here (in *Adonais*) the accents of poignancy are provided by two factors: thoughts of the brute finality of the ceasing-to-be, and the glory *and ardent interior* of the one who has ceased to be. Hence the lifelike quality of the following word-pictures of (invitations to) lamentation (*vibhāva*) that may be taken to parallel its bodily presentation on the stage:

a. Oh, weep for Adonais! *though our tears*
Thaw not the frost which binds so *dear a head!*[80]

79. *Master Poems*, p. 540.

80. Ibid., p. 527.

b. Oh, weep for Adonais — he is dead!

. . .

For he is gone, where all things wise and fair
Descend: oh, *dream not that the amorous Deep*
Will yet restore him to the vital air;[81]

. . .

c. *He will awake no more, oh, never more!*[82] —

But, one may ask, what are the *sañchārī* and *sāttvikabhāvas*, if any, in this poem? Now, one of these is *āvega* which we have already spoken of as the occasional swell of pathetic feeling in actual lamentation. What is more, the selfsame *bhāva* — along with some other *sañchārī* and *sāttvikabhāvas*, such as *moha, dainya,* and *maraṇa* (that is, attachment, wretchedness, and death or the act of dying) — is there also in such ardent, pathetic lines as the following:

1. Lament anew, Urania![83] . . .
2. . . . now, thy youngest, dearest one has perished
3. . . . , who grew
4. Like a pale flower by some sad maiden cherished,
5. And fed with true love tears, instead of dew;
6. Most musical of mourners, weep anew!
7. Thy extreme hope, the loveliest and the last,
8. The bloom, whose petals nipt before they blew
9. Died on the promise of the fruit . . .
10. The broken lily lies — the storm is overpast[84]

In these lines evocation of the *bhāvas* we have set out to trace is all clearly there in the only way that poetry admits of,

81. *Master Poems*.

82. Ibid., p. 528.

83. Urania is the muse of astronomy; and another name for Aphrodite, goddess of love and beauty in Greek mythology, daughter of Zeus. Its Roman counterpart in Venus.

84. *Master Poems*, p. 528.

that is, in terms of verbal meaning and word-bound images. The last three lines (8-10) bespeak *dainya*. It sure feels wretched to contemplate the premature passing away of a peaking genius; and the fourth and fifth lines clearly add to this feeling by providing a virtual picture of sadness. Words like *youngest*, (so) *dearest*, and *loveliest* smack of attachment (*moha*); and *has perished* and *died* are the poet's obvious words for what is called *maraṇa*. So, building on our innate disposition to grieve (*sthāyībhāva* of *śoka*) the poet adroitly interfuses the *vibhāva* of the premature death of a loved one with four transient emotions of *āvega*, *dainya*, *moha* and *maraṇa* to make us experience *karuṇa rasa*.

This *rasa*, we may note, is not the same thing as *our* feeling sad in real life, say, because of loss of prestige, riches, or a dear relative. Such unfortunate situations are only the *vibhāva* or apt occasions for sorrowing, though the easy rise of the experience here is due to our innate and abiding disposition to grieve (*sthāyībhāva* of *śoka*). Nor can the *rasa* in question be identified with our feeling moved spontaneously when we see someone suffering — say, due to sickness or sheer poverty — because, though the reaction here may well be wholly selfless, it can also cause some actual discomfort if, maybe because of the absence of needed resources, we are unable to give practical vent to our impulse to help. Further, insofar as the way *the object* appears to us, as distinguished from how *we* react to it, is not actively controlled here, our kindly attitude may vaporize the moment we are told that the misery of the person before us is a sequel to his own chronic and ruinous vices. What is more, though the actual impulsion to help is surely felt as a sweet expansion of our being, a sort of going out in love, this blissful core of the experience does not become *a steady object of contemplation for us*, because, though it can surely recur freely if one is committed to a life of helping the needy, its individual occurrences are all at the mercy of many contingencies.

Preoccupation with our own pressing problems may come in the way; or, as already indicated, some new information about the suffering one may dampen our very will to help.

Now, all this is quite transformed in the creative process of *rasa*-evocation as Bharata envisages it. One enters the theatre with the explicit intent to watch the presentation of a play; and what he sees on the stage — and hears what emanates therefrom, that is, the music and the dialogues — is all (in principle) such a compact blend (or *saṁyoga*) of *abhinaya* of different kinds that he is readily freed from the confines of his own joys and sorrows (*nijasuḥkhaduḥkhādivivaśibhāva*); and is enabled, in the case of a *karuṇa rasa* presentation, to relish the bliss of being perfectly in tune with what is presented (movingly) on the stage, and so to experience the particular *rasa*. Nothing that is presented on the stage is uniquely related to any one member of the audience. The various *bhāva*s are a part of everybody's being and behaviour in life, which is exactly what makes them easily and commonly intelligible. Yet the impact of the objective and integrated presentation of the various *bhāva*s on the stage (or in the text of a play) is *quite unlike our everyday experience* which is largely humdrum, often merely individual — at times even aggressively so; and rarely quite regulated. This is partly why *rasānubhūti* is said to be a beyond-the-world (or *lokottara*) experience.

But is not the poem avowedly about someone who *actually* lived? Sure, it is, about the poet, John Keats; but the way he is visualized in the present poem is such a palpitating blend of the real, the celestial, and the patently mythological; and the images that illumine the poem all along collocate quite disparate elements of our everyday experience in such novel and winsome ways that references to matters of fact nowhere seem to jar with what the poem seeks to do, that is, sanctifying the spirit of Keats[85] and making him appear virtually stellar in glory. This is why the reader just acquiesces in this movement away from real life.[86]

At the same time, in spite of its powerful, elegiac impact — and its recurring "invitations" to mourn, and abounding references to death and tears — the poem is by no means a vehicle of maudlin sentimentality. *Karuṇa rasa* is an exaltation *and no mere intensification* of the *sthāyībhāva* of *śoka*. The poem achieves this end partly by seeking to locate good poets in the heavens as stars, and partly by dotting the poem with such gems of philosophic solemnity as the following:

> The One remains, the many change and pass;
> Heaven's light forever shines, Earth's shadows fly;
> Life, like a dome of many-coloured glass,
> Stains the white radiance of Eternity,
> Until Death tramples it to fragments . . . [87]

Here, we seem to *see, and not merely to follow* what the poet says, if not in the way of watching a play. Indeed, as in reading Keats' *The Eve of St. Agnes*, the experience generated here is by and large immediate, or, as the *rasa* theorists would say, *sākṣātkārātmaka,* though not of course an actual *sakṣātkāra*.

What is said in the lines just cited from Shelley's poem is clearly of general significance. Further, of all the human beings visualized in the two poems we have dealt with, only one — that is, Keats — has actually lived; and (in *Adonais*) he too has been so beautifully idealized and framed in a setting of myth

---

85. *Master Poems*, p. 540.

86. See, here, references to Urania, the mythical goddess of love and beauty who is visualized as having her seat in Paradise (*Master Poems*, pp. 527-28) and also such pictures of real life as the periodic renewal or reappearance of "the airs and streams . . . ants, bees . . . swallows . . . fresh leaves and flowers" (Ibid., p. 532).

87. Ibid., p. 539.

that, instead of being disturbed by lack of historical detail, we just chime happily with this rarefaction of the real — a typically romantic device which is also at work where even some real life objects of Keats' poetic artistry are pictured as phantoms, so to say, and are thus half denuded of reality:

> . . . Desires and Adorations
> Winged Persuasions and veiled Destinies,
> Splendours, and Glooms, and glimmering Incarnations
> Of hopes and fears, and twilight Phantasies;
> And Sorrow, with her family of Sighs,
> And Pleasure, blind with tears
> Like pageantry of mist on an autumnal stream
> All he had loved, and moulded into thought
> From shape, and hue, and odour, and sweet sounds[88]

Yet, on the whole, the poem is no real strain on our credence. It only exalts the idiom of reality without quite deserting it. The vein of lament which is all along visible, and thus holds the poem pretty tightly as one, is so freely relieved by expressions of praise, love, and longing that the whole picture appears quite close to the common features of the way we all in fact tend to mourn the loss of our dear ones because of something admirable in them. There are some, it is true, who live through their heartaches in silence and solitude, whereas quite a few others choose to mourn quite openly and even so expressly for a definite period that they seem to be making a luxury of their grief.[89] These are, however, but individual differences; the common core of mourning is provided by the features we have listed. It is these that the poet builds upon; and it is precisely this seizure of essentials of both experience and expression that makes the picture of (say) grieving acceptable to all. What *rasa* theorists mean by *sādhāraṇīkaraṇa* is

---

88. *Master Poems*, pp. 530-31.

89. Say, like Olivia in Shakespeare's *Twelfth Night*.

no laboured simplification of what is originally obscure or profound. It is rather the device of so regulating an artistic presentation that, as a whole, it may neither appear related to any real person, nor to anybody's merely individual concerns; and may be positively relished by the *generality* of knowledgeable people. The whole process of *rasa*-evocation makes for both these ends, because *rasa* arises from an integration of situations and modes of expression which relate to human life *generally* and because what appears (in an exalted form) as the substance of the resulting (*rasa*-)experience is something that is already there *in one and all*, in the form of *sthāyībhāva*s.

Yet, as Abhinavagupta points out, the quality of being generally acceptable *and appealing* (or *sādhāraṇya*) is quite different from, and independent of, the *logical* concept of generality (*sāmānya*).[90] The logically general is that which is *understood or thought of* as being applicable to all or most members of a class or category. The aesthetically *sādhāraṇa*, on the other hand, is that which is not the private experience of any one individual but is accessible, as a *presentation*, to all those who are suitably equipped to attend to it; which is why the senses which enable a whole gathering of people to attend to the same art object at once — namely, the ear and the eye — are (for Bharata) pre-eminently aesthetic. A simple analogy should make the distinction clear. The *concept* of a public park *subsumes* all parks which are open to the public; an *actual* public park, on the other hand, *serves* as such simply because it is not any one individual's personal property. A stage presentation too, if it is to be experienced aesthetically, must be presented (according to Bharata) in such a manner that it may not appear as relating to any one real person alone, though its details may well be identified on the basis of our *general* experience of life

90. Gnoli, *The Aesthetic Experience According to Abhinavagupta*, 1st edn., p. 29, 5th footnote.

and reality. It is precisely because of this absence of explicit reference to our individual concerns that, while watching a play, we are able to attend to situations presented on the stage wholeheartedly, that is, without being disturbed by any such *purely individual* reactions on our part as could easily arise were we faced with similar situations in real life.

Here, again, we may take a simple example to make the point clear. If one of the two young and friendly neighbours one is known to be rather shy by temperament, and if he yet succeeds in carrying on with a lady in their locality, the other one may feel *happy* because, after all, his friend has been able to overcome shyness; *envious* because he has lost to one whom he had always regarded as inferior in love-making; or *angry* because the affair is likely to disturb the peace of their locality. But if the same shy young man impersonates an ardent lover in a dramatic performance, his friend will care only for the truth and subtlety of *abhinaya*; and, as a *sāmājika*, his attention to the play will not at all be disturbed by the real life reactions we have just visualized.

Yet, a little more care is needed to see how exactly the self is related to its object in aesthetic experience. On the one hand, it is surely not a state of indifference (or *tāṭasthya*); in fact it is rather "an active participation (*anupraveśa*) of the cognizing subject in the event represented."[91] How otherwise can we explain the fact that after we have witnessed a good play or dance recital, quite a few moving scenes or expressive postures continue to haunt the mind? Yet, on the other hand, our attention to what we see on the stage does not impel us into the broad, overt reactions of daily life. The whole point has indeed to be taken in a duly balanced way, partly by holding on to Bharata's own views on both aesthetic attitude and variety of aesthetic responses, along with due attention to the

91. Gnoli, op. cit., pp. xx-xxi. *Anupraveśa* means "entrance-into."

otherworldly character of *rasa* emphasized by commentators on his views. Bhaṭṭa Nāyaka insists that the essence of *rasa* is "a pleasure which has no relationship with any real individual"; and that

> the images contemplated on the stage or read in poetry are seen by the man of aesthetic sensibility independently of any relationship with his [own] ordinary life or with the [normal] life of the actor or of the hero of the play or poem; and appear, therefore, in a generalized [*sādhāraṇīkṛta*] way, that is to say, universally and released from individuality.[92]

Abhinavagupta goes even further when he says that during the course of aesthetic experience the individual raises himself above time, space and causality, and so also above the very basic character of practical life (or *saṁsāra*). He believes that such an experience, even "like . . . a flower born of magic, has, as its essence, solely the present; it is correlated neither with what came before nor with what comes after. This experience is therefore different both from the ordinary experience and from the religious one."[93]

Now, what is meant here simply is that we do not situate our aesthetic experiences in the space in which we actually move about or in the time by which we measure delays or premature ageing. Where a danseuse traverses the stage in a series of quick and tight-knit steps the space covered appears greater than it really is. Oppositely, if the recital is absorbing, the seventy-five minutes or so it usually takes may not appear as a *passage* at all. In neither case, it is true, the difference disturbs us. But, on the other hand, our reactions on such occasions can be *basically* quite true to life. It is true that "the proverbial unsophisticated yokel whose chivalrous interference in the play

---

92. Gnoli, op. cit.

93. Gnoli, *The Aesthetic Experience According to Abhinavagupta*, 2nd edn., Chowkhamba Sanskrit Series, vol. LXII, 1968, pp. xxiii, xxxvi.

on behalf of the hapless heroine [because he could not abstain from behaving as one is expected to, in response to a similar situation *in real life*] is not the ideal type of theatrical audience."[94] But, at the same time, the audience would be less than human if it reacted to emotive situations in a play *quite dissimilarly* to how we react to them in real life. Bharata does not visualize any such audience of bizarre onlookers; and where he speaks of the reactions of *prekṣaka*s (the audience) to presentations of different *rasa*s, he very rightly says that if the *rasa* evoked on the stage (effectively) is *adbhuta, śṛṅgāra* or *vīra*, the audience reacts with an audible *ahā* (or *vāh*, expressing wonder); and where the *rasa* is *karuṇa*, with tearful eyes or a mournful utterance of *hāi*.[95] What is more, with his uncanny eye for detail, Bharata even distinguishes the objects of aesthetic response from the viewpoint of age, sex and personality types. Children and ladies, we are told, generally react positively to a *hāsya rasa* presentation; and the elderly, to a religious or Purāṇic theme. By and large, however, Bharata's emphasis is on *prekṣaka*s of "parallel" sensitiveness:

> Only those should be provided as audience to a play who feel happy when they find a blessed person in the play and feel sad on seeing a grieving character in the play. . . . [96]

Such writing is clearly more enlightening than quite a few contemporary (and fairly sensible) definitions of the aesthetic attitude (and response) such as the following:

---

94. Edward Bullough's essay, "Psychical Distance" in M. Rader's *A Modern Introduction to Esthetics*. (Holt, Rinehart and Winston, 1979, 5th edn.) p. 350.

95. Śukla's *NŚ*, part III, 1st edn., 1983. *Sūtras*, 9-11, of chapter XVII, p. 324.

96. Ibid., *sūtra*, 54, p. 350.

> [The aesthetic attitude] is disinterested and sympathetic attention to and contemplation of any object of awareness whatever for its own sake alone.[97]

How the aesthetic attitude is disinterested in the sense of being free from determination *by the very basic character of reality* — that is, by distinctions of time and space, you and I, or subject and object, thereby providing release from our everyday concerns, if only for a while; and how it is "sympathetic" as vibrating with parallel sensitiveness to what is shown on the stage — all this is clear in Bharata's account concretely, that is, with due regard to details of artistic practice and art experience.

Drama and poetry in general, however, are not the only arts to which the theory of *rasa* seems relevant. As has been suggested by Hiriyanna, it may even be possible to construct, on the basis of *rasa* theory, an Indian aesthetics of fine art in general around the data provided by quite a few Sanskrit works on poetics, though "their set purpose is only to elucidate the principles exemplified in poetry and . . . drama."[98] Now, though the task here visualized has not been accomplished so far, it is undeniable that the theory in question is quite evidently at work in the majority of our classical dance-forms. Quite a few of them, in fact, regard *navarasamālikā* as an important number. Kathak, of course, is an exception to this. Indeed, of all the major classical dances of India it is probably the only one which has charmed its numberless fans without claiming that it derives its character or content from Bharata's *Nāṭyaśāstra*. A careful look, however, at the great variety of its representational and expressional numbers (that is, *nṛtya*) makes one wonder if it has not borrowed, if perhaps unconsciously, quite a good deal

---

97. Jerome Stolnitz's essay, "The Aesthetic Attitude" in *Introductory Readings in Aesthetics*, ed. John Hospers, The Free Press & Collier MacMillan, 1969, p. 19.

98. Hiriyanna, *Art Experience*, p. 2.

from the time-honoured classic of dramaturgy. A brief account of some such numbers — or *intra-forms*, as I prefer to call them[99] — as have been actually presented on the Kathak stage in contemporary India should make the point clear.

Consider, to begin with, that well-known *nṛtya* number which opens with the words, *Vṛndāvana kuñjana racho rāsa āli.* Here, the *sthāyībhāva* of *rati* is manifest pretty quickly not only because of the general awareness among Indians that a *rāsa* is essentially an artistic essay in playfulness, figural charm as manifest in dancing, and variform expression of love, but because of what the pattern in question itself actually provides. Thus, its very opening words that we have cited enable the *rasika* to visualize the relevant *vibhāva*, that is, a celebration of *rāsa* in Vṛndāvana featuring the Rādhā-Kṛṣṇa duo as *ālambana* and the verdant charm of a *kuñja* as *uddīpana vibhāva*. Further, along with quite a few *bol*s of pure dance — such as *dig, dig, trām* — the figural representation of such meaningful words as *laya gati dikhāvaṭ* or *chaplā si chamkat chandramukhī Rādhā* may be said to provide what Bharata speaks of as *anubhāva*; and, above all, the accordant dancing of details like *kasak-masak, chanchal nain bān*, and *bhanva-kaṭāksha* exemplify what he says about *vyabhichārī bhāva*s (as incidental to the evocation of *saṁyoga śṛṅgāra*) in chapter VI of his treatise.[100]

What is more, on a number of occasions even a close and balanced presentation of both *saṁyoga* and *vipralambha* (or *viyoga*)

99. My reason for this preference may be put thus. In so far as every Kathak number has to be internally well organized *and also* to appear self-completing (importantly because it follows a cyclic rhythm), it may be said to a *form* itself. But because a whole Kathak recital from the opening *thāṭ* to the closing *tatkār* — and including all the other "items" — is also (in principle) internally well organized, what it includes, that is, the individual numbers, may well be said to be *form within the recital's overall form*, or just *intra-forms*.

100. Śukla's *NŚ*, 2nd, part I, p. 308.

śṛṅgāra in terms of two separate compositions — and in fair accordance with Bharata's view of *rasa*-evocation — has been effectively presented in the Kathak idiom. This is how I recall the way it was done. [101]

The danseuse first picks a sad and moving composition for presentation. The text for singing (as accompaniment) is provided by a Mīrā *bhajan* which opens with the words, *horī piyā bin lāgey khāri*. *Khāri* may here be taken to express *glāni* which is one of the *vyabhichārī bhāva*s of *viyoga śṛṅgāra*.[102] The song is set in *rāga pūriyā* which is admirably suited to express how one pines in love unrequited, and lives through endless stretches of waiting for the dear one, here Murārī or Kṛṣṇa. The rhythm chosen is *tritāla* at a reposeful pace. The *sthāyībhāva* of *rati* is manifest straight away, because of the very opening line, a refrain throughout the course of dancing, which says that even a gay and *frolicsome* festival like *horī* feels distasteful *in the absence of the loved one*. The next line speaks of the loneliness that pervades the village — nay, the whole neighbouring region — and makes even the *saij* and *aṭārī* look forlorn, that is, sad and deserted.[103] Words such as these, we may note, lend extra explicitness to both *sthāyībhāva* and *vibhāva*, at once indicating how the two interrelate or colour each other in an actual situation. *Anubhāva* has, of course, to be there all along as *abhinaya*; and glimpses of *vyabhichārī bhāva*s are provided by such fleeting, but genuine indicators of an agonizing and seemingly unending wait as *andesā*[104] (or anxiety duly reflected

101. Pretty freely, by Rani Karnaa, winner of the prestigious Sangeet Natak Akademi Award for excellence in classical dance for 1997.

102. Śukla's *NŚ* 2nd part I, p. 309.

103. The Hindi words here are: "सूनो गांव, देस सब सूनो, सूनी सेज अटारी।"

104. Anxiety (or, चिन्ता), we may note, is (according to Bharata) one of the *vyabhichārībhāva*s in the evocation of *vipralambha* (or *viyoga*) *śṛṅgāra*. Sukla's *NŚ*, 2nd, part I, p. 309.

in the dancer's face) and the eventual disappearance of the very lines that segment the fingers because of incessant counting of days spent in forlornness.[105] The closing words duly signify a helpless admission of what must be endured, that is, lingering loneliness.[106]

The next composition which follows very quickly is an essay in evoking *saṁyoga śṛṅgāra*. The *rāga* chosen is *hindol*; the rhythm, *dhamār*, at *madhya laya*; the vocal form, also a *dhamār*; and the text of the song visualizes *holī*-playing at its sportive best, as indicated by the text of the very first line which runs thus: *khelat holī śyām chapal madmātī*. Quite a few other words like *abeer gulāl ki dhoom machi hai nāchat dey dey tālī* not only project the occasion or *vibhāva* (*holī*) and the *sthāyībhāva* of *rati* (as sheer rejoicing), but the *vyabhichārībhāva* of (an aspect of) dancing regarded as regulated movement of beauteous limbs.[107]

In respect of all such numbers, however, the following objection is possible:

It takes but a few minutes to complete their dancing; the staging of a play, on the other hand, lasts much longer; how then can we expect such dances to evoke the sustained emotive experience that *rasa* is said to be? Now, our answer may be that though the proper staging of a play is of course characterized by *saṁyoga* or due integration of the different *bhāvas*, good dancing is *more tightly* and more noticeably organized on the inside, and so is quicker in producing an impact than a play. The point may be argued as follows:

Rhythm in Hindustānī (north Indian) music is necessarily cyclic in character; and so, because it here envelops and

105. This is my translation of the following words in the *bhajan* in question: "गिणता गिणता घिस गई रेखा, आंगुरिया की सारी".

106. Signified by the words, "अबंहु न आये मुरारी."

107. Or, "ललित अंगो का परिचालन". Śukla's *NŚ*, part I, 2nd edn., p. 308.

regulates both music and the dancing, the entire presentation appears visibly gathered. This appearance is also determined, in part, by the fact that the rhythm here is not a mere cycle, but a cycle with a distinct centre, namely, the *sama*, from where the *laya*-flow begins and to which it returns, *directing the rasika*'s *attention accordingly*. Above all, the two senses which are eminently aesthetic according to Bharata — namely, the ear and the eye — are much more conjointly and continually tickled by the dances we have referred to than by a play. No mere dialogues here detract from the fascination of senses; and the ideal content — that is, the meaning of the text of the songs — is generally too familiar to *rasika*s to make any heavy demands on their understanding. The *rasa* here evoked may not last long, but so long as it does, its impact is definite; and its character, quite easy to identify.

To turn, now, to classical music, in our talk about this art we freely — and confidently — speak of the *rasa*s of (at least) some *rāga*s. It is quite widely accepted that a recital of *rāga Adānā* has to evoke a semblance of *vīra rasa*, or at least of aggressiveness; and that the proper singing of *Jogīyā* and *Sohnī* has to wear a look of *karuṇa rasa*. But, on the other hand, there is a good deal in the forms, structural features, and practice of our (Hindustānī or north Indian) music today which distances the art from the *rasa* theory. What we call *sthāyī* in our *dhruvapad* and *khayāl* singing is not at all the same thing as *sthāyībhāva*. Whereas such a *bhāva*, we have seen, is an innate disposition to have *emotional* experiences of a particular kind, a *sthāyī* in vocal music is, for theory, just the first (steadfast) line of a composition and in practice the *structural* anchor of a whole recital. The text of a *khayāl-sthāyī* may have nothing to do with emotion; and even where it has some emotive import, like the well-known *Sadaraṅg* composition (in *rāga Miyān ki Malhār*), *Karīm Nām Tero*, its opening devotionl air may be, in fact it usually is, quickly dissipated by the *taan*s in which a *khayāl* recital usually abounds.

Further, *tarānā*s which only use mnemonic syllables, and no words at all, do not aim at evoking any emotion; and the whole genre of *ṭappā* singing is distinguished only by the vocalist's ability to execute quite sudden and difficult vocal turns, and not at all by evocation of emotions.

Yet this is undeniable that where our *classical* singing — specially as *ālāpa* of the *dhruvapad* manner and *vilambit khayāl*-singing — is really top class it *is* able to provide us with an experience which is delightful and unruffled by distinctions that characterize our everyday experience; which lifts us, temporarily, above the concerns of our real life; and, above all, which leaves us finally, if momentarily, with the feeling that we, who were just a random gathering of separate listeners at the start of the recital, have somehow become not merely akin, but one in the fellowship of art contemplation. How the evocation of this experience results from an integration of the various *bhāva*s which the *rasa sūtra* speaks of is extremely difficult, if not impossible, to trace in respect of *our music today*; but as to the quality of the experience it *can* evoke, what we have just said is indubitable. This should become clear as we turn to consider how the experience of *rasa* actually feels — a task which calls for a fair amount of phenomenological analysis. Happily, our task is made easy by such succinct accounts of what *rasa* distinctively is as the following one by Vishvanath:

> *sattvodrekād akhaṇḍasvākāsānandachinmayaḥ* ।
> *vedyāntarasparśaśūnyo brahmāsvādasahodaraḥ* ॥
> *lokottarachamatkāraprāṇaḥ kaiśchit pramāṭrbhiḥ* ।
> *svākārvad abhinnatvenāyam āsvādyate rasaḥ* ॥[108]

Gnoli translates the above as follows:

> *Rasa* is tasted by the qualified persons. . . . It is tasted by virtue of the emergence of *sattva*. It is made up of a full Intelligence, Beatitude and Self-luminosity. It is void of contact

108. R. Gnoli, *The Aesthetic Experience According to Abhinavagupta*, 2nd edn., p. 47, f.n. 1a.

> with any other knowable thing, [and is the] twin brother to the tasting of *Brahman*. It is tasted as if it were our being, in indivisibility.[109]

Now, this translation may well be true to the essential features of *rasa*, but it is unable to account for their being interrelated in the unity of *rasa*-experience. Perhaps we could make it a little more enlightening too by reflecting as under:

There are three basic considerations which have to be borne in mind. First, however different it be from our everyday emotional experiences, *rasa* is not *alaukika* in the sense of being *utterly* independent of *every* kind of context, though, as Abhinavagupta insists, aesthetic experience does disconnect us, if temporarily, from the spatio-temporal awareness and utilitarian interests of our everyday life. It is emphatically said to happen *as the result of* a proper integration of the different *bhāva*s in the presentation of a play, in good poetry or in a dance recital — all as contemplated by a *rasika*. Second, though *rasa* is surely dominated by *sattva*, as against *rajas* and *tamas*, we cannot hope to see how the operation of the three *guṇa*s interrelates in the blissful experience which *rasa* is, because it is (insistently said to be) thoroughly unified or *niravacchinna*. Further, the locus of *rasa* is always the state of *tādātmya*, that is, the *rasika*s' imaginative self-identification with what they see on the stage or read in a play. Finally, though the experience of *rasa* may well be taken to release the *rasika*s (temporarily) from preoccupation with their own individual lives and problems, it does not efface their temperamental characteristics and ingrained likes and dislikes, and sense of values, which is precisely why Bharata thinks it necessary to point out that *sāmājika*s do not all react identically to plays projecting different *rasa*s, and that differences of sex, age, and individual tastes

109. R. Gnoli, op. cit.

necessarily determine their aesthetic responses. We have to resist being swept off the ground by references to light, beatitude, and composure (*viśrānti*);[110] and to refrain from the temptation to think that *rasa* is a kind of luminous cloud floating all by itself in mid air.

Bearing all these precautionary attitudes in mind, let us now turn to the first keyword in Vishvanath's definition, that is, *sattvodrekād*. *Udreka* is here to be interpreted as predominance, not mere abundance; for to say that a quality is abundant is only to mean that it is there in plenty, not necessarily that it also rules over other qualities. *Sattva* must here be taken to dominate *rajas* and *tamas*; otherwise it will not be possible to relate *sattvodrek* with other attributes that are made to qualify *rasa*. But how is *sattva* to be taken as distinct from *rajas* and *tamas*? According to the *Gītā*,[111] *sattva* makes for purity, light as heightened awareness and keener powers of apprehension, right knowledge, overall purity, and so for happiness. *Rajas* is at the root of self-serving actions, (hence) attachment to consequences, greed, fickleness of mind, desire for sense-indulgence; and so it causes *duḥkha*. The third *guṇa*, *tamas*, is regarded as the principle of *pramād* (or useless, wasteful activity), ignorance, and *moha*. Therefore, *sattvodrek* or ascendance of *sattva* over *rajas* and *tamas* here means that, as experience, *rasa* is characterized by purity (as freedom from cravings, sensuous desires, and mental fickleness), and so by

---

110. "*Viśrānti*, rest, denotes the fact of our being absorbed in something, immersed in it, to the exclusion of every other thing (*vigalitavedyāntaratayā*), without, that is, having any mental movement, any extraneous desire (in other words, no obstacle, *vighna*) which . . . [may come] to break into that state of consciousness. In . . . the . . . language [of aesthetics] *viśrānti* denotes, at the same time, the fact of being absorbed in the aesthetic object, and the sensation of pleasure *sui generis* which accompanies that state of consciousness."

111. Chapter XIV.

composure and beatitude, because (as according to Sāṁkhya) it is *aviśrānti* (or lack of composure) which is the *immediate* cause of *duḥkha*. But, we may note, the ascendance in question does not mean that *rajas* and *tamas* are thereby made inoperative for good, or even for the duration of *rasa*-experience itself. It is an obvious fact that after the most gripping aesthetic experience the normal tenor of our selfish pursuits, cravings and dissatisfaction — with spells of sheer lethargy and boredom — reappears pretty soon. What is more, even during the course of *rasa*-experience *rajas* and *tamas* do not become entirely ineffective. The luminous character of *rasa*-experience is not to be confused with the inert, changeless glow of a torch. *Wondrous* though it is surely said to be, *rasa* is not to be regarded as a *benumbing* experience. Nor is it accompanied by the incredulous feeling, *how could it happen*, which is partly why *rasa* is said to be a miracle *of a quite uncommon kind*. In spite of being very different from our everyday experiences it elicits credence because what it builds on, basically, is a *sthāyībhāva*, a disposition which we readily identify as our own. What is more, it is a *course* of blissful experience; and it cannot but be so because it is largely confluent with our attention to the stage presentation, or with our reading of a play, both alike sequential necessarily. Now, this pervasive fluidity (*druti*) is provided by a contact of *sattva* with *rajas*.[112] Where *sattva* operates by itself — that is, where its sway is absolute — the resulting state of consciousness is *vikās* or expansion; but where its working is tempered with a touch of *tamas*, we get moments of mere dilatation or *vistār*.[113] This distinction, which can be drawn only by *recalling* how we felt in experiencing *rasa*, and not *during* the course of the experience itself, may be clarified thus:

First, out of this world though it may well be, *rasa* is after all an emotional experience; and, in point of fact, every emotion

112. Ibid., p. 46, footnote 1a.

113. Ibid.

can be felt in two ways; as a flow, so long as it is allowed to express itself; and as a trifle uneasy block-cum-swell if it is denied due vent. Now, where the stage presentation appears to be heading for a denouement, and the *prekṣaka* holds his breath in *mounting suspense* or apprehension, the passing arrest in the varying flow of experience is due to the impact of *tamas* on *sattva* (or is *vistār*, a mere bloating of the present state of experience, so to say); and the moment uncertainties are clarified, and previously unresolved problems and mysteries are unravelled, *sattva* may be said to reassert its supermacy over *tamas*, undoing the hold on the flow of experience, providing fuller understanding (*vikās*) and deepening *viśrānti*.

The ascendancy of *sattva* over *rajas* — the *guṇa* which is the cause not only of overly oriented activity, but of haste, impatience, and unrest — accounts for the presence of tranquillity, as also for the absence of willed overt activity in the experience of *rasa*. As we have already hinted, some reflex bodily changes, such as bated breath and accelerated heartbeat, may well occur in *rasānubhūti*, but here we do not *seek to do* anything; and, generally, serene contemplation of what is presented to us is our only intentional or effortless activity.

Some features of *rasa*, however, relate directly to *sattva* itself. This *guṇa* is commonly regarded as the principle of *purity*; but here this quality cannot be said to characterize our motives and conduct. It has rather to be taken in a sense which is partly, but importantly negative. Just as *ālāpa* of the *dhruvapad* way of singing is said to be pure music because it is free from admixture with language and beat-measured rhythm, so the purity which *sattva* lends to *rasa* means that the experience here is not at all ruffled by preoccupation with one's *own* joys and sorrows (*nijasukhaduḥkādiviveśibhāva*) and cravings and desires, because of the *sādhāraṇīkaraṇa* brought about by the aesthetic configuration of different *bhāvas*; and is therefore *chinmaya* or consisting of pure awareness.

But, one may ask, what exactly is the point in relating this awareness to *prakāsh* and *ānand*? Here, we may answer thus:

It is quite proper and surely not uncommon to speak of feeling lit up with understanding, say, after we have given close and fruitful attention to an intricate train of argument. Now, though quite differently evoked, this feeling is importantly there in *rasa*-experience as well, because of the tightly focused and so exclusive quality of our attention. We feel gripped by the integrated and expressive form of what is presented on the stage, as also by its appeal as much to the ear and the eye as to understanding, not a little because of *āhārya abhinaya*. Further, by virtue of being authentic *rasika*s, we are not merely willing but *able* to follow the presentation. This ability is due to two main factors: first, our own past training and experience in watching plays; and, second, the passing release from preoccupation with our *own* joys and sorrows presently brought about in the way already indicated, so that our attention is here "exclusive" in the sense of not being ruffled at all by concern with any other object of knowledge (*vedyāntarasparśa śūnyo*). Be that as it may, this is a matter of actual experience that one who tastes *rasa* rests in a state of pure contemplation bereft of all practical interest (*saṁvit*), which is at once a feeling of composure (*viśrānti*). Such tranquil and undivided attention naturally makes for very clear perception which enlivens understanding. What is, in this context, spoken of as *prakāsh* is obviously no physical light, but

> The inner radiation of being which accompanies delighted understanding, a joyous state of heightened awareness.[114]

Correspondingly, Bharata's characterization of *rasa* as *ujjvalaveśātmakaḥ* may be translated as "whose essence is a look of splendour and clarity (rather than of *burning*!)" The italicized

---

114. S.K. Saxena, *Aesthetical Essays*, Delhi: Chanakya Publications, 1981, p. 159.

word within brackets has been taken from S.K. De's translation (of the Sanskrit word) which runs thus: "whose essence is an appearance of burning." By way of explaining what this *burning* is he has cited the case of "inflamed" passions. Now, this interpretation creates a problem if we take *it*, obviously a way of characterizing *rasa*, along with De's other view that *rati*, the *sthāyībhāva* of *śṛṅgāra rasa*, is "physical passion."[115] Are we to believe that *śṛṅgāra rasa*, as *ujjvalaveśātmakaḥ*, is simply the inflamed or violently excited (because *burning*) evocation of an animal appetite?

Anyway, to turn now to *prākash* and *viśrānti*, important though they surely are, these terms do not exhaust the meaning of *ānand* in Visvanatha's definition of *rasa*. Taken along with *sattvodrek*, *ānand* cannot be interpreted as everyday happiness, and surely not as sensual pleasure, though these are both acknowledged meanings of the word. The "emergence of . . . *sattva*, limpid and mirror-like" always makes for a clearer reflection of "the light and beatitude proper to the self."[116] So, taken in the light of this truth, *ānand* can here be taken to mean pure happiness alone, that is, happiness which is utterly free from impulses to do or to get, and from all domination by pull of the senses. It is this beatitude — that is, happiness with absolute peace — which brings *rasa* very close to the bliss of realizing *Brahman* (*Brahmānand sahodaraḥ*), for *ānand* (as we have interpreted it) is also regarded as one of the three attributes of *Brahman*. Another clue to this closeness is provided by the fact that just as *brahmānubhav* is a very deeply satisfying experience because it answers a basic need of the *ātman*, so is *rasa* because of its grounding in *sthāyībhāva*s which are a part of our native equipment of tendencies to have emotional experiences of

115. Cf. S.K. De, *Sanskrit Poetics as a Study of Aesthetic*, p. 109.

116. Gnoli, *The Aesthetic Experience According to Abhinavagupta*, 2nd edn., p. 46.

specific kinds. In neither case does the blissful experience appear as the attainment of a merely objective end.

This is, we may note, not only an important emphasis of the theory in question but a point of some theoretical value, insofar as it enables us to meet an obvious and quite sensible objection. Can we not experience, one may ask, utter and blissful tranquillity even in looking at a beautiful detail of natural beauty, be it even a little foam on the moonlit bank of a lake? We surely can. What is more, intense and reverent communion with nature has even enabled some sensitive poets, such as Wordsworth and Sūrdās, to receive (or elicit) some quiet, but ennobling impulses of vital moral significance.[117] Yet such experiences cannot be summarily likened to *rasa* because of two clear differences. First, our attention to a beautiful object of nature can hardly ever be *so sustained and so manifestly engaging to the mind* as our knowledgeable contemplation of a dramatic presentation which does not merely tickle our eyes and ears, but provides, as a rule, a full-blown plot packed with almost every element of real life, namely, thought, emotion, and variform interplay of character with situations. Secondly, to receive elevating influences from outside is not the same thing as seeing something that is essential to our own being reflected in an outer object with charm and convincingness, as really

---

117. Wordsworth, for instance, voices the faith that

> One impulse from a vernal wood
> May teach you more of Man;
> Of moral evil and of good
> Than all the sages can.

And, in a much more enlightening *bhajan* which opens with the words: "वृक्षन से मति ले मन तू", Sūrdās reads in the existence and function of trees quite a few moving messages of selfless service and transcendence of the duality of aversion and attachment; for, do not these stately objects of Nature drop fruits precisely for those who throw pebbles at them; and do they ever get angry with those who cut them or attached to those who water them?

happens when we witness plays which present our own *sthāyībhāvas* as creatively exalted for objective contemplation. It is this projection of what is intrinsically within us as human beings which enables us to taste *rasa* with a degree of intimacy which is hardly ever there in Man's communion with Nature, except perhaps in the case of some religious mystics. There *are* moments when we feel perfectly *at peace with* the beauty that Nature presents, but the beauteous objects of Nature are surely not felt *as reflecting us*; and it is no mere rhetoric to say, as Vishvanath does, that "*rasa* [alone] is tasted as if in indivisibility."

Our experience of listening (knowledgeably) to good music can perhaps be said to be closer to Vishvanath's characterization of *rasa* than our contemplation of Nature. There are reasons why I refer to such experiences again. They have a definite and illustrative, if yet partial, value for the purpose of this essay. So far as I know, in independent India just one explicit attempt has been made to *relate drama* to the *rasa* theory. This happened in 1980 when Shyamanand Jalan tried to explore the theory with a multi-disciplinary production of *Abhijnānaśākuntalam* with the assistance of Guru Kelucharan Mohapatra as choreographer and Girija Devi as music composer — a venture which subsequently enabled Jalan to organize comprehensive workshops such as Indian Dance Traditions and Modern Theatre (1983) with seminarists, classical dancers and theatre actors. I have no idea of the result of this creative effort. Further, because the dramatic art of Bharata's day to which the *rasa* theory might well have been very relevant, is no longer accessible to us, and also because it is not the general practice of our playwrights and directors of today to consciously adhere to all the injunctions of Bharata, we may turn to a visualized instance of listening to a top class music recital for getting some idea of how the various qualities distinguished by Abhinavagupta in his succinct characterization of *rasa* could in fact interrelate in a single experience.

With such an instance in mind we may proceed quite simply, say, as follows:

The clear *and discriminating* perception (by a knowledgeable listener) of sweet-sounding (and correctly placed) *svaras* as making the distinct wholeness of a single *rāga* provides some joy *and* also a little thinking simultaneously. What is clearly and appealingly perceived at once makes the listener feel enlivened or (so to say) lit up on the inside (*prakāsh*). All this is aided by intenseness of attention which is, in turn, helped not only by the ability and willingness of the (qualified) listener to care for nothing but the music (*vedyāntarasparśaśūnyo*) but (in principle) by the pull of the music itself. This perfect accord of *what* he listens to and *how* he does so makes for the undivided (*akhand*) quality of the experience which is wondrous (or of the nature of a miracle, *chamatkāra*) because it is quite unlike our everyday experiences insofar as it is not all disturbed by considerations of utility, or of location in real space or time and is therefore *vītavighna*. It may well be — in fact it often is — quite without the semblance of *a distinct full blown emotion* (which is not the same thing as a little happy wonderment); and this is indeed what prevents it from becoming an exact parallel of *rasānubhūti*. But this is incontrovertible that, as I have already said earlier, at least for a while after the listening is over, or even during the course of listening, such an experience lifts one out of the sense of being just a limited "I" as opposed to the others.

Yet, in spite of all that is said for it, *rasa*-experience is only very similar to, or a twin brother of (*sahodaraḥ*) so to say, but not exactly identical with the bliss of realizing *Brahman*; and the differences are easy to see. Even our most fascinated watching of a play is quickly followed by a return to the humdrum tenor of life; the recurring eclipse of *sattva* by the other two *guṇas* begins all over again; and, as we resume it, our normal living generally does not show any marked improvement in its moral tone. The bliss of realizing *Brahman*, on the other hand, ennobles our lives markedly and loosens our bondage (more or less) to sheer worldly concerns. What is more, besides of course a modicum of moral decency — say, by way of discipline as members of an audience — no such rigorous psycho-ethical disciplines are needed for experiencing *rasa* as are generally essential for achieving the relish of Brahmānanda.

However, the

> limitations of the experience of art, to which we have just alluded, do not affect the conclusion that it is of the same [*sattva*-dominated] order as . . . the ideal [spiritual] state; . . . [what is more, it even makes *that state* appear feasible] . . . art experience [as visualized by the *rasa* theory] is well adapted to arouse our interest in the ideal state by giving us a foretaste of it, and thus to serve as a powerful incentive to the pursuit of . . . [that] state. . . . It is not given to the ordinary man to transcend [merely individual concerns] . . . ; art by its impersonalized forms appears the best means for a temporary [yet educative] escape from the ills of life arising from such [self-serving interests].[118]

Such a view which posits an essential relation between art experience and humanity's ethico-religious interests is obviously a far cry from those trends in present-day aesthetics which seek to *dehumanize* art completely; but though it seems most clearly relevant only to the more systematic of our classical dances today, it has surely been the traditional Indian conception of art.

---

118. Hiriyanna, *Art Experience*, Mysore: Kavyalaya Publishers, pp. 13, 28.

Bibliography

Abraham, Abu, "Unsupporting Cast" in *The Hindustan Times* (New Delhi), 20 February 1983.

Alperson, Philip, "Musical Time and Music as an 'Art of Time", the *Journal of Aesthetics and Art Criticism* (*JAAC*) Summer 1980.

Archer, W.G., *Indian and Modern Art*, George Allen & Unwin, 1959.

Attenborough's, Richard, "Gandhi: An Essay in Understanding", *Journal of Comparative Literature and Aesthetics*, vol. V, nos. 1-2, 1982.

Audi, Robert (ed.), *The Cambridge Dictionary of Philosophy*, Cambridge University Press, 2nd edn., 1999.

Barfield, Owens, *What Coleridge Thought*, London: OUP, 1972.

Beardsley, M.C., *Aesthetics — Problems in the Philosophy of Criticism*, Harcourt, Brace & World, Inc. 1958.

Bell, Clive, *Art*, Grey Arrow Edn. 1961.

Best, David, "Reply to My Critics", *The British Journal of Aesthetics*, vol. 23, no. ?, Spring 1983.

Blanshard, Brand, *On Philosophical Style*, New York: Greenwood Press, 1969 rpt.

Budd, Malcolm, "The Repudiation of Emotion — Hanslick on Music", *The British Journal of Aesthetics*, vol. 20, no. 1, Winter 1980.

Bullough, Edward, "Psychical Distance" in M. Rader ed., *A Modern Book of Esthetics*, 4th edn.; New York: Holt, Rinehart Winston, 1973.

Bush, Douglas (ed.), *Milton: Poetical Works*, London: OUP, 1968.

Chaitanya, Krishna, "A halation of beauty" in *The Hindustan Times*, 14.6.1987.

Chatterjee, Margaret, *Contemporary Indian Philosophy*, Series Two, London: George Allen & Unwin, 1974, pp. 194-214.

Coleman, Earle, "On Saxena's Defense of the Aesthetic Attitude" *Philosophy East and West*, 29, no. 1 January, 1979.

Collingwood, R.G., *The Principles of Art*, Oxford: Clarendon Press, 1955 rpt.

Coomarasway, A.K., *The Transformation of Nature in Art*, Harvard, 1934.

Coomaraswamy, Ananda, *The Dance of Śiva*, Asia Publishing House, 3rd printing, 1956.

De, S.K., *Sanskrit Poetics as a Study of Aesthetic*, OUP, 1963.

Dewey, John, *Art as Experience*, New York: Capricorn Books, 1958, 7th impression.

Dickie, George, Richard Scalfani, and Ronald Rabbin (eds.): *Aesthetics — A Critical Anthology*, Boston and New York: Bedford/ St. Martin's, 2nd edn., 1989.

Dickie, George, "The Myth of the Aesthetic Attitude", *Introductory Readings in Aesthetics*.

Dutt, Utpal, *Contemporary Indian Theatre: Interviews with Playwrights and Directors*, New Delhi: Sangeet Natak Akademi, 1989.

Elton, E. (ed.), *Aesthetics and Language*, Oxford: Basil Blackwell, 1970.

Feezell, R.M., "The Aesthetic Attitude Debate: Some Remarks on Saxena, Coleman, and a Phenomenological Approach to the Issue", *Philosophy East and West*, January 1980.

Flew, Antony, *A Dictionary of Philosophy*, Pan Books Ltd., 1984 edn.

Fry, Roger, *Vision and Design*, London: Chatto and Windus, 1920.

Frye, *Anatomy of Criticism*, Princeton University Press, 1957, (PB).

Gandhi, M.K., *In Search of the Supreme*, vol. II, compiled and edited by V.B. Kher, Ahmedabad: Navajivan Publishing House, 1961.

Gargi, Balwant, "I Live for Today", an encounter with Satish Gujral, in *The Hindustan Times* (New Delhi), 30 November, 1980.

Gatt, Giuseppe, *Turner*, A Dolphin Art Book, Thames and Hudson, 1968.

Gilani, Malti and Quratulain Hyder (eds.), *Ustād Bade Ghulam Ali Khan: His Life and Music*, New Delhi: Harman Publishing House, 2003.

Gnoli, R., *The Aesthetic Experience According to Abhinavagupta*, Varanasi: Chowkhamba Sanskrit Series Office, 2nd edn., 1968

Goodman, Nelson, *Languages of Art*, Indianapolis: Hackett, 1976.

Hammermeister, Kai, *The German Aesthetic Tradition*, Cambridge University Press, 2002.

Hanslick, *The Beautiful in Music*, tr. Gustav Cohen, London & New York, 1891.

Hiriyanna, M., *Art Experience*, Mysore: Kavyalaya Publishers, 1954.

Hospers, John, "The Concept of Artistic Expression", in John Hospers (ed.), *Introductary Readings in Aesthetics*, The Free Press, Collier MacMillan Publishers, 1969.

———, "The Esthetic Attitude" in *A Modern Book of Esthetics*, 4th edn., p. 398.

Joseph, Margolis, "A Strategy for a Philosophy of Art", *JAAC*, U.S.A., Summer 1979.

Kaji, C., *Prayer*, edited and compiled by Navajivan, 1977.

Kaviraja Vishvanatha, *Sāhityadarpaṇa*, ed. Satyavrata Singh, Varanasi: Chowkhamba Vidya Bhawan, New edn., 1992.

Kivy, Peter, *Music Alone*, Cornell University Press, 1st printing, Cornell Paperbacks, 1991.

Krishnamoorthy, K., "Traditional Indian Aesthetics in Theory and Practice" in *Indian Aesthetics and Art Activity*, Shimla: Indian Institute of Advanced Study, 1968.

Langer, Susanne K., *Feeling and Form*, London: Routledge and Kegan Paul Ltd., 1963, Third Impression.

———, *Mind: An Essay on Human Feeling*, vol. I. Baltimore and London: The John Hopkins University Press, Second printing (paper) 1975.

———, *Problems of Art*, London: Routledge & Kegan Paul, 1957.

———, *Reflections on Art*, ed. Baltimore: The Johns Hopkins Press, 2nd printing 1960.

Maritain, Jacques, *Art and Scholasticism and the Frontiers of Poetry*, tr. J.W. Evans, University of Notre Dame Press.

Mothersill, Mary, *Beauty Restored*, Oxford Clarendon Press, 1984.

Nwodo, C.W., "Philosophy of Art *vs* Aesthetics", *The British Journal of Aesthetics*, Summer 1984.

Osborne, Harold, *The Art of Appreciation*, London: OUP, 1970.

Pandey, K.C., *Comparative Aesthetics*, vol. I (Indian Aesthetics), 2nd edn. 1959, Varanasi: Chowkhamba Sanskrit Series Office,

Prabhu, R.K. and U.R. Rao (ed.), *The Mind of Mahatma Gandhi*, Ahmedabad: Navajivan Publishing House, 1967.

Puppi, Lionello, *El Greco*, A Dolphin Art Book, London: Thames and Hudson, 1967.

Pyarelal, *The Last Phase*, Ahmedabad: Navajivan Publishing House, 1958.

Read, Herbert, "A Definition of Art", in L.A. Jacobus ed., *Aesthetics and the Arts*, McGraw Hill Book Co., 1968.

Reid, L.A., *Meaning in the Arts,* London: George Allen & Unwin, 1969.

Sartwell, Crispin, "Aesthetic Dualism and the Transfiguration of the Commonplace" in *JAAC*, Summer 1988.

Sauvage, M., "Notes on the Superposition of the Temporal Modes in Works of Art", in S.K. Langer ed., *Reflections on Art*, Baltimore: The John Hopkins Press, 2nd printing, 1960.

Saxena, Sudhir Kumar, *The Art of Tabla Rhythm: Essentials, Tradition and Creativity,* New Delhi: Sangeet Natak Akademi and D.K. Printworld (P.) Ltd., 2nd Impression, 2008.

Saxena, Sushil Kumar, *Aesthetical Essays*, Delhi: Chanakya Publications, 1981.

———, "Aesthetic Theory and Hindustani Rhythm", *The British Journal of Aesthetics*, Summer 1976, vol. 16, no. 3, rpt.

———, "Essentials of Hindustānī Music" *Diogene*, 45, Paris, 1964.

———, "Form and Content in Hindustani Rhythm", *Sangeet Natak*, no. 18, October–December 1970.

———, "Reply to My Critics" *Philosophy East and West* 29, no. 2, April 1979.

———, "The Aesthetic Attitude" (*Philosophy East and West*, 28, no. I, Jan. 1978).

———, "The Aesthetic Attitude Debate: Reply to Some New Criticisms", *Philosophy East and West*, April, 1980.

———, "The Concept of *Laya* in Hindustānī Music", *Indian Philosophical Quarterly*, Pune, vol. I. no. 2, January 1974.

———, "The Fabric of Aamad — A Study of Form and Flow in Hindustānī Music" *Sangeet Natak*, no. 16, April–June, 1970.

———, "The Spiritual and Hindustānī Music" *Sangeet Natak*, nos. 131-32, 1999.

———, *The Winged Form: Aesthetical Essays on Hindustani Rhythm*, Sangeet Natak Akademi, Delhi, 1979.

Schott, Rolf, *Michelangelo*, London: Thames and Hudson, 1st edn., 1964.

Selincourt, "Music and Duration", in *Reflections on Art*.

Shakespeare's *Hamlet*, Act I, Speeches 10, 11.

Shelley, *Epipsychidion*, lines 94, 95.

Snoeyenbos, M.H., *Philosophy East and West*, January 1980.

Snoeyenbos, Milton H., "Saxena on the Aesthetic Attitude", *Philosophy East and West*, vol. 29 no. 1, January, 1979.

Spender, Stephen, *World within World*, London: Hamilton, 1951.

Stolnitz, Jerome, *Aesthetics and Philosophy of Art Criticism*, Boston: Houghton Mifflin, 1960.

———, "The Aesthetic Attitude, in the Rise of Modern Aesthetics" *JAAC*, U.S.A., Summer 1978.

———, "The Aesthetic Attitude" in John Hospers ed., *Introductory Readings in Aesthetics*, The Free Press and Collier MacMillan, 1969.

Tralbaut, M.E., *Van Gogh — A Pictorial Biography*, London: Thames and Hudson, 1959.

Tripathi, Radhavallabh, review of Prof. Kapil Kapoor's book, *Literary Theory — Indian Conceptual Framework*, in *Journal of Indian Council of Philosophical Research*, March 2002.

Vajpeyi, Ashok, (ed.), *Kumar Gandharva*, New Delhi: Rajkamal Prakashan, 1st edn., 1982.

Whittick, Arnold, "Towards Precise Distinctions of Art and Craft", *The British Journal of Aesthetics*, Winter 1984.

Williams, Oscar, *Master Poems of the English Language*, ed. New York: Trident Press, 1966.

Index of Names

Index of Concepts, Viewpoints and Accents of Reflection